おべんとう Obento

SUPREME ❯ STUDENT BOOK

4th EDITION

Kyoko Kusumoto
Ayako Lyons
Jacqueline Brown
Anne Fisher
Jean Swinyard

NELSON
CENGAGE Learning

Australia • Brazil • Japan • Korea • Mexico • Singapore • Spain • United Kingdom • United States

NELSON
CENGAGE Learning·

Obento Supreme Student Book
4th Edition
Kyoko Kusumoto
Ayako Lyons
Jacqueline Brown
Anne Fisher
Jean Swinyard

Publishing editor: Jana Gabriel
Editor: Danielle Dominguez
Senior editor: Penny Analytis
Senior designer: Miranda Costa
Cover designer: Studio Pounce
Photo researcher: Wendy Duncan
Production controllers: Tanya Wasylewski and Jem Wolfenden
Illustrations: Hannah Malcom, Fiona Lee, James Hart, Yuko Fujita
Reprint: Jess Lovell
Typeset by Polar Design

Any URLs contained in this publication were checked for currency during the production process. Note, however, that the publisher cannot vouch for the ongoing currency of URLs.

Acknowledgements
The Publisher would like to thank contributing editor Luciano di Gregorio. The Publisher would also like to credit and acknowledge the following sources for photographs: Contents: Getty Images/AID/a.collectionRF, p. viii (left); Getty Images/Patrice Hauser, p. viii (centre); Getty Images/Ryuhei Shindo, p. viii (right); Shutterstock.com/Nobusuke Oki, p. ix (left); Getty Images/Dex Image, p. ix (centre); Alamy/Giovanni Mereghetti, p. ix (right); Alamy/Payless Images, p. x (left); Corbis, p. x (centre); Alamy/Jochen Tack, p. x (right); Corbis, p. xi (left); Getty Images/BLOOM image, p. xi (centre); Getty Images/Laurence Mouton, p. xi (right); design images: yellow robot, aqua robot, green robot Shutterstock.com/Charles Taylor; green tea in white cup Shutterstock.com/sai0112; sushi Shutterstock.com/withGod; red and black Japanese shoes, black and beige Japanese shoes Shutterstock.com/Blinka, orange koi Shutterstock.com/Eric Isselée, red and white koi Shutterstock.com/Kroko, single strand of cherry blossom Shutterstock.com/piyato, view of Tokyo city Shutterstock.com/Attila JANDI, autumn leaves Shutterstock.com/sea-walker, green soybeans Shutterstock.com/Pigdevil Photo; Ken Hutchinson

For product information and technology assistance,
in Australia call **1300 790 853**;
in New Zealand call **0800 449 725**

For permission to use material from this text or product, please email
aust.permissions@cengage.com

National Library of Australia Cataloguing-in-Publication Data
Obento Supreme Student Book / Kyoko Kusumoto ... [et al.].

ISBN 9780170198271

1. Japanese language--Textbooks for foreign speakers--English.

495.682421

Cengage Learning Australia
Level 7, 80 Dorcas Street
South Melbourne, Victoria Australia 3205

Cengage Learning New Zealand
Unit 4B Rosedale Office Park
331 Rosedale Road, Albany, North Shore 0632, NZ

For learning solutions, visit **cengage.com.au**

Printed in China by China Translation & Printing Services.
8 9 10 11 12 13 21 20 19 18 17

Welcome!

Welcome to *Obento Supreme*, the second book in the Obento series.

This book contains 12 units that introduce a variety of interesting topics. The topics are relevant to your everyday world and range from fashion and media, to hobbies such as reading manga and what you do in your free time. You will learn to communicate with Japanese students your own age – to talk about your home life, leisure activities, friends and school life – and to function in the Japanese-speaking world.

As with all the books in the Obento series, you are encouraged to use every aspect of language learning to communicate in Japanese. In each unit you will find sentence patterns, vocabulary and exercises that equip you to communicate in Japanese. Even so, you do not need to understand everything you hear or read – situations requiring guesswork and gestures play an important part in conversation.

In addition to the above features, the *Obento Supreme Student Book* is supported by a Workbook, Audio Pack, Teacher's Edition, an app and the Obento website, which can be found at **www.nelsonlanguages.com.au**

Please use this book and its components to enjoy your study of the Japanese people and their language.

この本で 日本ごの べんきょうを たのしんで ください。

Getty Images/Image Source

Foreword

In 1990, Japanese became the number one language taught in Australian secondary schools and a prominent offering in primary schools across all states. Most of our universities offer Japanese language programs, strongly sustained by Australian teachers, materials and research in collaboration with various agencies in Japan. Supporting the presence of Japanese language and culture in our educational institutions, *Obento Deluxe* and *Obento Supreme* are an outstanding example of what Australian expertise has pioneered in Japanese language education.

Commercial, cultural and personal relations with the people of Japan have stimulated interest and growth in the study of Japanese language in Australia. The last two decades can be seen as a 'golden age' of Japanese foreign language education with significant advances in the teaching of Japanese in foreign contexts, amply evident in the Obento series.

Teaching Japanese as a foreign language raises the challenge of identifying the most appropriate approach for the acquisition of its fascinating orthography. Teachers will inevitably adapt and innovate as they search among many methods for the best ways to meet the needs of individual students. All good teaching is a combination of the principled and the eclectic; there will never be only one correct method to the absolute exclusion of all alternatives.

The suite of offerings in the Obento series is characterised by its distinctive solution to the central challenge of teaching script. For English learners of cognate foreign languages that use an alphabetic writing system (especially those that use roman script such as most European languages, Indonesian and others), there is little additional orthography to acquire. For languages which use ideographic scripts, particularly Japanese with its mixed systems of ideographs (*kanji*) and two syllabaries (*hiragana* and *katakana*), teachers need the guidance that both research and prior experience can offer. They now have this with Obento!

Obento is designed to reproduce as far as possible the successful sequences of natural or first language learning: listening, speaking, recognising significant single characters, recognising words, and finally writing characters. This is achieved without ever suspending oral-based teaching. There is extensive use of Japanese instructions to introduce the two *kana* and selected *kanji*, enabling students to immediately recognise words without having to depend on *rōmaji*.

The backbone of the Obento approach consists of the scope of what to cover in limited class time, the sequence of how to order and arrange the material to promote learning, and the wise preference for the polite です／ます forms. Rather than being entirely prescriptive, the Obento authors acknowledge that some but not all students will have studied Japanese in primary school, resulting in a range of ability and interest levels and a variety of preferred learning styles. This variation is well catered for in Obento. The innovative design builds familiarity and aural/oral recognition of key words before students are required to read them, developing the new learners' confidence.

The excellent student materials in the Obento series link to superb teacher support and extensions, and stimulus content that is reinforced online and in audio and video. In studying these materials, I was impressed by the clever linking of cultural items and information to points of general knowledge and culturally authentic content that will appeal to teenagers. Teachers can set the pace for introduction of items and there are ample opportunities for students to become architects of their own learning within the linked student materials.

Whether print or digital, oral or aural, the materials in the Obento series are integrated with a sophistication that encourages interest and facilitates learning. Obento has been conceived to correlate directly with the pathways and expectations of the Australian Curriculum, supporting cross-disciplinary skills, intercultural education and Asian studies.

The diverse resources in the Obento series guarantee a methodologically rich program that shows good use of the practical insights and research evidence of experienced teacher writers. Teachers can be confident that the recommendations and scope and sequence in the teacher materials are the result of deep reflection on effective practice. The pages of the Obento course books unfold beautifully, providing students with not only linguistic but also aesthetic offerings as they progress. Obento is a sound and visually appealing program for both students and their teachers, one which makes sense pedagogically and provides rich reward for exploration. This is surely what all excellent teaching should be and do.

Dr Joseph Lo Bianco, AM
Professor of Language and Literacy Education,
Graduate School of Education, University of Melbourne, Australia
President, Tsinghua Asian-Pacific Forum on Translation and
Intercultural Studies
Immediate Past President, Australian Academy of the Humanities

About the series

Student Book

The Student Book is clearly structured and well paced. It suits students of all levels and presents all the skills needed for language learning. It includes lively cartoon spreads, images of Japan, activities and reading passages, and it also provides plenty of opportunities for intercultural reflection and discussion.

NelsonNetBook

The *Obento Supreme* NelsonNetBook is an ebook that can be used online or offline. It has interactive links and 'hot spots' that give you access to a variety of multimedia resources via the Web. Students can add notes, weblinks and audio recordings, and teachers can use it to share their personalised version with the class.

Please note that complimentary access to the NelsonNetBook is only available to teachers who use the accompanying student book and workbook as a core educational resource in their classroom. Contact your sales representative for information about access and conditions.

Workbook, CD & DVD

The *Obento Supreme* Workbook offers a wealth of consolidating and reinforcing exercises to revise language and structures, plus:
- a CD with the audio recordings for the listening tasks
- a DVD of cultural videos as well as unit theme videos (with and without subtitles) that exemplify the language covered.

ISBN 9780170198271

Audio Pack

The Audio CDs are recorded with native speakers and contain recordings of:
* selected texts from the Student Book (including songs!)
* listening exercises for the Workbook
* listening exercises for the unit tests and study guides.

Teacher's Edition & DVD

* A full colour wraparound version of the Student Book with handy margin notes on how to conduct the lessons; suggested pathways; extension activities; as well as references to the Worksheet, Workbook and digital resources
* A DVD with unit tests, worksheets, audio transcripts and Workbook solutions
* Access to the teacher website, which includes chapter PDFs of the Student Book, access to the NelsonNetBook (for adopting schools), and comprehensive unit teaching plans and curriculum grids.

Note: additional teaching material is available on the DVD with the Teacher's Edition.

Obento Website

The *Obento Supreme* website at **www.nelsonlanguages.com.au** offers a comprehensive suite of engaging digital resources for students, and includes:
* a variety of interactive activities
* Play 'n' Say (featuring hundreds of words and phrases for listening and speaking practice)
* Kana-chan game (for *hiragana*, *katakana* and *kanji* practice)
* *Manga* Movies (animated *manga*)
… to name just a few!

Obento App (iPhone, iPad and iPod Touch)

The Obento Supreme App is a great way to revise the Obento core vocabulary, and it's easy and fun!

You can download the app directly from iTunes. For more information, contact the relevant state sales representative.

About this book

Obento Supreme is divided into 12 units.

The first page of each unit introduces the topic and outlines what you can expect to achieve on completion of the unit. It is both an introduction and a summary of the unit.

Getting started

The first section of the unit covers a variety of text types, from letters and emails to phone conversations and manga. In this section, which introduces the unit theme and key language, you get started – you listen to the CD, look at the images and try to guess what the people are saying and doing.

れんしゅう

These pages give examples of the sentence patterns introduced in the unit. Here you will find speaking and listening practice for all the key elements of the unit. The patterns are also provided on audio tracks to give you maximum practice.

かんじ

These sections deal with Japanese writing. Each character or *kanji* is shown with its stroke order, pronunciation (as appropriate), meaning and example words or phrases.

にほんぶんか

The Japanese culture section gives you important and interesting information about Japanese culture, thereby expanding your understanding of the Japanese people. Cultural knowledge is just as important as language in helping you to communicate.

だいはっけん

The breakthrough section covers intercultural language learning. It features a variety of stimulus material, and provides you with strategies to explore these points further via class discussion or homework investigations. This section is designed to help you develop a rich understanding of how languages and cultures influence each other, and how they relate to other languages and cultures.

ぶんぽう

This section provides the language foundation (or grammar) of each unit. The grammar is introduced through example sentences. To this, we add たんご (vocabulary) to give the grammar its flavour. The core vocabulary for the unit is listed, along with extra vocabulary relevant to the topic.

ISBN 9780170198271

ぶんぽうプラス

Here you will find detailed explanations of the grammar points introduced in each unit. This section provides extra examples and draws attention to the tricky aspects of the sentence patterns introduced.

エクストラ

This section features further Japanese text types, such as conversations, emails, invitations and letters, and gives you the opportunity to produce them yourself.

At the back of the book is a handy reference section, in which the grammar of each unit is summarised with examples, and there is a complete list of all the vocabulary learnt.

Icons used in this book

This book contains the following icons to guide you to extra material and resources.

This icon directs you to an audio recording that is in the Audio Pack, and is hotspotted in the NelsonNetBook.

This icon directs you to manga movie animations on the website.

This icon directs you to external websites in order to learn more about a topic or to complete an activity.

This icon directs you to the Play 'n' Say on the website where you can listen to these words and phrases, record yourself saying them and play back your recording to compare.

This icon directs you to a relevant cultural slideshow on the Teacher's Edition DVD.

This icon directs you to a relevant video clip on the Student Workbook DVD.

This icon directs you to the website to complete a drag-and-drop or similar interactive task.

This icon means there are worksheets, activity sheets, puzzles or research tasks. They are located on the Teacher's Edition DVD and are hotspotted in the NelsonNetBook.

Contents

ISBN 9780170198271

ISBN 9780170198271

The Obento song

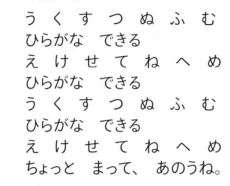

Verse 1

あ か さ た な は ま
ひらがな、　かたかな
い き し ち に ひ み
ひらがな、　かたかな
あ か さ た な は ま
ひらがな、　かたかな
い き し ち に ひ み
にほんごは　すごい。

Chorus

にほんごは　たのしい
おべんとうは　おいしい
1、2、3、4、5
さあ、　おべんとう
にほんに　いきましょう
ともだちに　あいましょう
1、2、3、4、5
さあ、　おべんとう。

Verse 2

う く す つ ぬ ふ む
ひらがな　できる
え け せ て ね へ め
ひらがな　できる
う く す つ ぬ ふ む
ひらがな　できる
え け せ て ね へ め
ちょっと　まって、　あのうね。

Verse 3

お こ そ と の ほ も
みんな、　おべんとう
にほんご　やさしい
みんな、　おべんとう
お こ そ と の ほ も
みんな、　おべんとう
にほんご　やさしい
みなさん、　いっしょに!

ISBN 9780170198271

ゆきさんのカラオケパーティー

In this unit, you will learn to:

- tell the time
- say what time you do an activity
- use other words indicating time
- say where you do an activity
- invite someone to do something and respond to an invitation
- recognise and write the *kanji* characters 何, 時, 分 and 半

In this unit, you will learn about:

- Japanese culture: when to use polite, humble and casual speech
- intercultural understanding: punctuality
- text types: invitation cards, map

Getty Images/AID/a.collectionRF

Yuki is moving away from Tokyo to a town in the south of Japan called Yamaguchi. Kenichi has invited everyone to a farewell party for Yuki.

月曜日、がっこうの　あとで

free time

Won't you come?

to move house

I will miss her.

I can't wait / I'm looking forward to it.

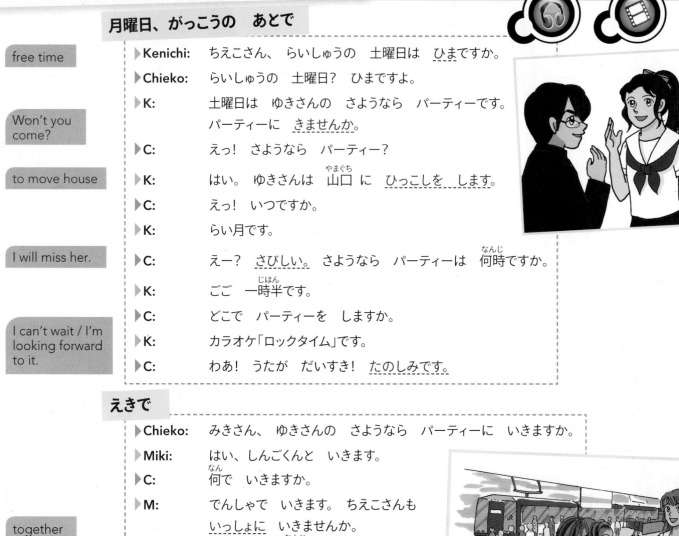

▷Kenichi: ちえこさん、　らいしゅうの　土曜日は　ひまですか。

▷Chieko: らいしゅうの　土曜日？　ひまですよ。

▷K: 土曜日は　ゆきさんの　さようなら　パーティーです。
パーティーに　きませんか。

▷C: えっ！　さようなら　パーティー？

▷K: はい。　ゆきさんは　山口に　ひっこしを　します。

▷C: えっ！　いつですか。

▷K: らい月です。

▷C: えー？　さびしい。　さようなら　パーティーは　何時ですか。

▷K: ごご　一時半です。

▷C: どこで　パーティーを　しますか。

▷K: カラオケ「ロックタイム」です。

▷C: わあ！　うたが　だいすき！　たのしみです。

えきで

together

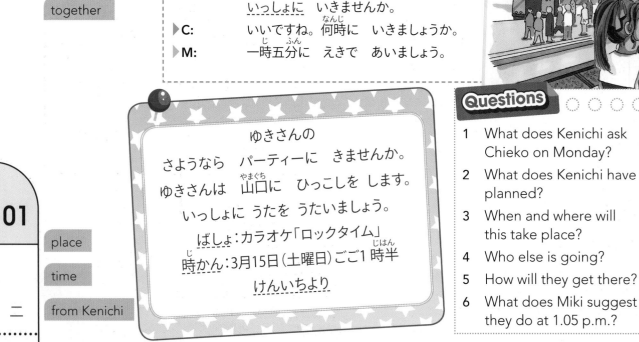

▷Chieko: みきさん、　ゆきさんの　さようなら　パーティーに　いきますか。

▷Miki: はい、しんごくんと　いきます。

▷C: 何で　いきますか。

▷M: でんしゃで　いきます。　ちえこさんも
いっしょに　いきませんか。

▷C: いいですね。何時に　いきましょうか。

▷M: 一時五分に　えきで　あいましょう。

ゆきさんの
さようなら　パーティーに　きませんか。
ゆきさんは　山口に　ひっこしを　します。
いっしょに　うたを　うたいましょう。
ばしょ：カラオケ「ロックタイム」
時かん：3月15日（土曜日）ごご1時半
けんいちより

place

time

from Kenichi

Questions

1 What does Kenichi ask Chieko on Monday?

2 What does Kenichi have planned?

3 When and where will this take place?

4 Who else is going?

5 How will they get there?

6 What does Miki suggest they do at 1.05 p.m.?

01

二

ゆきさんのカラオケパーティー

ISBN 9780170198271

れんしゅう

1 Asking and telling the time

A:	いま　何時ですか。
B:	Timeです。
A:	パーティーは　何時ですか。
B:	パーティーは　timeです。
一	いま　何時ですか。
	八時です。
二	いま　何時ですか。
	いま　ごご　三時五分です。
	いま　ごぜん　十時半です。

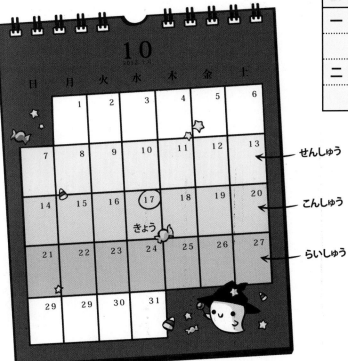

せんしゅう

こんしゅう

らいしゅう

2 Asking and saying what time you do an activity

A:	何時に　おきますか。
B:	Timeに　おきます。
一	何時に　バスに　のりますか。
	八時に　のります。
二	きのう、何時に　おきましたか。
	きのう、ごぜん　七時十五分に　おきました。

3 Asking and saying when you do an activity

A:	いつ　しゅくだいを　しますか。
B:	Time word　します。
一	いつ　しゅくだいを　しますか。
	あした　します。
二	いつ　プレゼントを　かいましょうか。
	らいしゅう　かいましょう。
三	いつ　コンサートに　いきましたか。
	せん月　いきました。

たんご

7.00 a.m. ／ごぜん　七時	きょう
9.30 a.m. ／ごぜん　九時半	せんしゅう
4.15 p.m. ／ごご　四時十五分	らい月
11.50 p.m. ／ごご　十一時五十分	ことし

Which do you say: 6.55 or five to seven?
六時五十五分　*or*
七時五分まえ?
*Japanese people these days
tend to use the digital way.*

ISBN 9780170198271

ゆきさんのカラオケパーティー

01

三

Alamy/Ian Nolan

4 Asking and saying where you do an activity

A:	どこで　しますか。
B:	Placeで　します。
一	どこで　パーティーを　しますか。
	ともだちの　うちで　します。
二	どこで　ひるごはんを　たべましたか。
	レストランで　たべました。

Be careful! Don't forget to check if your time word needs the past tense.

5 Inviting someone to do something and responding

A:	〜ませんか。
B:	はい、　〜ましょう。
	いいえ、　〜は　ちょっと…
一	あした　としょかんに　いきませんか。
	はい、　いきましょう。
二	いっしょに　でかけませんか。
	はい、　でかけましょう。
三	コーラを　のみませんか。
	すみません。　コーラは　ちょっと…

たんご

こうえん	あいます
えいがかん	うたを　うたいます
みせ	べんきょう　します

Getty Images/Gary Conner

Getty Images/Koichi Kamoshida

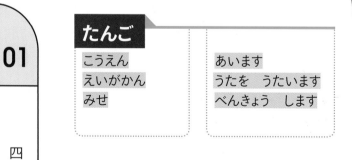

Getty Images/Justin Guariglia

四

4

ゆきさんのカラオケパーティー

ISBN 9780170198271

These are the *kanji* and their readings introduced in this unit.

なに／なん what

何　何

Two people are saying 'What's in the box?'

ノ	イ	亻	仃	佰	佰	何	

何を　しましょうか。　→　なにを　しましょうか。　→　What shall we do?

何で　いきますか。　→　なんで　いきますか。　→　By what transport will you go?

何時　→　なんじ　→　What time?

何曜日　→　なんようび　→　What day of the week?

とき／ジ time/o'clock

時　時

Saturday and Sunday – time for a little fun!

丨	冂	月	日	日一	日十	旪	旹
時	時						

いま　六時です。　→　いま　ろくじです。　→　It is 6 o'clock now.

四時に　→　よじに　→　at 4 o'clock

ひまな時に　→　ひまなときに　→　in my free time

フン／プン minute

分

In the clock, there is a minute man pointing to the minutes.

ノ	八	分	分				

十五分　→　じゅうごふん　→　15 minutes

二十分　→　にじゅっぷん　→　20 minutes

三時五十五分に　→　さんじごじゅうごふんに　→　at 3.55

二時十分です。　→　にじじゅっぷんです。　→　It is 2.10.

ハン half

半

A karate black-belt chopping three boards by hand and breaking them exactly in half. He calls out, 'Han!'

丶	丷	丷	兰	半			

いま　十時半です。　→　いま　じゅうじはんです。　→　It is now 10.30.

五時半に　いきます。　→　ごじはんに　いきます。　→　I will go at 5.30.

ISBN 9780170198271

ゆきさんのカラオケパーティー

01

にほんぶんか

In Japanese, as in English, we choose our language based on whether we find ourselves in a formal or informal situation. Depending on the situation, a Japanese person may have to choose not only between polite and casual, but also between polite and humble speech. Polite and humble speech are not the same thing. In English we use polite and casual speech, particularly with friends and family, but what is humble speech?

Polite versus casual speech

In invitations

Polite

～しませんか。	Won't you do ...?
～しましょう。	Let's do ...
たのしみに しています。	I am looking forward to it!
ぜひきて ください。	Please come.
まっています。	I am waiting!

ばしょ	place/venue
時かん	time
日時 (にちじ)	date and time
もってくるもの	things to bring
へんじは 金曜日までに。	RSVP by Friday.

すごい。	It is amazing.
とても たのしいよ。	It will be a lot of fun.
きてね。	You must come!
わすれないで!	Don't forget!
でんわ してね!	Call me!
へんじ かいてね!	Write me a reply!
Eメールしてね。	Send me an email.
まってます／まってるよ。	I am waiting!

Casual

Polite

クリーン　アップ　ジャパン

クラスの　みなさんへ

五月二十日は　クリーン　アップ　ジャパン
デーです。

みんなで　かわの　そうじを　しましょう。

時かん: 五月二十日(日曜日)一時三十分

ばしょ: がっこうで　あいましょう。

そうじの　あとで、　みんなに　アイスクリームを
プレゼントします。

ぜひ、　きて　ください。　まっています。

へんじは　金曜日までに　おねがいします。

せんせいより

Shutterstock.com/CLM

Casual

あやかちゃんへ

すしパーティー!　すしパーティー!　すしパーティー!

二月十九日は　わたしの　たんじょうび!

たんじょうびパーティーを　します。

すしの　りょうりコンテストを　します。

たくさん　たべましょう。　きてネ。

ばしょ: わたしの　うち

時かん: 2月21日(土曜日)ごご4時半

金曜日までに　でんわしてネ。

たのしみ!

みかより

ゆきさんのカラオケパーティー

Polite versus humble speech

Talking about family

The differences between polite and humble speech can be tricky, but only at first.

Polite speech shows respect to the person you are talking to. Humble speech shows you are being modest about yourself.

There are three situations to think about here:

1 when you are talking to or about members of someone else's family
2 when you are talking to members of your own family
3 when you are talking about members of your own family to someone else.

Look at the table below showing family members.

The polite terms in the second column are used in the first and second situations above.

The terms in the third column are not as polite. They are not used in the first situation, when you are talking to or about someone else's family, or in the second situation, when you are talking to your family members. They are used in the third situation, when talking about your own family to others, and they show you are being humble.

English	Someone else's family (polite terms)	Your family (humble terms)
grandfather	おじいさん	そふ
grandmother	おばあさん	そぼ
father	おとうさん	ちち
mother	おかあさん	はは
uncle	おじさん	おじ
aunt	おばさん	おば
older brother	おにいさん	あに
older sister	おねえさん	あね
younger brother	おとうとさん	おとうと
younger sister	いもうとさん	いもうと
cousin	いとこさん	いとこ

Corbis/Hill Street Studio

Getty Images/artparadigm

ISBN 9780170198271

ゆきさんのカラオケパーティー

01

七

Punctuality

Punctuality is one of those abstract concepts that depend on context. For example, if you arrange to meet up with one of your friends, it might be fine to turn up a little late. However, if you are late for a job interview, you could ruin your chances of getting the job.

When concepts such as punctuality differ between cultures, it can lead to situations where people become confused or uncomfortable, or even behave in culturally inappropriate ways without realising it.

The definition of punctuality can also change depending on what country you are in. How do you think an Australian would define 'a little late' and 'late'? How do you think a Japanese person would define ちこく (lateness).

In many instances, particularly informal ones, it would probably be fair to say that a 10-15 minute buffer would be considered acceptable to Australians. However, in Japan, there is a deep-seated cultural belief that a person's time is valuable, so being late or arriving too early effectively means that you are wasting the other person's time (and money). Japanese people therefore have a reputation for being punctual, but of course some are and some aren't. It depends on the personality of the person as well. So where did the reputation for punctuality come from? What are some examples of punctuality and tardiness in Japanese culture that might prove or disprove this reputation?

By investigating the answers to these questions, you can use what you learn about Japanese culture to improve your Japanese, see where a stereotype may come from and gain insights into your own culture.

OBENTO ELECTRIC RAILWAY

遅延証明書
（ＪＲ東日本）
12月20日（土曜日）
10分

電車が　以上の　とおり、
おくれたことを　証明します。
誠に　申し訳ございませんでした。

Questions

1 Things can be on time, early or late. For example, find out about Japanese train services. Do they generally run on time? Do people expect them to run on time?

2 What are some other factors that a Japanese person might value in a train service? For example, what is a 遅延証明書? (An example of one is shown above). Who might this be given to?

3 Compare the information you found for questions 1 and 2 with your own local public transport service. In what ways are they similar? In what ways do they differ?

4 People can be on time, early or late. Give some examples of people you know who have different attitudes towards punctuality.

5 What factors might influence these attitudes?

6 How can social pressure affect our decision to be punctual or to take a more casual approach to punctuality?

7 Do you value punctuality or do you take a more relaxed approach? Why?

8 Why do you think it is important to understand that cultures might have different attitudes to punctuality?

ゆきさんのカラオケパーティー

ISBN 9780170198271

1 What three important things about punctuality would you tell a Japanese person coming to Australia that would make their stay easier?

2 If you were in Japan, what situations can you imagine yourself in that would require you to take into account Japanese social attitudes to punctuality?

Using the sentences below, categorise each situation as either 'important to be on time for' (O) or 'don't worry about being on time for' (X) in Australia and Japan.

- (The train leaves at 1.30 p.m.) でんしゃは　ごご一時半に　でます。

- (I must be at the airport at 6.00 a.m.) ごぜん六時に　くうこうに
つかなければなりません。

- (School starts at 8.30 a.m.) がっこうは　ごぜん八時半に　はじまります。

- (Basketball practice starts at 5.00 p.m.) バスケットボールの　れんしゅうは
ごご五時に　はじまります。

- (The dentist appointment is at 2.30 p.m.) はいしゃの　よやくは
ごご二時半です。

- (I will meet friends at 11.00 a.m. on Saturday.) 土曜日の十一時に　ともだちに
あいます。

- (I will be home at about 4.00 p.m.) 四時ごろ　うちに　かえります。

- (The school concert is at 8.00 p.m.) がっこうの　コンサートは　ごご八時です。

- (The Australian Open tennis game starts at 7.00 p.m.)
オーストラリア　オープンの　テニスの　しあいは　ごご七時に　はじまります。

- (Grandma's birthday party is from 5.30 p.m.)
そぼの　たんじょう日パーティーは　五時半からです。

- (My part-time job starts at 6.30 p.m.)
アルバイトは　六時半からです。

- (The shop closes at 9.00 p.m.)
みせは　ごご九時に　しまります。

Getty Images/Toby Burrows

文法
ぶんぽう

1 Asking and telling the time

いま　何時ですか。	What time is it now?
いま　ごぜん　十時十五分です。	It is 10.15 a.m. now.
パーティーは　何時ですか。	What time is the party?
パーティーは　ごご八時四十五分です。	The party is at 8.45 p.m.

2 Asking and saying what time you do an activity

何時に　ともだちに　あいますか。	What time will you meet your friend?
一時に　ともだちに　あいます。	At 1 o'clock, I will meet my friend.

3 Asking and saying when you do an activity

いつ　テニスを　しますか。	When will you play tennis?
らいしゅう　テニスを　します。	I will play tennis next week.

4 Asking and saying where you do an activity

どこで　ともだちに　あいましたか。	Where did you meet your friend?
がっこうで　ともだちに　あいました。	I met my friend at school.

5 Inviting someone to do something

あした、　いっしょに　でかけませんか。	Won't you go out with me tomorrow?
わたしの　バナナケーキを　たべませんか。	Won't you have some of my banana cake?

6 Responding to invitations

はい、　でかけましょう。	Yes, let's go out.
すみません。　バナナケーキは　ちょっと…	Sorry. I am not really keen on banana cake.

Getty Images/Mlenny
Photography

Shutterstock.com/nevenm

Note how the meaning changes:

ましょうか　Shall we?
ましょう　let's
ませんか　Won't you?
ません　I don't/I won't

Shutterstock.com/Helenlbuxton

ゆきさんのカラオケパーティー

ISBN 9780170198271

Time (o'clock)

ごぜん	一時	いちじ	1 o'clock	a.m.
ごご	二時	にじ	2 o'clock	p.m.
	三時	さんじ	3 o'clock	
	四時	よじ	4 o'clock	
	五時	ごじ	5 o'clock	
	六時	ろくじ	6 o'clock	
	七時	しちじ	7 o'clock	
	八時	はちじ	8 o'clock	
	九時	くじ	9 o'clock	
	十時	じゅうじ	10 o'clock	
	十一時	じゅういちじ	11 o'clock	
	十二時	じゅうにじ	12 o'clock	

Shutterstock.com/sizov

Time (minutes)

五分	ごふん	5 minutes
十分	じゅっぷん	10 minutes
十五分	じゅうごふん	15 minutes
二十分	にじゅっぷん	20 minutes
二十五分	にじゅうごふん	25 minutes
三十分	さんじゅっぷん	30 minutes
三十五分	さんじゅうごふん	35 minutes
四十分	よんじゅっぷん	40 minutes
四十五分	よんじゅうごふん	45 minutes
五十分	ごじゅっぷん	50 minutes
五十五分	ごじゅうごふん	55 minutes

Time (half-past)

一時半	いちじはん	half-past one
二時半	にじはん	half-past two

Getty Images/RUNSTUDIO

Time words

いつ	when				
Past		**Present**		**Future**	
きのう	yesterday	きょう	today	あした	tomorrow
せんしゅう	last week	こんしゅう	this week	らいしゅう	next week
せん月 (げつ)	last month	こん月 (げつ)	this month	らい月 (げつ)	next month
きょねん	last year	ことし	this year	らいねん	next year

Do not use に with this group of time words.

01

Shutterstock.com/tororo reaction

Shutterstock.com/Norikazu

Getty Images/PNC

Getty Images/PhotoAlto/ Laurence Mouton

Places

うみ	beach
えいがかん	movie theatre
えき	station
がっこう	school
きっさてん	coffee shop
こうえん	park
としょかん	library
ともだちの　うち	a friend's house
まち	town/city
みせ	shop
レストラン	restaurant
やま	mountains

Verbs

たべます	eat
のみます	drink
みます	look
ききます	listen
よみます	read
かきます	write
かいます	buy
つくります	make
とります	take (photos)
うたいます	sing
します	do
おきます	wake
ねます	sleep
のります	ride
でかけます	go out
あいます	meet
いきます	go
べんきょう（を）します	study

ゆきさんのカラオケパーティー

ISBN 9780170198271

A puzzling question

Look at this invitation:

あした　ぼくの　うちに　きませんか。　(Won't you come to my house tomorrow?)
はい、いきます。　(Yes, I'll go.)

Did you notice that the invitation uses the verb きませんか, but the response is 「はい、いきます」? In English, we usually say, 'Would you like to come to my house?' and the reply is 'Yes, I would like to come'. However, it is more logical to answer 'Yes, I will go' to show you are going to someone else's house.

Particle panic!

When do you use で, に, と and を?

で

Means of transport
でんしゃで　いきました。

Places where you did something
としょかんで　よみました。

に

Places you went to
としょかんに　いきました。

Specific times when you do things
二時に　いきましょう。

と

Doing something with someone or with a pet
ともだちと　でかけました。
いぬと　あそびました。

Something you do/did

ほん　　　　　よみます
えいが　　　　みます
すし　　　　　たべます
コーラ　　　　のみます
てがみ　　　　かきます
テニス　　　　します
CD　　　　　ききました
プレゼント　　かいました

Handy hints

In both English and Japanese, building a long sentence is like lining up blocks of information. Look at this example:

Yuki → went → to the beach → with her friend by train → on Sunday.

ゆきさんは → 日曜日に → ともだちと → でんしゃで → うみに → いきました。

01

ISBN 9780170198271
ゆきさんのカラオケパーティー

スペースワールドにいきましょう!

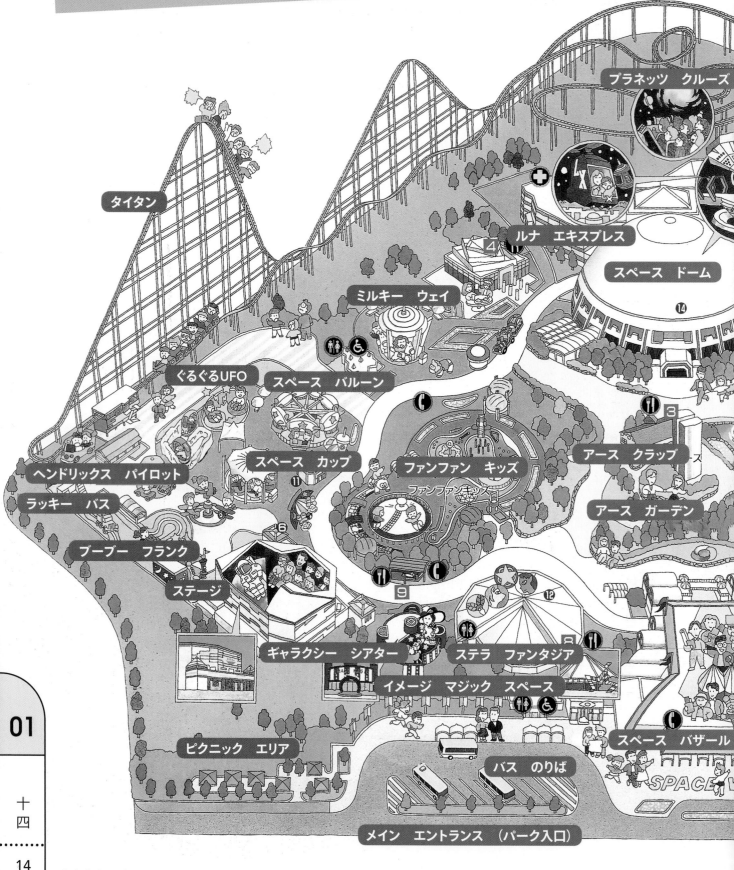

プラネッツ　クルーズ

タイタン

ルナ　エキスプレス

スペース　ドーム

ミルキー　ウェイ

ぐるぐるUFO　　スペース　バルーン

アース　クラブ

ヘンドリックス　パイロット　　スペース　カップ　　ファンファン　キッズ

ファンファンキッズ

アース　ガーデン

ラッキー　バス

ブーブー　フランク

ステージ

ギャラクシー　シアター　　ステラ　ファンタジア

イメージ　マジック　スペース

スペース　バザール

ピクニック　エリア

バス　のりば

SPACE

メイン　エントランス　（パーク入口）

ゆきさんのカラオケパーティー

ISBN 9780170198271

Look for the following places in the Space World Guide. As you find the places, read them aloud in Japanese.

Main Entrance
Galaxy Theatre
Super Planet
Black Hole Scramble
Star Shaker
Space Camp
Milky Way
Lunar Express
Lucky Bus
Fun Fun Kids
Earth Club
Stage
Space Cup

Cosmo Fighter
Space Lodge
Picnic Area
Planet Cruise
Lunar Swing
Space Balloon
Space Dome
Earth Garden
Venus
Bus Stop
Clipper
Free Fall
Stellar Fantasia

Cosmo Pier
Taxi Stand
Image Magic Space
Cosmic Eye
Vroom Vroom Frank
Titan
Hendrix Pilot
Spinning UFO
Space Coaster
Space Bazaar
Discovery Square

1.6

ブラック　ホール　スクランブル

コスモ　ピア

スター　シェイカー

スーパー　プラネット

コスモ　ファイター

スペース　コースター

コズミック　アイ

フリー　フォール

ディスカバリー　スクエア

クリッパー

スペース　ロッジ

ルナ　スウィング

スペース　キャンプ

スペースロッジ

ヴィーナス

タクシーのりば

ISBN 9780170198271

ゆきさんのカラオケパーティー

すごろくをしませんか

スタート

Say that you will go to school at 7.00 a.m.

Say that you will do your homework tomorrow.

Name four activities that you do on the weekend.

Read the clock face.

Ask what time it is and then answer: 2.25 p.m.

Invite someone to go to the park with you.

Fill in the missing particles:
土曜日＿＿＿ともだち＿＿＿でかけました。

Say in Japanese: 'Yesterday, today, tomorrow, last week, this week, next week.'

せんしゅうの　金曜日に
としょかんで　べんきょうを　しました。
What did you do? Where? When?

Say that you ate sushi at a Japanese restaurant.

Ask a friend to have lunch with you tomorrow.

＿＿＿に　テレビの　ニュースを　みます。
Supply a time for the sentence.

Name four places you can go after school.

Suggest to a friend that you go to town at 10.30 a.m.

Invite someone to come to your home next week.

Say in Japanese: 'Last month, this month, next month, last year, this year, next year.'

ごご　四時五分に　こうえんで　あいましょう。
What is it suggested you do? When? Where?

Invite a friend to sing a song with you.

ゴール

How many questions can you answer?

14–18	9–13	0–8
すごいですね! Congratulations! You are a champion!	もうちょっと… Nearly there! Go over the questions that you got wrong.	がんばって! Go over the ぶんぽう and たんご pages and try again. Good luck!

ゆきさんのカラオケパーティー

ISBN 9780170198271

ひっこし!

In this unit, you will learn to:
- say that something or someone is there
- say where something or someone is
- describe what something is like
- describe what is in your room
- recognise and write the *kanji* characters 上, 下, 中 and 前

In this unit, you will learn about:
- Japanese culture: Japanese architecture – how building design and features reflect cultural practices and environmental influences
- intercultural understanding: what makes Australian and Japanese homes distinctive
- text types: postcard, letter

Yuki has moved from Tokyo to Yamaguchi.
She sends a postcard and a letter to her friend
Daisuke to tell him about her new home.

「みて! はがきです。ゆきさんから!」

moved house

address

Please come over.

ひっこしを しました。
あたらしい じゅうしょです。
あそびに きてください。
〒753-0046
山口県 山口市 本町 １９０５番地
電話 083-973-0472

だいすけくんへ、
こんにちは。おげんきですか。
わたしは いま あたらしい うちに すんでいます。
とても すてきです。わたしの あたらしい うちは 山口に あります。
山口は しずかな まちです。東京の アパートは とても せまかったです。
でも、あたらしい うちは とても ひろいです。いまも だいどころも
おおきいです。ちいさい たたみの へやも あります。きれいな にわも
ありますよ。にわの しゃしんを みてください。いもうとと いぬが います。
いぬの なまえは ポチ です。かわいい いぬでしょう。

very

both ... and ...

Don't you
think?

わたしの へやは とても あかるいです。へやに ベッドと つくえと
いすと 本だなと テレビと DVDプレーヤーが あります。ベッドの
上に ぬいぐるみが たくさんあります。くまや パンダ などです。わたしは
ぬいぐるみが だいすきです。つくえの よこに 本だなが あります。
本だなの 中に まんがや ざっしや DVDが たくさん あります。
つくえの 上に でんき スタンドや コンピューターが あります。
わたしは あたらしい うちが だいすきです。でも、まだ ともだちが
いません。ちょっと さびしいです。みんなに また あいたいです。
だいすけくん、みんなと いっしょに あそびに きませんか。
じゃあ、またね
3月17日 金曜日
まつだ ゆきより

a lot

bear

but

sad

Won't you
come over?

not yet

I want to see
you again.

〒194-0021
東京都 町田市 中町 ５丁目485-9
本田 だいすけ 様

AIR MAIL

ひっこし!

ISBN 9780170198271

While unpacking her belongings, Yuki misplaces several items.

おかあさん、ふでばこは どこに ありますか。

ちいさい はこの 中に あります。

あれ？ おかあさん、でんき スタンドは どこに ありますか。

つくえの 上に あります。

おかあさん、ぬいぐるみは どこに ありますか。

本だなの 前に あります。

おかあさん、ざっしは どこに ありますか。

ベッドの 下に ありますよ。

おかあさん、ポチは どこに いますか。

うちの そとに います。

ねえ、ねえ、おかあさん、わたしの けいたいでんわは…

うるさいなあ… しりませんよ。

Comic by Mami Yamanaka

しりませんよ　I don't know

Questions

1　Where is Yuki's new home?
2　How does she compare her old and new homes?
3　What is her new home like?
4　Describe Yuki's room. What is on her bed?
5　What is on the bookshelf? What about on Yuki's desk?
6　How is Yuki feeling?
7　When did Yuki write the letter?
8　What is Yuki looking for?

02

十
九

19

ISBN 9780170198271

ひっこし！

れんしゅう

1 Asking and saying something or someone is there

A:	Placeに person/animalが います か。
A:	Placeに itemが あります か。
B:	はい、います。 いいえ、いません。
B:	はい、あります。 いいえ、ありません。
一	うちに いぬが いますか。
	いいえ、いません。ねこが います。
二	へやに テレビが ありますか。
	いいえ、ありません。コンピューターが あります。

2 Asking or saying where something or someone is

A:	Person/animalは どこに いますか。
A:	Itemは どこに ありますか。
B:	Person/animalは ～の ～に います。
B:	Itemは ～の ～に あります。
一	おかあさんは どこに いますか。
	おかあさんは テレビの よこに います。
二	ごみばこは どこに ありますか。
	つくえの 下に あります。

たんご

わしつ	上
だいどころ	前
にわ	うしろ

ひっこし!

ISBN 9780170198271

3 Describing what is in your room

A:	Placeに　なにが　ありますか。
B:	Itemや　itemや　itemなどが　あります。
一	へやに　何が　ありますか。
	コンピューターや　とけいや　ごみばこなどが　あります。

4 Describing what something or someone is like

A:	どんな　へやですか。
B:	Adjectiveい　へやです。 Adjectiveな　へやです。
一	どんな　へやですか。
	あかるい　へやです。
二	どんな　ひとですか。
	べんりな　ひとです。

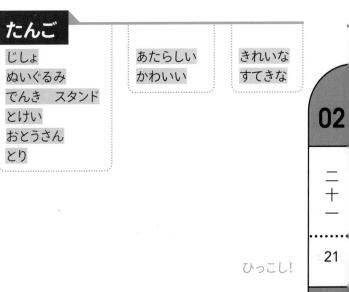

たんご

じしょ ぬいぐるみ でんき　スタンド とけい おとうさん とり	あたらしい かわいい	きれいな すてきな

02

二十一

21

ISBN 9780170198271

ひっこし！

These are the *kanji* and their readings introduced in this unit.

うえ／ジョウ on top/above

上

A ninja is standing above the line.

一	卜	上					

上に → うえに → above/on top of
テーブルの　上に → テーブルの　うえに → on top of the table
はこの　上に → はこの　うえに → above the box
水上スキー → すいじょうスキー → water skiing

した under/below

下

A ninja is hanging upside down below the line.

一	丅	下					

下に → したに → below/under
ベッドの　下に → ベッドの　したに → below the bed
テレビの　下に → テレビの　したに → under the TV
つくえの　下に　あります。 → つくえの　したに　あります。 → It is under the desk.

なか／チュウ inside/in the middle

中

A ninja is standing in the middle of a circle.

丶	冂	口	中				

中に → なかに → in the middle of/inside
はこの　中 → はこの　なか → inside the box
中学 → ちゅうがく → junior high school
じゅぎょう中 → じゅぎょうちゅう → during class

まえ／ゼン in front of/before

前

Two people are standing in front of a house.

丶	丷	亠	广	屰	前	前	前
前							

うちの　前に → うちの　まえに → in front of the house
あさごはんの　前に → あさごはんの　まえに → before breakfast
な前 → なまえ → name
ご前 → ごぜん → a.m.

ひっこし!

ISBN 9780170198271

日本文化
にほんぶんか

Traditional housing

Japan has a diverse range of housing, from traditional houses with wood and paper screens (しょうじ), to small apartments (アパート、マンション), popular with singles and university students.

All housing styles have some things in common. These pages give you an idea of the types of houses you might expect to find in Japan.

Naomi's grandmother's house

なおみさんの　おばあさんの　うちは　でんとうてきな　うちです。

In the formal entrance (げんかん) you remove your shoes and step up a level. Put on the slippers waiting for you, but don't step onto the lower floor without shoes.

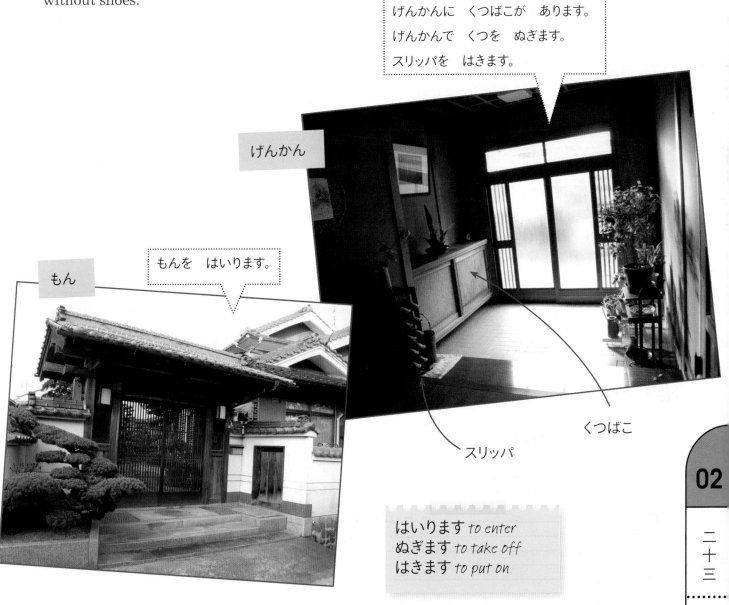

げんかんに　くつばこが　あります。
げんかんで　くつを　ぬぎます。
スリッパを　はきます。

げんかん

もんを　はいります。

もん

くつばこ

スリッパ

はいります *to enter*
ぬぎます *to take off*
はきます *to put on*

02

二十三

23

ISBN 9780170198271

ひっこし！

Awareness of nature is central to Japanese aesthetics. Sliding doors open wide to bring the outside in. The verandah (えんがわ) is a place to relax and enjoy the garden. Heavy glass doors keep the cold and rain out.

A traditional house emphasises the use of wood and natural materials. Rooms are small, but screens and sliding doors (ふすま and しょうじ) can be removed or opened to make the rooms bigger.

There may be rooms with tables, sofas and chairs, but a たたみ room (わしつ) does not use chairs with legs. In わしつ you might find a こたつ used as both furniture and heating.

Japanese rooms are measured by the number of たたみ mats, not in metres. Even apartments often have a space with たたみ.

えんがわ

わしつは　たたみの　へやです。
わしつに　たたみと　ざぶとんが　あります。
そして、　とこのまが　あります。

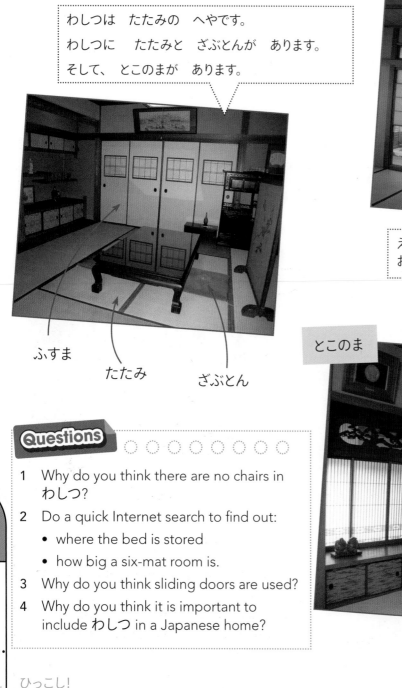

ふすま
たたみ
ざぶとん

えんがわで　にわを　みます。
おちゃを　のみます。

とこのまに　かけじくと
いけばなが　あります。　きれいです。

とこのま

Questions ◦◦◦◦◦◦◦◦◦

1 Why do you think there are no chairs in わしつ?

2 Do a quick Internet search to find out:
   - where the bed is stored
   - how big a six-mat room is.

3 Why do you think sliding doors are used?

4 Why do you think it is important to include わしつ in a Japanese home?

ひっこし！

ISBN 9780170198271

Modern housing

Naomi's sister's apartment

なおみさんの　おねえさんの　アパートは　ちいさいです。
おねえさんは　一人で　アパートに　すんでいます。

In a small studio apartment, favoured by many Japanese
students, you have everything you need in a compact space.
As you can see from the photos, space is an issue in Japanese
homes and needs to be used effectively.

ふろばです。
おふろに　はいります。
はを　みがきます。

おふろ

シャワー

げんかんです。
ちいさいとだなが　あります。

トイレも　せまいです。　でも、
べんりです。　あたらしい　トイレです。
水を　リサイクルします。

トイレ

てを　あらいます。

とだな

とだな *cabinet/closet*

だいどころは　とても　ちいさいです。
おねえさんは　りょうりが　きらいです。
よく、　レストランに　いきます。

トイレ

だいどころ

しんしつです。
ベッドの　下に　おおきい　たなが　あります。
つくえの　上に　テレビが　あります。

ベッド

たな

しんしつ

ステップ

Questions ○○○○○○○○○○○

1 List the design features that maximise
   space.
2 Create a visual presentation of your
   home or ideal house, in Japanese.

二十五

ISBN 9780170198271

ひっこし！

だいはっけん

Home design and features

Japanese homes are as varied in their design as Australian homes. Nonetheless, there are some features that make Japanese homes distinctive, reflecting the lifestyles and living conditions in Japan.

Consider some of the typical features of Japanese houses – where and how they are built, what they are made of and what you might find inside.

Quirks and perks

To provide a safe and comfortable lifestyle, houses need to be built according to the environment and climate in which they are located. This can result in some interesting quirks, such as wooden foundations and elevated flooring to avoid moisture build-up.

While elevated flooring in Japan originated to accommodate the environment, raised floors on the inside of a home can sometimes help to indicate when you need to take your shoes or slippers off. For example, when you enter a home in Japan, the floor around the entrance (げんかん) may be raised by around 15 centimetres or more, which signals that you need to swap your shoes for house slippers. A tatami room (わしつ) may be raised by a few centimetres, meaning that you need to remove your slippers. When you use the toilet in a traditional Japanese home, you may also be asked to swap your house slippers for special toilet slippers. These customs all originated from the very practical wish to keep the home clean.

Shutterstock.com/Neale Cousland

ひっこし!

ISBN 9780170198271

Questions

1 Research two other interesting quirks of Japanese houses. (There are many!) Look at a variety of housing in rural, city and coastal areas in Japan. You might like to use an online street-view map to find examples. Share your findings with a classmate and, together, create a brief slideshow presentation to show your findings to the rest of the class.

2 Choose a house in Japan and compare its features with your own home. You can do this in a table. For ideas, refer to task 23 in the *Obento Supreme Workbook*.

3 List the things you couldn't live without from one room in your house (for example, the kitchen, living room or study) and find out if these are the same essentials in a Japanese house.

Shutterstock.com/Dementeva
Marina&NatashaNaSt

Have a think

1 Investigate some of the customs and language related to entering and leaving a Japanese home. Can you identify any customs that relate to the different housing styles?

2 How would a person in Japan answer the following questions? Use the Internet to research the answers.
   • Where do you put your shoes?
   • What shoes do you wear around the house?
   • How do you make your bed?
   • When do you have a bath?

3 Would the answers to question 2 differ if someone in Australia was answering them? If yes, how would they differ?

Have a go

With a partner, role-play a scenario where you are either entering or leaving a Japanese home. Make sure you use the new language you have learnt, and that you behave according to Japanese custom. Some example scenarios that you could role-play in Japanese are:
• arriving at a friend's home
• entering a friend's home
• leaving a relative's home
• saying farewell to someone leaving your home.

Shutterstock.com/Hinochika

ひっこし！

ぶんぽう

Shutterstock.com/WEGO Pics

1 Asking and saying if something or someone is there

A:	へやに　しゃしんが　ありますか。	Are there photos in the room?
B:	はい、　あります。 (non-moving things)	Yes, there is/are.
B:	いいえ、　ありません。	No, there isn't/aren't.
A:	にわに　いぬが　いますか。	Is there a dog in the garden?
B:	はい、　います。 (living things)	Yes, there is/are.
B:	いいえ、　いません。	No, there isn't/aren't.

2 Asking or saying where something or someone is

A:	コンピューターは　どこに　ありますか。	Where is the computer?
B:	コンピューターは　つくえの　上に　あります。	The computer is on top of the desk.
A:	ねこは　どこに　いますか。	Where is the cat?
B:	ねこは　いすの　下に　います。	The cat is under the chair.

3 Describing what is in your room

A:	へやに　何が　ありますか。	What is in the room?
B:	へやに　しんぶんと　ざっしと　本が　あります。	There are newspapers, magazines and books in the room.
B:	つくえの　上に　ふでばこや　でんき　スタンド　などが　あります。	On the desk there is a pencil case and a lamp, among other things.

4 Describing what something or someone is like

A:	どんな　うちですか。	What kind of house is it?
B:	ひろい　うちです。	It is a spacious house.
B:	すてきな　うちです。	It is a wonderful house.

は and が

は and が have no English meaning, but they are important grammar tools in Japanese.

Where do the particles appear in a sentence?

Placeに　itemが　あります／います。

いまに　テレビが　あります。　There is a TV in the living room.

Itemは　placeに　あります／います。

テレビは　いまに　あります。　The TV is in the living room.

You can recognise the particles through English cues.

There is/there are　→　use が

にわに　ねこが　います。　There is a cat in the garden.

The item/thing is　→　use は

ねこは　にわに　います。　The cat is in the garden.

ひっこし！

ISBN 9780170198271

たんご

iStockphoto/karam miri

Houses and rooms

うち	house
アパート	flat/unit/apartment
マンション	apartment/apartment building
いま	living room
だいどころ	kitchen
トイレ	toilet
にわ	garden
へや	room
たたみの　へや	tatami room
しんしつ	bedroom
ようしつ	Western-style room
わしつ	Japanese-style room

Furniture and objects found in a room

つくえ	desk
ベッド	bed
コンピューター	computer
ＤＶＤ　プレーヤー	DVD player
テーブル	table
テレビ	TV
でんき　スタンド	lamp
とけい	clock
けいたいでんわ	mobile phone
ざっし	magazine
じしょ	dictionary
しゃしん	photo
しんぶん	newspaper
ぬいぐるみ	soft toy
はがき	postcard
えんぴつ	pencil
けしゴム	eraser
ものさし	ruler
はこ	box
ふでばこ	pencil case
ごみばこ	rubbish bin
本ばこ／本だな	bookcase/bookshelf
ふとん	Japanese bed
ざぶとん	Japanese-style cushion

Corbis

Shutterstock.com/szsz

Locations

上	above
いすの　上に	on top of the chair
下	below
ベッドの　下に	under the bed
前	in front of
本だなの　前に	in front of the bookshelf
うしろ	behind
つくえの　うしろに	behind the desk
中	inside
はこの　中に	in the box
そと	outside
うちの　そとに	outside the house
よこ	next to
テレビの　よこに	next to the TV
となり	next to
にわの　となりに	next to the garden

Shutterstock.com/
Anton Balazh

Shutterstock.com/Tomislav Stajduhar

Shutterstock.com/siraphat

Describing words

どんな	what kind of ...?
どんな　ひと	what kind of person?
あかるい	bright
くらい	dark
あたらしい	new
ふるい	old
いい	good
わるい	bad
ひろい	spacious
せまい	narrow
おおきい	big
ちいさい	small
かわいい	cute
きたない	dirty
うるさい	noisy
しずか（な）	quiet
きれい（な）	pretty/clean
すてき（な）	wonderful
べんり（な）	convenient
すき（な）	likable (favourite)
きらい（な）	unlikable

The past tense of いい *is* よかった.

三十

ひっこし！

ISBN 9780170198271

ぶんぽうプラス

あります and います

These two words mean the same thing, so how are they different? Can you guess from the examples on the right?

あります is used for inanimate objects – things that can't move around by themselves. This includes trees and plants.

います is used for animals and people – even if they are not alive any more!

うち	ぬいぐるみ	つくえ
	あります	
へや		えんぴつ
	ほん	

	ともだち	
ねこ		おかあさん
	います	
おにいさん		いぬ

Adjectives

Some adjectives end in い. For others you need to use な between the adjective and the noun.

This is important to remember as the two types of adjectives have different grammatical rules. How are they used?

- Something they have in common → both can be followed by です.

  おおきいです。　　　　　　(It is big.)

  しずかです。*　　　　　　(It is quiet.)

- Something different → you need to use な when an adjective is used before a noun.

  おおきい　うちです。　　　(It is a big house.)

  すてきな　うちです。　　　(It is a wonderful house.)

*You cannot say しずかなです because な here is not followed by a noun.

It isn't easy to remember which type is which, but if an adjective ends in い then it usually doesn't use な. It is useful to remember the exceptions. There aren't many – they look like い-adjectives but actually take な: きれい, きらい, ゆうめい and とくい.

Getty Images/DAJ

Shutterstock.com/Luftikus

Particle panic!

と and や both mean 'and', but the difference is:

- と means you have to name all the items
- や means you only have to name some of them.

For example:

テーブルの　上に　ペンと　えんぴつと　はさみと　けしごむと　ものさしと　ふでばこが　あります。
(On the table there are pens, pencils, scissors, an eraser, a ruler and a pencil case.)

テーブルの　上に　ペンや　けしごむや　ものさしなどが　あります。*
(On the table there is a pen, eraser, ruler, etc.)

*など (etc.) can be dropped at any time.

Shutterstock.com/DiverS-VectoR

ISBN 9780170198271

02

三十一

ひっこし！

エクストラ

Daisuke's reply

Daisuke writes a letter to Yuki.

ゆきさんへ、

おげんきですか。

てがみを　どうも　ありがとう。

ゆきさんの　あたらしい　うちの　しゃしんを　みました。

あたらしい　うちは　いいですね。　ぼくの　うちは　せまいです。

へやに　コンピューターが　ありますね。　いいなあ。

ポチは　かわいい　いぬですね!

せんしゅう　けんいちくんと　いっしょに　えいがに　いきました。

えいがは　とても　よかったです。　でも、　ゆきさんが　いません。

だから、　けんいちくんは　ちょっと　さびしそうです。

ゆきさんの　あたらしい　Eメール　アドレスは　何ですか。

はやく　へんじを　くださいね。

ごかぞくの　みなさんに　どうぞ　よろしく。

じゃあ、　また。

三月二十一日　火曜日

本田　だいすけより

very

that's why

seems sad

Useful phrases for letters and emails

ゆきさんへ、	Dear Yuki
おげんきですか。	How are you?
ひさしぶりですね。	It has been a long time.
ながい　あいだ、　てがみを　かかなくて、　すみませんでした。	I am sorry I haven't written to you for a long time.
てがみを　どうも　ありがとう　ございました。	Thank you very much for your letter.
てがみを　ください。	Please send me a letter.
おへんじを　かいてください。	Please write back.
おへんじを　たのしみに　しています。	I am looking forward to your reply.
ごかぞくに　どうぞ　よろしく。	Give my regards to your family.
おからだに　きを　つけて。	Take care of yourself.
じゃあ、　また。	See you later.

Getty Images/© UnderConcept, Atsushi Hasegawa, Ph.D.

02

三十二

32

ひっこし!

ISBN 9780170198271

あたらしい学校

In this unit, you will learn to:

- talk about school grades
- talk about school subjects
- use から and まで when talking about specific times
- use the negative
- compare things (say the best and the most)
- give reasons
- write an article about your school, teachers and friends
- recognise and write the *kanji* characters 学, 校, 年 and 生

In this unit, you will learn about:

- Japanese culture: introduction to a Japanese high school, and what school life is like
- intercultural understanding: everything that you would tell a Japanese exchange student about an Australian school to make their stay easier, and vice versa
- text types: interview, timetable, personal profile

Getty Images/Ryuhei Shindo

Yuki went to an orientation day at her new school. She was interviewed by the principal.

インタビュー

▶ **Principal:** ゆきさんは 何年生ですか。

▶ **Yuki:** わたしは 中学 三年生です。

▶ **P:** あ、三年生ですか。どんな かもくを べんきょう していますか。

▶ **Y:** えいごと こくごと れきしと すう学と か学と おんがくと びじゅつと たいいくを べんきょう しています。

▶ **P:** そうですか。ちりを べんきょう していますか。

▶ **Y:** いいえ、ちりを べんきょうしていません。

▶ **P:** そうですか。でも、あたらしい 学校で らいしゅうから ちりを べんきょう しますよ。

▶ **Y:** ああ、そうですか。ちりは むずかしいですか。

▶ **P:** いいえ、むずかしくないです。たのしいですよ。一ばん とくいな かもくは 何ですか。

▶ **Y:** ええと、一ばん とくいな かもくは えいごです。

▶ **P:** あら、そう？ どうしてですか。

▶ **Y:** えいごの せん生は とても おもしろかったです。きびしくなかったです。そして、えいごの うたを うたいました。それから、ゲームも しました。だから、えいごが だいすきです。

▶ **P:** そうですか。あたらしい えいごの せん生も とても やさしいですよ。

▶ **Y:** えー。よかった。

▶ **P:** 一ばん にがてな かもくは 何ですか。

▶ **Y:** たいいくです。あまり とくいじゃないです。

▶ **P:** そうですか。たいいくの せん生も やさしいですよ。じゃあ、しつもんが ありますか。

▶ **Y:** はい、あります。学校は 何時から 何時までですか。

▶ **P:** 学校は ご前 八時四十分から ごご 三時三十五分までです。これは 時かんわりです。どうぞ。

▶ **Y:** ありがとう ございます。

the study of your mother tongue

Oh, really?

(We) also played games.

Do you have questions?

This is your timetable.

Questions

1 What school grade is Yuki in? What subjects is she studying now?

2 What is Yuki's favourite subject? Why? What is her weakest subject?

3 What question does Yuki ask the principal?

あたらしい学校

ISBN 9780170198271

れんしゅう

		月曜日	火曜日	水曜日	木曜日	金曜日
	南　中学校　時かんわり					
ホームルーム	8.40–8.50					
一時かんめ	8.55–9.45	か学	すう学	ちり	えいご	こくご
二時かんめ	9.55–10.45	れきし	えいご	こくご	か学	びじゅつ
三時かんめ	10.55–11.45	ちり	か学	ほけん	すう学	れきし
四時かんめ	11.55–12.45	こくご	おん学	すう学	かていか	えいご
ひる休み	12.45–1.20					
五時かんめ	1.25–2.15	すう学	たいいく	かていか	こくご	すう学
六時かんめ	2.25–3.15	えいごコミュニケーション	びじゅつ	か学	おんがく	たいいく
ホームルーム／そうじ	3.15–3.35					

(南 = みなみ、中 = ちゅう)

1 Talking about school grades

A:	何年生ですか。
B:	Year 年生です。
一	何年生ですか。
	中学　三年生です。
二	だいすけくんは　何年生ですか。
	こうこう　一年生です。

2 Talking about school subjects

A:	どんな　かもくを　べんきょうしていますか。
B:	Subjectや　Subjectや　Subjectなどを　べんきょうしています。
一	どんな　かもくを　べんきょうしていますか。
	えいごや　すう学や　日本ごなどを　べんきょうしています。

3 Saying from what time to what time

A:	学校は　何時から　何時までですか。
B:	学校は　timeから　timeまでです。
一	一時かんめは　何時からですか。
	八時五十五分からです。
二	ひる休みは　何時までですか。
	ごご　一時二十分までです。
三	キャンプは　いつから　いつまでですか。
	水曜日から　金曜日までです。

Ioan-Liviu Orletchi

たんご

しょう学　六年生 だい学　一年生	たいいく　　ちり びじゅつ　　休み れきし	六時かんめ	2.25から 9.45まで 金曜日から　金曜日まで

03

三十五

ISBN 9780170198271

あたらしい学校

4 Using the negative

A:	すう学は　い-adjective くないです。
A:	すう学は　な-adjective じゃないです。
一	すう学は　むずかしくないです。
二	たいいくの　せん生は　きびしくないです。　やさしいです。
三	日本ごの　クラスは　あまり　しずかじゃないです。
四	ゆきさんは　スポーツが　ぜんぜん　とくいじゃないです。

5 Comparing things
(saying the best and the most)

A:	一ばん　い-adjective せん生は　～です。
A:	一ばん　な-adjectiveな　かもくは　～です。
一	一ばん　きびしい　せん生は　えいごの　せん生です。
二	一ばん　すきな　かもくは　日本ごです。

6 Giving reasons

A:	どうして　日本語が　すきですか。
B:	日本語は　たのしいです。　だから、　日本語が　すきです。
一	どうして　おんがくが　すきですか。
	うたを　うたいます。　だから、　おんがくが　です。
二	どうして　かていかは　たのしいですか。
	おいしい　りょうりを　つくります。　だから、　かていかは　たのしいです。
三	どうして　きのう　おべんとうを　かいませんでしたか。
	おべんとうは　たかかったです。　だから、　かいませんでした。

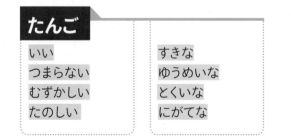

たんご

いい	すきな
つまらない	ゆうめいな
むずかしい	とくいな
たのしい	にがてな

ISBN 9780170198271

Getty Images/Ryuhei Shindo

漢字
かんじ

These are the *kanji* and their readings introduced in this unit.

ガク to learn

学　学

A child, with arms out, stands under a roof with three rain drops.

、	゛	ツ	⺌	丷	学	学	学

中学 → ちゅうがく → junior high school
すう学 → すうがく → maths
か学 → かがく → science

コウ school

校

Every school has trees and students.

一	十	才	木	朾	栌	栌	栌
栌	校						

学校 → がっこう → school
こう校 → こうこう → senior high school

とし／ネン year

年

Once a year, you can cut your birthday cake.

ノ	⺊	乍	匞	年	年		

一年 → いちねん → one year
二年半 → にねんはん → two and a half years
何年 → なんねん → How many years?
こ年 → ことし → this year

セイ student

生

A student has a pen in his hand.

ノ	⺊	牛	牛	生			

何年生 → なんねんせい → What school grade?
九年生 → きゅうねんせい → Year 9
中学生 → ちゅうがくせい → junior high school student
学生 → がくせい → university student

03

三十七

ISBN 9780170198271

あたらしい学校

わたしは　あやかです。
高校二年生です。　わたしの
<ruby>高校<rt>こうこう</rt></ruby>二年生です。
学校の　な前は
ふじみがおか学えんです。
わたしの　学校は　<ruby>女子校<rt>じょしこう</rt></ruby>です。

girls' high school

わたしの　学校は　とうきょうの　しぶやに　あります。
わたしの　学校に　中学校と　<ruby>高校<rt>こうこう</rt>があります。

きょうしつは　とても　きれいです。
ホームルームの　あとで　そうじを　します。

学校は　ご前　八時二十五分から　ごご
四時十五分　までです。
げんかんに　くつばこと　かさたてが　あります。
そして、　ロッカーが　あります。

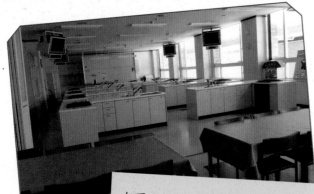

かていかを　べんきょうします。
キッチンと　ダイニングルームが
あります。　りょうりの　あとで、
ダイニングルームで　たべます。
りょうりは　たのしいですよ。

生ぶつの　きょうしつです。
せん生は　とても　きびしいですよ。
そして、　しゅくだいが　たくさん　あります。
生ぶつは　いちばん　おもしろい　かもくです。

ISBN 9780170198271

tea ceremony room

ちゃしつも　あります。
ちゃしつで　さどうを　します。
おちゃを　のみます。
そして、おかしを　たべます。
ちゃしつは　わしつです。
とこのまが　あります。

when you are sick

nurse

ほけんしつです。びょうきの　とき、
ほけんしつで　ねます。
かんごしの　たかだせん生は
やさしいです。

ざぶとんに　すわりましょう。

ソーラーパネルで
クリーンエネルギーを
つくります。

わたしの　学校で　まいにち
リサイクルを　します。
リサイクルのかみで
トイレットペーパーを　つくります。

としょかんで　まいにち
コンピューターを　つかいます。

Have a go ○ ○ ○ ○ ○ ○ ○ ○ ○ ○ ○

In pairs, ask and answer the following questions.
1　あなたの　学校は　どんな　学校ですか。
2　何時から　何時まで　ですか。
3　どんな　きょうしつが　ありますか。
4　あなたの　学校で　リサイクルを　しますか。

たいいくかんです。たいいくかんで、
バスケットボールや　バレーボールが
できます。
学校の　あとで　からての　クラブを
します。

ISBN 9780170198271

Alamy/MBI

Education

As you might expect, there are some significant differences between the education systems and the school environments in Australia and Japan.

To find out more about the differences investigate and compare lunch menus, timetables, maps, pictures, school brochures, subject lists, school rules, textbooks, uniforms and more from both countries. You will find school websites a particularly handy reference. Choose a few to look at closely, but don't worry if you can't understand all the Japanese you see or hear.

One aspect of school life to compare is lunchtime. Many Japanese public high schools offer 給食 (*kyushoku*), which is school lunch funded by the local government. 給食 is a nutritionally balanced school lunch, sometimes with a different menu each day on a regular rotation. Each region has its own selection of meals that make up the 給食. While in the past they included only traditional Japanese dishes, today they also include international food such as sandwiches and spaghetti. However, not every Japanese region offers 給食. There are also schools that offer fixed canteen menus (offering hot food such as ラーメン, うどん and カレーライス, for example). Also, many students choose to bring their own lunch from home.

An example of a menu that appears on a weekly rotation is shown below.

Corbis/TWPhoto

ひるごはんのメニュー

月曜日	火曜日	水曜日	木曜日	金曜日
ハンバーガー ミルク デザート	てんぷらうどん おちゃ ヨーグルト	サンドイッチ ジュース デザート	カレーうどん みず ヨーグルト	ホットドッグ サラダ　ミルク

Photos by Shutterstock.com/Dan Peretz, Shutterstock.com/ifong, Shutterstock.com/stocksolutions, Shutterstock.com/Norikazu, Shutterstock.com/Brenda Carson

あたらしい学校

ISBN 9780170198271

Take a closer look at the menu on the previous page. Some differences between your school menu and this menu are the types of dishes and the variety of food on offer. For example, some of the dishes are examples of traditional Japanese cuisine (e.g. てんぷらそば), while others (ホットドッグ) are more modern examples of international foods. How does this compare with your school's canteen menu? Does your school have a menu? Would it be true to say that most Australian schools don't work on a rotational menu as some Japanese schools do, but instead offer the same choices each day? The answers to these questions will help you to piece together some observations about differences between school life in Japan and in Australia.

Language challenge: show and tell

1   Go back to the original list of information that you could research, on the previous page. Choose another example to investigate online, and then make some further key observations. Depending on your resources, you might look into classroom sizes, school grounds and buildings, curriculum, sport and activities, assessment, study, student attitudes, expectations of students, learning English in Japan, and so on.

2   Develop your findings into a presentation that identifies differences and similarities between your own education and education in Japan. You could present your findings in a chart, a poster, a visual diary, a manga or a slideshow with captions.

Photo Japan/Kenneth Hamm

Fairfax Syndication

Have a go

1   Imagine Yuki is a Japanese exchange student coming to your school next week. To help her adjust, make a list of things to tell her about school in Australia.

2   You have just arrived in Japan on an exchange. The students are keen to hear what school life is like in Australia, so the teacher asks you to do a one-minute talk. What will you tell them? Because your time is short, make sure that you highlight the key differences.

03

四
十
一

ISBN 9780170198271

あたらしい学校

iStockphoto/zhu difeng

1 Talking about school grades

何年生ですか。	わたしは　中学　三年生です。
What school grade are you?	I am a Year 3 student at junior high school (Year 9).

2 Talking about school subjects

どんな　かもくを べんきょうしていますか。	えいごや　すう学や　れきしなどを べんきょう　しています。
What subjects are you studying?	I am studying English, Maths, History, etc.

3 Saying from what time to what time

学校は　何時から　何時までですか。	学校は　ご前　八時半から ごご　三時二十五分までです。
What time does school start and finish?	School is from 8.30 a.m. to 3.25 p.m.

4 Using the negative

日本ごは　むずかしくないです。
Japanese is not difficult.
おんがくの　クラスは　しずかじゃないです。
Music class is not quiet.

Getty Images/Michael Hitoshi

5 Comparing things (saying the best and the most)

一ばん　おもしろい　かもくは　か学です。
The most interesting subject is Science.
一ばん　すきな　かもくは　びじゅつです。
My favourite subject is Art.

Alamy/Ian Shaw

6 Giving reasons

どうして　日本ごが　すきですか。	ゲームを　します。　だから、　日本ごが　すきです。
Why do you like Japanese?	We play games. That's why I like Japanese.

ISBN 9780170198271

3, 2, 3, 6

Subjects

えいご
English

おんがく
Music

日本ご
Japanese

ちり
Geography

フランスご
French

れきし
History

イタリアご
Italian

けいざい
Economics

コンピューター
Computer (Information Technology)

びじゅつ
Art

すう学
Maths

ぎじゅつ
Design and Technology

か学
Science

たいいく
Physical Education

かていか
Home Economics

ほけん
Health and Human Development

03

四十三

3.4, 3.8

Timetable terms

ホームルーム	homeroom
一時かんめ	period 1
二時かんめ	period 2
三時かんめ	period 3
四時かんめ	period 4
ひる休み	lunch break
五時かんめ	period 5
六時かんめ	period 6
そうじ	clean up
クラブ　かつどう	club activity
ほうかご	after school

School

しょう学校	primary school
中学	middle school/ junior high school
こう校	senior high school

い-adjectives

いい	good	よくない	not good
うるさい	noisy	うるさくない	not noisy
おもしろい	interesting	おもしろくない	not interesting
きびしい	strict	きびしくない	not strict
たのしい	fun	たのしくない	not fun
つまらない	boring	つまらなくない	not boring
むずかしい	difficult	むずかしくない	not difficult
やさしい	kind/easy	やさしくない	not kind/easy
わるい	bad	わるくない	not bad

School grades

Japanese school grades		English	Australian school grades	
しょう学校	一年生 二年生 三年生 四年生 五年生 六年生	primary	Yr 1 Yr 2 Yr 3 Yr 4 Yr 5 Yr 6	一年生 二年生 三年生 四年生 五年生 六年生
中学	一年生 二年生 三年生	junior high	Yr 1 Yr 7 Yr 2 Yr 8 Yr 3 Yr 9	七年生 八年生 九年生
こう校	一年生 二年生 三年生	senior high	Yr 1 Yr 10 Yr 2 Yr 11 Yr 3 Yr 12	十年生 十一年生 十二年生
だい学	一年生 二年生 三年生 四年生	university	Yr 1 Yr 1 Yr 2 Yr 2 Yr 3 Yr 3 Yr 4 Yr 4	一年生 二年生 三年生 四年生

な-adjectives

きらい (な)	dislike	きらいじゃない	don't dislike
きれい (な)	pretty/clean	きれいじゃない	not pretty/not clean
しずか (な)	quiet	しずかじゃない	not quiet
すき (な)	like/favourite	すきじゃない	don't like
すてき (な)	nice	すてきじゃない	not nice
でんとうてき (な)	traditional	でんとうてきじゃない	not traditional
とくい (な)	good at	とくいじゃない	not good at
べんり (な)	convenient	べんりじゃない	not convenient
にがて (な)	bad at	にがてじゃない	not bad at
ゆうめい (な)	famous	ゆうめいじゃない	not famous

あたらしい学校

ISBN 9780170198271

There is a subtle difference between these pairs of words.

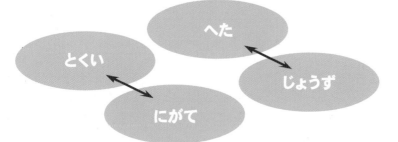

Do you remember learning じょうず and へた? These words describe your skill level.
じょうず = good at
へた　　 = bad at

The new words とくい and にがて describe a person's personal strengths and weaknesses. とくい is for a person's strong points, and にがて is for a person's weak points. The good thing to remember is that all these words are な-adjectives.

Particle panic!

Take a look at the following sentence pattern.

	は		が		です。
スコットくん	は	たいいく	が	にがて	です。

は is used to talk about a person or a topic, while が tells you something about that person or topic. We are talking about Scott and we are saying that Physical Education is his weak point.

Words of frequency

まい日　every day	よく　often	時どき　sometimes

These words are all used with positive verb endings.

まい日　あさごはんを　たべます。　　　　　(I eat breakfast every day.)
よく　コンピューターを　つかいます。　　　(I often use the computer.)
時どき　ともだちに　でんわをします。　　　(Sometimes I phone my friend.)

あんまり not much	ぜんぜん not at all

These words are used with negative endings.

ケーキが　すきじゃないです。　だから、　あんまり　たべません。
(I don't like cakes. So, I don't eat them much.)

だから、ぜんぜん　たべません。　(So, I don't eat them at all.)

まい, meaning 'every', has other applications
(see examples on the right).

まいあさ	every morning
まいばん	every night
まい日	every day
まいしゅう	every week
まい月	every month
まい年	every year

03

四
十
五

エクストラ

Shutterstock.com/East

ぼくの学校

こんにちは。　ぼくは　にしむら　たかしです。

ぼくは　こうりつ　こう校の　一年生です。

まい日、　九時から　二時まで　アルバイトを　しています。

きっさてんの　アルバイトです。　シェフの　しごとです。　だから、　ぼくは

てい時せいの　こう校で　べんきょう　しています。

てい時せいの　こう校は　ごご　五時半から　九時までです。

学校で　すう学や　こくごや　か学や　ちりを　べんきょう　しています。

学校の　あとで　しゅくだいを　します。　たいへんです。

でも、　がんばります。

public high school

working part time

work

part-time high school

hard

I do my best.

Getty Images/Rubberball/
Mike Kemp

せん生　しょうかい

ぼくの　せん生を　しょうかい　します。

トンプソンせん生です。　一ばん　おもしろい　えいごの　せん生です。

オーストラリアから　きました。　三十六さいです。　えいごの　クラスは

とても　たのしいです。　時どき　ゲームを　します。

だから、　えいごの　クラスは　しずかじゃないです。　トンプソン

せん生は　ちょっと　きびしいです。　だから、みんな　かならず

えいごの　しゅくだいを　します。

introduction

without fail

Getty Images/DAJ

一ばん　すきな　ともだち

ぼくの　一ばん　すきな　ともだちは　まさひろくんです。　いま、

ラサールこう校で　べんきょうしています。　こう校　一年生です。

ラサールこう校は　しりつの　学校です。　とても　でんとうてきな

学校です。

まい日　しゅくだいが　たくさん　あります。　せん生も　きびしいです。

まさひろくんの　一ばん　とくいな　かもくは　すう学です。

だから、　まさひろくんは　すう学が　だいすきです。　でも、　すう学は

むずかしいです。　だから、　時どき　まさひろくんは　ぼくの　しゅくだいを

します。　いいですね。

private school

03

四十六

46

あたらしい学校

ISBN 9780170198271

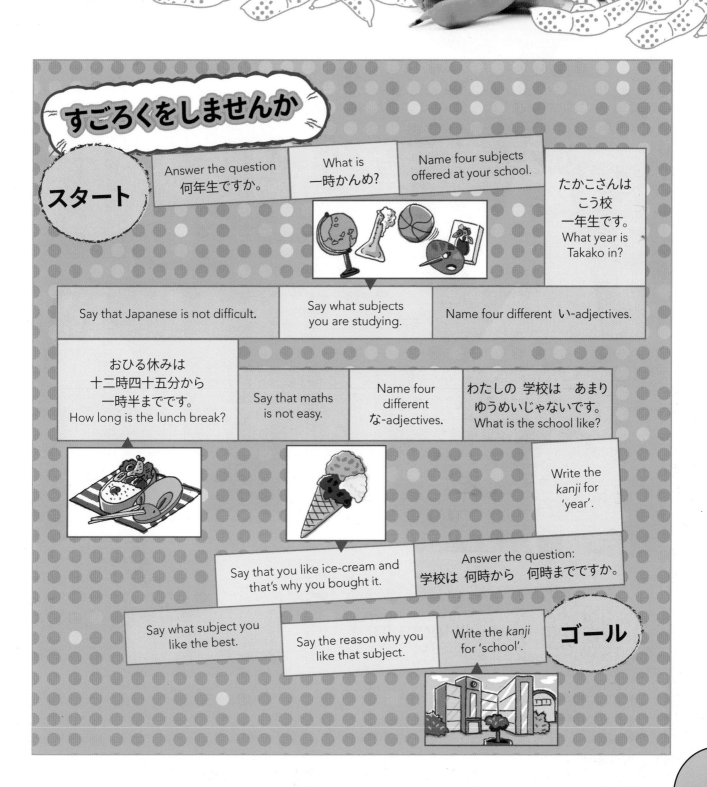

すごろくをしませんか

スタート

Answer the question 何年生ですか。

What is 一時かんめ?

Name four subjects offered at your school.

たかこさんは こう校 一年生です。 What year is Takako in?

Say that Japanese is not difficult.

Say what subjects you are studying.

Name four different い-adjectives.

おひる休みは 十二時四十五分から 一時半までです。 How long is the lunch break?

Say that maths is not easy.

Name four different な-adjectives.

わたしの 学校は あまり ゆうめいじゃないです。 What is the school like?

Write the *kanji* for 'year'.

Say that you like ice-cream and that's why you bought it.

Answer the question: 学校は 何時から 何時までですか。

Say what subject you like the best.

Say the reason why you like that subject.

Write the *kanji* for 'school'.

ゴール

How many questions can you answer?		
13–17	**8–12**	**0–7**
すごいですね! Congratulations! You are the champion!	もうちょっと… Nearly there! Go over the questions that you got wrong.	がんばって! Go over the ぶんぽう and たんご pages and try again. Good luck!

ISBN 9780170198271

あたらしい学校

Unit 4

きせつ

In this unit, you will learn to:
- talk about seasonal activities
- say you are going to do an activity
- describe the weather
- say what the weather was like
- predict the weather
- discuss temperature
- say what you want to do
- recognise and write the *kanji* characters 春, 夏, 秋 and 冬

In this unit, you will learn about:
- Japanese culture: Japanese onomatopoeia, haiku poetry, proverbs relating to the weather, seasonal traditions in Japan and natural disasters
- intercultural understanding: responding to natural disasters
- text types: brochures, greeting cards, haiku, recounting

Shutterstock.com/Nobusuke Oki

Tsubasa and his family planned a holiday this year. They looked at brochures to help them decide when and where to go. Afterwards, Tsubasa wrote a report describing their trip.

きせつ

春

はなみツアー

九州（きゅうしゅう）の　春（はる）の　てんきは　いいですよ。
さくらを　みに　いきませんか。
4日かんの　りょこう：
一人　¥80 000から
まい日　いろいろな　こうえんに
いきます。　きれいな　さくらの　はなを
みましょう。　ともだちと　いっしょに
ピクニックを　しませんか。
カラオケ　パーティーも　あります。

4日かん	four days
いろいろな	many different
さくらの　はな	cherry blossoms

夏（なつ）

南（みなみ）中学校の　ニュース

つばさくんの　夏休（なつ）みレポート

七月二十一日から　二十七日まで

月曜日: あつかったです。　だから、　十時まで　ねました。
ごご、　けんいちくんと　うみに　およぎに
いきました。

水曜日: けんたくんと　かわに、　つりに　いきました。
たのしかったです。　ぼくと　けんたくんは
つりが　だいすきです。　でも　さかなが
つれませんでした。　ざんねんでした。

日曜日: かぞくと　たまがわで　はなびを
みました。　かきごおりを　たべました。

七月二十八日から　八月三日まで

火曜日: ちえこさんの　おとうさんの　ボートで
水上スキーを　しました。　とても　よかったです。

木曜日: ぼくの　たん生日でした。　ちちと
ははから　あたらしい　じてんしゃを
もらいました。
ごご、　みんなで　こうえんに　あそびに
いきました。　サイクリングを　しました。

土曜日: ちちの　ともだちの　うちで　バーベキューを
しました。　おいしかったです。
ステーキと　サラダを　たべました。　ジュースと
コーラを　のみました。
にわで　いぬと　あそびました。
その　あとで　ちちの　くるまで
ドライブに　いきました。

Getty Images/Wataru Yanagida

つれませんでした	I couldn't catch any
ざんねんでした	it was disappointing
かきごおり	shaved ice treat
水上スキー	waterskiing
もらいました	received
その　あとで	after that

ISBN 9780170198271

秋

ほっかいどう
北海道キャンプ
じょうばや　やまのぼりや　ハイキングなどが
できます。
北海道の　秋は　すばらしいです。
こくりつこうえんで　いろいろな　ことを
しましょう。　やまに　こうようを　みに
いきませんか。　おんせんも　あります。
どうぞ　北海道に　きてくださいね。
スケジュール
一日め: ひこうきで　東京から　さっぽろへ
二日め: ごぜん:　じょうば　ごご:　ピクニック
　　　　こうようの　しゃしんを　とりましょう
三日め: こくりつこうえんで　やまのぼり
四日め: ごぜん:　じゆうこうどう
　　　　ごご:　東京に　かえります
　　　　一人　￥60 000

こくりつこうえん	national park
いろいろな　こと	various things
こうよう	the changing colour of autumn leaves
一日め	the first day
さっぽろへ	to Sapporo
じゆうこうどう	free time

冬

わくわく　おんせん
さむい　冬が　きました。
あたたかい　おんせんは
どうですか。　きもちが　いい
ろてんぶろに　はいりませんか。
からだに　いいですよ。
3日かんの　りょこう:
一人　￥60 000から
しょくじつき
ばんごはんは　わしょく
あさごはんは　ようしょく
まい日　リラックス　しましょう。

Photos by Corbis/amanaimages/© Masaaki Tanaka, Shutterstock.com/Hywit Dimyadi, Shutterstock.com/Olena Mykhaylova

わくわく	exciting
きもちが　いい　ろてんぶろ	a relaxing outdoor bath
からだに　いい	good for your body
3日かん	three days
しょくじつき	meals included
わしょく	Japanese food
ようしょく	Western food
リラックス　しましょう	let's relax

Questions

1 Look at the travel brochures and report. How much does each tour cost and what activities are available?

2 What is the schedule for the camping tour of Hokkaido?

3 What kind of holiday did Tsubasa's family finally take?

4 Describe four activities he did during his holiday.

ISBN 9780170198271

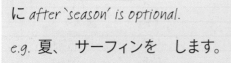

1 Talking about seasonal activities

A:	春、	はなみを	します。	
一	秋、	こうようの	しゃしんを	とります。
二	冬、	おんせんに	はいります。	

に after 'season' is optional.

e.g. 夏、　サーフィンを　します。

2 Saying you are going to do an activity

A:	しゅうまつ、	どこに	いきますか。	
B:	うみに	activity に	いきます。	
一	夏休みに	やまに	いきますか。	
	はい、	やまに	ハイキングに	いきます。
二	あした	何を	しますか。	
	まちに	あそびに	いきます。	いっしょに	いきませんか。

3 Describing the weather

A:	きょうの	てんきは	どうですか。
B:	きょうは	weather	です。
一	きょうの	てんきは	どうですか。
	あめです。		
二	きょうの	てんきは	どうですか。
	いいてんきですよ。	はれです。	

たんご

かわ	つり	くもり　のち　あめ
うみ	およぎます	はれ　のち　くもり
こうえん	はなびを　みます	ゆき

ISBN 9780170198271

きせつ

4 Saying what the weather was like

A:	きのうの　てんきは　どうでしたか。
B:	きのうは　〜でした。　むしあつかったです。
一	せんしゅうは　いいてんきでしたか。
	いいえ、　いやな　てんきでしたよ。　かぜが　つよかったです。

5 Predicting the weather

A:	あしたの　てんきよほうです。　広島（ひろしま）は　weatherでしょう。
一	大阪（おおさか）は　あめ　のち　くもりでしょう。　ごごは　かぜが　つよいでしょう。
二	北海道（ほっかいどう）　くもり　ときどき　ゆき。
三	東京（とうきょう）　はれ　のち　くもり。

6 Discussing temperature

A:	きのうの　きおんは　何どでしたか。
B:	〜どでした。　あつかったですね。
一	きょうの　さいていきおんは　何どですか。
	れいどです。　とても　さむいですね。
二	あしたの　さいこうきおんは　何どでしょうか。
	十六どでしょう。　すこし　すずしいでしょう。

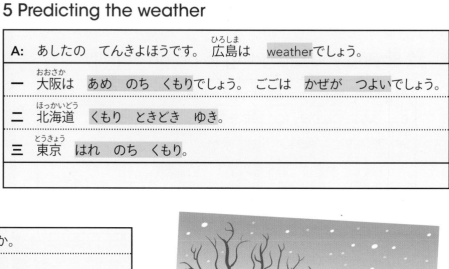

7 Saying what you want to do

A:	あめです。　何を　したいですか。
B:	DVDを　〜たいです。
一	夏休みに　何を　したいですか。
	りょこうを　したいです。
二	いいてんきですね。　テニスを　しましょう。
	テニスですか。　あまり　したくないです。

たんご

25 ℃	くもり　のち　あめ	きょう	みます
10 ℃	あめ　ときどき　ゆき	きのう	いきます
32 ℃		あした	ひきます
			でかけます

きせつ

ISBN 9780170198271

かんじ

4.9

These are the *kanji* and their readings introduced in this unit.

はる spring

春　春

Three people are in the sun.

一	二	三	声	夫	夫	春	春
春							

春休み　→　はるやすみ　→　spring holiday
春子　→　はるこ　→　Haruko (female name)
春まき　→　はるまき　→　spring roll
春が　すきです。　→　はるが　すきです。　→　I like spring.

なつ summer

夏　夏

Think of setting up your umbrella and towel and seat in the summer sun. Go 'nuts' on the beach in summer.

一	一	厂	万	百	百	百	頁
夏	夏						

夏休み　→　なつやすみ　→　summer holiday
夏の　いろ　→　なつの　いろ　→　summer colours
夏子　→　なつこ　→　Natsuko (female name)
夏は　あついです。　→　なつは　あついです。　→　Summer is hot.

あき autumn

秋　秋

Autumn leaves are fiery red.

ノ	二	千	千	秆	禾	利	秋
秋							

秋まつり　→　あき　まつり　→　autumn festival
秋子　→　あきこ　→　Akiko (female name)
秋は　きれいです。　→　あきは　きれいです。　→　Autumn is pretty.

ふゆ winter

冬　冬

Two people are skiing on the slopes in winter. 'Who' is skiing? 'You'!

ノ	ク	夂	冬	冬			

冬休み　→　ふゆやすみ　→　winter holiday
冬の　たべもの　→　ふゆの　たべもの　→　winter food
冬が　すきです。　→　ふゆが　すきです。　→　I like winter.
冬は　さむいです。　→　ふゆは　さむいです。　→　Winter is cold.

04

五十三

日本文化
にほんぶんか

冬　　　　　　　　　春

Corbis/Natsuki Sakai

ひなにんぎょう Girl's Day dolls

学校の　あとで　パーティーを　しましょう。

These dolls are displayed on Girl's Day (三月三日) and represent the emperor and empress. They are displayed to pray for the happiness and good health of the girls in the family.

おせちりょうり New Year food

おいしい！　おしょう月の　たべものです。　たべませんか。

Special New Year food is eaten cold. This allows everyone to relax on New Year's Day. The food is beautifully presented in a four-tiered lacquer box.

おはなみ Flower viewing

はなみを　しましょう。　いっしょに　ピクニックを しませんか。　カラオケで　うたを　うたいました。 はずかしかったです。

This is a time for outdoor picnics to celebrate the coming of spring.

あけまして
おめでとう ございます

New Year cards

Japanese people often send Christmas cards these days, but the really important tradition is the sending of New Year cards. Look at these examples.

ことしも　よろしく
おねがい します。

Corbis/Dai Kurokawa

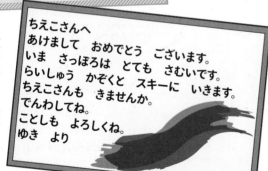

ちえこさんへ
あけまして　おめでとう　ございます。
いま　さっぽろは　とても　さむいです。
らいしゅう　かぞくと　スキーに　いきます。
ちえこさんも　きませんか。
でんわしてね。
ことしも　よろしくね。
ゆき より

五月にんぎょう
Boy's Day decorations

五月五日は　休みでした。
たのしかったですよ。

These dolls include samurai armour or helmets and other items needed to fight battles in olden times. They are displayed to pray for the bravery and courage of the boys in the family.

Alamy/J Marshall

04

五十四

54

きせつ

ISBN 9780170198271

夏

Shutterstock.com/Hiroshi Ichikawa

秋

Photo Japan/Kenneth Hamm

はな火 Fireworks

一ばんすきな　きせつは　夏です。
たのしいです。　はな火が　たのしみです。

Fireworks are a traditional part of summer festivals.

ぶんかさい Cultural day

学校に　あそびに　いきましょう。

Schools all over Japan celebrate learning by arranging displays, games and food stalls for visitors who come to the school on this open day.

Getty Images/Masahiro Hayata

たなばた Star festival

おもしろい　はなしですよ。　おりがみで　ほしを　つくりましょう。

This is the one day of the year when the weaver princess star crosses the path of the cowherd star. These stars were lovers and were separated by the river of heaven (the Milky Way), and on this night they renew their love for each other.

Getty Images/Tibor BognÁjr

秋まつり Autumn harvest festival

一ばん　おもしろい　おまつりは　秋まつりです。

This is a celebration of a good harvest, which means a time of prosperity for everyone. It is the traditional way to give thanks.

Shutterstock.com/akiyoko

うちわ Fans

夏まつりに　いきましょう。

These are often available at festivals and are designed with many colourful traditional patterns and logos.

お月み Moon viewing

お月みが　すきです。
お月みは　たのしいです。

When the moon is full in autumn, many families like to admire it in the cool of the evening. Decorations of rice dumplings, pampas grass and autumn fruit are displayed.

04

五十五

55

ISBN 9780170198271

Getty Images/Datacraft Co Ltd

きせつ

日本のしぜん

春一ばん

春一ばん are strong winds that blow during spring. The word was originally used by Japanese fishermen because of the rough seas caused by the wind. It is now a commonly used term to describe weather.

かみなり

かみなり (lightning) often occurs in electrical storms, bringing rain and sudden drops in temperature. かみなり is an old favourite in Japanese folk tales. It was believed that かみなり liked to take children's belly buttons! This story encourages children to cover their tummies when they are having an afternoon nap.

つなみ

Tidal waves are produced by earthquakes under the ocean. The word つなみ is now used internationally. つなみ travel faster in deeper water. For example, at depths of 1 kilometre, the water's speed is the same as that of the しんかんせん, which travels at over 300 kilometres per hour.

Getty Images/Hiroshi Watanabe

Shutterstock.com/Fesus Robert

つゆ

In early summer, cold winds from the north-east and warm air from the south-west come together over Japan bringing heavy rain. This rainy season is called つゆ and normally lasts about a month. Although this season is considered a nuisance by some people, it is essential for farmers' crops.

Getty Images/AFP/Sadatsuqu Tomizawa

きせつ

ISBN 9780170198271

じしん

Earthquakes are one of the most feared natural disasters in Japan. Japan is situated on the intersection of three tectonic plates and is therefore prone to earthquakes. Japan has more than 1000 earthquakes every year.

たいふう

Tropical depressions sometimes develop into tropical storms. A large-scale storm in Asia is called a たいふう (typhoon).

Shutterstock.com/Vladislav Gurfinkel

Getty Images/Ben Simmons

Three of Japan's most notable earthquakes are the great Kanto earthquake (1923), the Kobe earthquake (1995) and the Tohoku earthquake (2011). The Tohoku earthquake was the most powerful known earthquake to strike Japan, measuring 9.0 on the Richter scale and triggering tsunami waves of up to 40 metres.

火ざん

Japan has a number of active volcanoes. ふげんだけ in the north of Kyushu erupted in 1990 after being dormant for over 200 years. In June 1991, it erupted again. Thirty-nine people were killed, including some famous vulcanologists who were studying the mountain. Houses were burned under the lava and the area was severely damaged. Mt Fuji is a dormant 火ざん. It last erupted in 1707.

AFP Photo/INFN

Questions ○○○○○○○○○○○○○○○

1 オーストラリアで　いちばん　おおきい　おまつりは なんですか。　いつですか。

Compare your answer with Japan's おしょうがつ.

2 オーストラリアでも　つなみや　じしんや　かざんが ありますか。

Name a recent Australian natural disaster. How has it influenced the way we respond to natural disasters?

3 オーストラリアの　休みの日は　いつですか。

Each seasonal change is very exciting for Japanese people. Why do you think this is so? Which season do you most look forward to? Why?

だいはっけん

Natural disasters in context

The types of natural disasters that affect Japan and Australia are influenced by very different environmental factors. Japan lies on a tectonic fault line, so it has endured many earthquakes throughout its history, as well as major disasters like the 2011 tsunami. Some areas of Japan are also more densely populated than anywhere in Australia, so when these disasters strike, they can affect the lives of millions of people.

How people prepare for and respond to natural disasters, both in their actions and in their attitudes, can vary just as much as the contributing environmental factors. To prepare for natural disasters, fire drills are regularly practised in Australian schools and companies, while in Japan, earthquake drills are practised. For an earthquake drill, students are instructed to act quickly to switch off the electricity and gas, open all doors and take shelter under furniture until the earthquake stops.

When a major natural disaster strikes (such as a flood or bushfire), the Australian media often reports how the nation has responded. During times of catastrophe, Australians talk about 'mateship' and 'pitching in' to help each other 'get back on our feet'. This is seen as part of being an Australian.

During the 2011 tsunami in Japan, media worldwide reported on the quiet dignity of those devastated by the tsunami – how everyday Japanese people helped each other to share food, clothing and shelter, and how they endured it all with an uncomplaining resolve.

Getty Images/AFP/Jiji Press

きせつ

ISBN 9780170198271

Another point to consider is how different people will respond to the same environmental effect, depending on where they live and what climate they're used to. For instance, a temperature of 36°C might be considered a hot summer's day in south-eastern Australia, but it might be seen as an average day in other parts of Australia. What about Japan – do the temperatures there get that high, and how would such heat be considered by the locals?

Getty Images/Jim Holmes

Questions ○○○○○○○○○○○○○○○○○○○○○○○

Look at some weather charts for Japan on the Internet.

1 Do the Japanese use degrees Celsius (like in Australia) or Fahrenheit (like in the USA) to measure temperature?
2 Where in Japan might you encounter temperatures of 36°C? When and how often would they occur?
3 How humid is it likely to be on a 36°C day in Japan?
4 Which parts of Japan are likely to experience colder weather than the majority of Australia?
5 How might a Japanese person react to average winter temperatures of 15°C?

Have a think ○○○○○○○○○○○○○○○○○○○

1 Research the Pacific Ring of Fire. How does it affect the likelihood of natural disasters in Japan? Present your findings to a classmate.
2 What geographical factors can you think of that might make Australia prone to natural disasters?

Have a go ○○○○○○○○○○○○○○○○○○○○○

1 Imagine you are talking to someone who is not Australian. How would you define 'mateship' to them?
2 Imagine that Yusuke is a Japanese exchange student visiting your school. Using the climate information you have gathered, explain some of the differences between weather in Australia and Japan.
3 Discuss what Japan and Australia are doing to cooperate in combating climate change.

04

五
十
九

59

ISBN 9780170198271

きせつ

ぶんぽう

1 Talking about seasonal activities

夏、うみに いきます。
In summer, I go to the beach.

2 Saying you are going to do an activity

ともだちの うちに あそびに いきます。
I will go to my friend's house to play.

3 Describing the weather

きょうの てんきは どうですか。	いい てんきですよ。 きょうは はれです。 さむくないです。
What is today's weather like?	It is good weather. Today is sunny. It is not cold.
	いやな てんきですよ。
	It is awful weather.

4 Saying what the weather was like

きのうの てんきは どうでしたか。	きのうは むしあつかったです。
What was yesterday's weather like?	Yesterday was hot and humid.
せんしゅうは いい てんきでしたか。	いいえ、いやな てんきでした。
Was it good weather last week?	No, it was awful weather.

5 Predicting the weather

あしたの てんきは どうでしょうか。	くもりでしょう。
What will tomorrow's weather be like?	It will probably be cloudy.

6 Discussing temperature

きょうの さいこう きおんは 何どですか。	さいこう きおんは 三十五どです。
What is the highest/maximum temperature today?	The highest temperature is 35 degrees.
きのうの さいてい きおんは 何どでしたか。	さいてい きおんは れいどでした。
What was the lowest/minimum temperature yesterday?	The lowest temperature was zero degrees.

7 Saying what you want to do

きょうは あめですね。 何を したいですか。	水えいを したいです。
It's raining today. What do you want to do?	I want to swim.
りょうりを したいですか。	りょうりを したくないです。
Do you want to cook?	I don't want to cook.

Photos by Shutterstock.com/Tristan Scholze, Shutterstock. com/Hinochika, Shutterstock.com/ Sergej Razvodovskij

六十

きせつ

ISBN 9780170198271

Seasons

きせつ	seasons/season
春 (はる)	spring
夏 (なつ)	summer
秋 (あき)	autumn
冬 (ふゆ)	winter

Weather

はれ	sunny
くもり	cloudy
あめ	rain/rainy
ゆき	snow/snowy
あらし	stormy
ふぶき	blizzard
たいふう	typhoon
かぜが　つよい	strong wind
あめ　ときどき　ゆき	rain and occasional snow
はれ　のち　くもり	sunny and cloudy later

Temperature

さいこう　きおん	highest temperature
さいてい　きおん	lowest temperature
何ど	what temperature?
ど	degrees (Celsius)
れいど	zero degrees

Adjectives

むしあつい	hot and humid
あつい	hot
あたたかい	warm
すずしい	cool
さむい	cold
いい	good
わるい	bad
すごい	amazing
いそがしい	busy
すばらしい	wonderful
いや（な）	undesirable

04

六十一

きせつ

ISBN 9780170198271

The many faces of に

You have learnt to use the particle に in various ways. For example:

- to express a specific time: 六時**に**　おきます。
- to express going to a place: やま**に**　いきます。
- to say where something is: へや**に**　あります。

However, に can also be used when you are going to a place to do an activity. For example:

Place に activity に　いきます。

Study the examples below:

- やま**に**　ドライブ**に**　いきます。　　(I am going to the mountains for a drive.)
- うみ**に**　およぎ**に**　いきます。　　(I am going to the beach to swim.)

> The activity can be a noun or a verb stem, such as あそび *from* あそびます *or* およぎ *from* およぎます.

です／でしょう

When you use です, you are saying the situation 'is'. For example:

きょうは　あめです。　　　　　　(It is rainy today.)

However, when you use でしょう, you are saying the situation 'probably will be'. でしょう is used to indicate uncertainty. For example:

あしたは　あめでしょう。　　　　(It will probably rain tomorrow.)

I want to/I don't want to

When you want to say 'I want to' or 'I don't want to' do something, you can use the following:

- いきます。　　　　　　　　(I will go.)
- いきたいです。　　　　　　(I want to go.)
- いきたくないです。　　　　(I don't want to go.)

Using past and negative

Analyse the similarities and differences between the endings used by each type of describing word. Both use ない and なかった and the past endings all have た. Once you see the pattern, look for a clue to help you remember the differences.

い-adjectives	
あつい	is hot
あつくない	is not hot
あつかった	was hot
あつくなかった	was not hot

な-adjectives	
いや	is awful
いやじゃない	is not awful
いやでした	was awful
いやじゃなかった	was not awful

きせつ

ISBN 9780170198271

Activities you might do during the different seasons

Alamy/Stock Connection Distribution

Alamy/Stock Connection Distribution

春	こうえんに　はなみに　いきます。	I will go to the park to go flower viewing.
	おんせんに　はいります。	I will get into a hot spring.
	サイクリングを　します。	I will ride a bicycle.
	こくりつこうえんで　じょうばを　します。	I will ride a horse in a national park.
	りょこうを　します。	I will travel.
	にわで　ねます。	I will sleep in the garden.
	りょうりを　します。	I will cook.
	さんぽを　します。	I will take a walk.
	ハイキングを　します。	I will hike.
	やまのぼりを　します。	I will climb up the mountain.

夏	うみに　サーフィンに　いきます。	I will go to the beach to surf.
	はな火を　みに　いきます。	I will go to see the fireworks.
	かわに　つりに　いきます。	I will go to the river to fish.
	ボートに　のります。	I will ride in a boat.
	水上スキーを　します。	I will water-ski.
	うみで　およぎます。	I will swim at the beach.
	水えいを　します。	I will have a swim.
	ともだちと　あそびます。	I will play with my friend.
	ともだちと　でかけます。	I will go out with my friend.
	エアコンを　つけます。	I will switch on the air conditioner.
	せんぷうきを　けします。	I will switch off the fan.
	かさを　かいます。	I will buy an umbrella.

04

六十三

ISBN 9780170198271

きせつ

Alamy/Photo Japan

秋		
	やまに　ドライブに　いきます。	I will go to the mountains for a drive.
	秋まつりで　やきいもを　たべます。	I will eat roasted sweet potato at an autumn festival.
	やまのぼりを　します。	I will climb up the mountain.
	しゅうがくりょこうに　いきます。	I will go on a school excursion.
	やまに　こうようを　みに　いきます。	I will go to the mountains to see the autumn leaves.
	こんや　お月みを　します。	I will do moon-viewing tonight.

冬		
	おもちを　たべます。	I will eat rice cakes.
	おかしを　たべます。	I will eat sweets.
	スキーを　します。	I will ski.
	スノーボードを　します。	I will snowboard.
	ゆきだるまを　つくります。	I will make a snowman.
	トランプを　します。	I will play cards.
	ピアノを　ひきます。	I will play the piano.
	としょかんに　いきます。	I will go to the library.
	ヒーターを　つけます。	I will switch on the heater.

ISBN 9780170198271

はいく

Originating in the fourteenth century, haiku poetry conveys rich imagery using very few words. It is often used to write about the seasons and has evolved to become a three-line poetic form made of five, seven and five syllables per line. Here are some examples in English and Japanese.

Beautiful sunshine
I lie on a picnic rug
Feeling so happy

The park is changing
Autumn turns red and yellow
A carpet of leaves

春かぜで
さくらの はなが
ちりました

秋まつり
よいやさ よいさ
にぎやかね

夏の うみ
あかい ボートに
のりました

あつい 夏
アイスクリーム
たべたいよ

ともだちと
はな火を みます
すばらしい

ゆきだるま
かわいそうだね
さむいから

さむいから
あついおもちを
たべましょう

秋の いろ
もみじの はっぱ
うつくしい

きせつ

Onomatopoeia

Here are some onomatopoeic words relating to the weather.

1 ぽかぽか

2 ぎらぎら

3 たらたら

4 ぼつぼつ

5 しとしと

6 ざあざあ

7 びゅーびゅー

8 さむざむ

9 ぶるぶる

10 こんこん

11 カチンコチン

1 warmth
2 pulsating heat from the sun
3 sweating
4 light drops of rain
5 sprinkling rain
6 heavy rain
7 strong wind
8 chilly/draughty
9 shivering
10 heavy snow
11 freezing up

きせつ

ISBN 9780170198271

たん生日のプレゼント

In this unit, you will learn to:

- count to a million
- ask and say how much an item costs
- ask for an item (これ, それ, あれ)
- ask and say which one (この, その, あの)
- ask someone to do something
- recognise and write the *kanji* characters 百, 千, 万 and 円

In this unit, you will learn about:

- Japanese culture: different types of shops and markets in Japan, vending machines and Japanese service
- intercultural understanding: Japanese currency, counting without zero and counting large numbers
- text types: manga

たん生日のプレゼント

ISBN 9780170198271

These are the *kanji* and their readings introduced in this unit.

ヒャク／ビャク／ピャク 100

百

One hundred jelly beans are in a jar.

一 ア ア 百 百 百

三百	→	さんびゃく	→	300
四百	→	よんひゃく	→	400
六百	→	ろっぴゃく	→	600
八百	→	はっぴゃく	→	800

何百ですか。 → なんびゃくですか。 → How many hundreds?

セン／ゼン 1000

千

Think of the *katakana* letter チ giving 1000 cheers.

ノ 二 千

三千	→	さんぜん	→	3000
六千	→	ろくせん	→	6000
八千	→	はっせん	→	8000

何千ですか。 → なんぜんですか。 → How many thousands?

マン 10 000

万

A man is rollerskating.

一 フ 万

一万	→	いちまん	→	10 000
五万	→	ごまん	→	50 000
百万	→	ひゃくまん	→	1 000 000

何万ですか。 → なんまんですか。 → How many tens of thousands?

エン yen (¥)

円

A Japanese safe has two drawers.

｜ 冂 冂 円

九十円	→	きゅうじゅうえん	→	¥90
二百十円	→	にひゃくじゅうえん	→	¥210
千二百円	→	せんにひゃくえん	→	¥1200
百万円	→	ひゃくまんえん	→	¥1 000 000

1 Asking and saying how much something is

A:	Itemは いくらですか。
B:	Itemは　price円です。
	Itemは　priceドルです。
一	いくらですか。
	十八万五千円です。
二	アイスクリームは　いくらですか。
	三ドル五十セントです。

2 Asking for an item

A:	Itemを ください。
一	どれですか。
	これです。
二	これを　ください。
三	コーラを　ください

120円

たんご

ざっし	六百四十円
コンピューター	千三百ドル
くるま	二百五十万円
それ	
あれ	
コーヒー	

230円

たん生日のプレゼント

ISBN 9780170198271

3 Asking and saying which one

A:	どの	itemが	すきですか。
B:	この	itemが	すきです。
一	どの	ふでばこが	すきですか。
	この	ふでばこが	すきです。
二	どの	CDを	かいたいですか。
	あの	CDを	かいたいです。
三	その	ケーキは	おいしいですか。
	はい、	おいしいです。	

4 Asking someone to do something

A:	Verbてください。
一	その　くつを　みせてください。
二	サインしてください。
三	どうぞ、　はいってください。

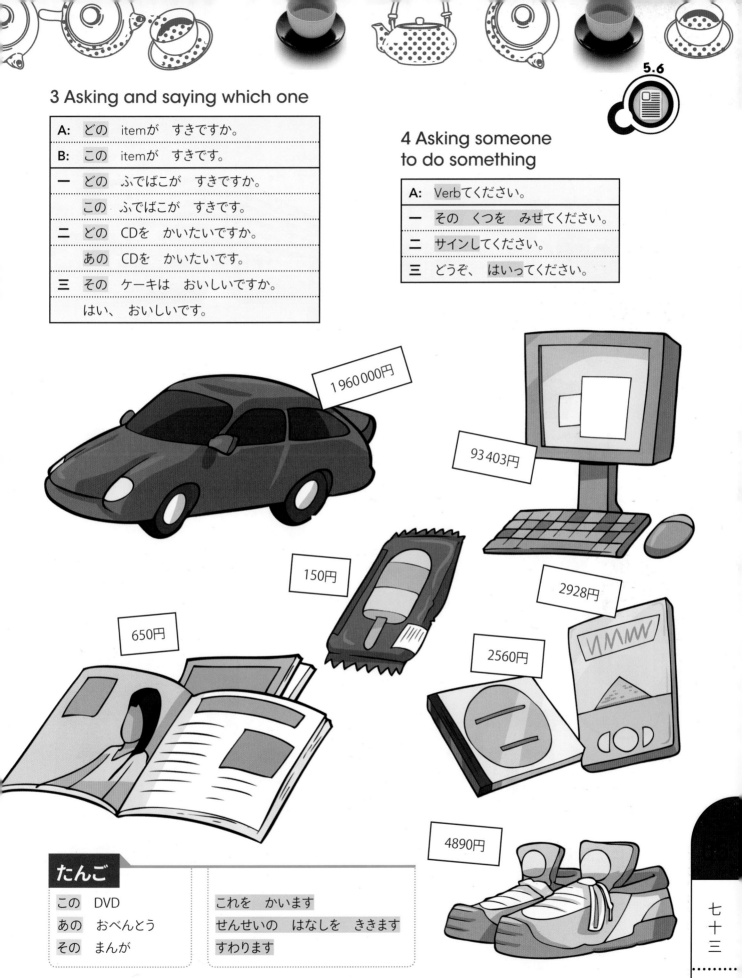

1960000円

93403円

150円

2928円

2560円

650円

4890円

たんご

この	DVD		これを　かいます
あの	おべんとう		せんせいの　はなしを　ききます
その	まんが		すわります

ISBN 9780170198271

たん生日のプレゼント

七十三

日本文化
にほんぶんか

日本でかいものをしましょう

Street market stalls

はらじゅくと　アキバの　みせは
とても　おもしろいです。
ブティックや　へんな
きっさてんや　でんきせいひんの
（electrical goods）みせなどが　あります。

フリーマーケットに　いきましょう。
おもしろい　ものが
ありますね。

はらじゅくの　ブティック

アキバの　メィドカフェ

アキバ is a nickname
for あきはばら.

Photos by Alamy/Nic Cleave Photography, Alamy/David L Moore, Glow Images/Ben Simmons, Alamy/Picture Contact BV, Alamy/Adam Eastland, Shutterstock.com/Radu Razvan

05

七十四

74

たん生日のプレゼント

ISBN 9780170198271

コンビニで　何が　できますか。

FamilyMart

町一番街店

おべんとうや　おかしや
のみものを　かいます。

コンビニは　べんりですよ。

しゃしんが　プリント　できます。

宅急便

たくはいびん
delivery service

ISBN 9780170198271

たん生日のプレゼント

ひゃくえんショップ

（ほんとうは 105 円！— 100 円＋ 5 ％GST）

ボウル	プレート	おさら
たっきゅうの ラケットと　ボール	スイミングゴーグル	おりがみ
巻き尺	ペン	シール

たん生日のプレゼント

ISBN 9780170198271

05

じどうはんばいき

Japan has the highest number of vending machines per capita, with about one machine for every 23 people. The variety of items you can buy from vending machines in Japan is truly amazing.

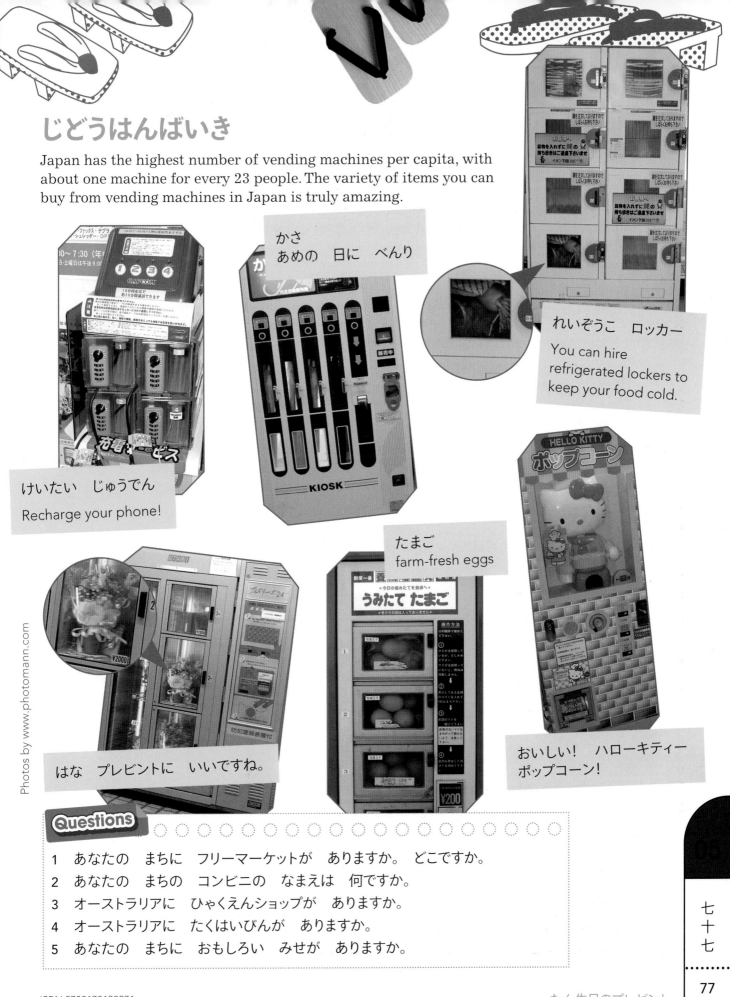

かさ
あめの　日に　べんり

れいぞうこ　ロッカー
You can hire refrigerated lockers to keep your food cold.

けいたい　じゅうでん
Recharge your phone!

たまご
farm-fresh eggs

おいしい!　ハローキティー
ポップコーン!

はな　プレゼントに　いいですね。

Photos by www.photomann.com

Questions

1　あなたの　まちに　フリーマーケットが　ありますか。　どこですか。
2　あなたの　まちの　コンビニの　なまえは　何ですか。
3　オーストラリアに　ひゃくえんショップが　ありますか。
4　オーストラリアに　たくはいびんが　ありますか。
5　あなたの　まちに　おもしろい　みせが　ありますか。

ISBN 9780170198271

たん生日のプレゼント

Counting without zero

For centuries, the Japanese have used a counting system based on the Chinese system, which does not use zero. Yet historically, Japanese people traded, kept accounts, measured distances and developed sophisticated mathematics. How was this possible without zero? Essentially, there is more than one way to think about numbers and counting, and so people from different cultures can count in different ways.

Making it work without zero

In the Japanese system, the counter for the place has to be said each time (e.g. 10 or 100). In English, we don't pronounce the zero in numbers like 405, and in Japanese, you simply don't say or write anything where the zero would go.

- The number 45 is thought of as 4 x 10 + 5, so that is what you write: 四十五.
- The number 405 has no tens, so it is 4 x 100 + 5: 四百五.

Tongue-twisting numbers

Learning how Japanese numbers have been written historically sheds light on the modern system of counting. The trick is to remember that regardless of how you write the number, it is pronounced the same way according to the Japanese counting system.

Here is an example:

2 459 763 = 二百四十五万九千七百六十三

Both are pronounced:

にひゃく　よんじゅう　ごまん　きゅうせん　ななひゃく　ろくじゅう　さん

Millions	100s of 1000s	10s of 1000s	1000s	100s	10s	Units
2	4	5	9	7	6	3
二百	四十	五万	九千	七百	六十	三
100s of 10000s	10s of 10000s	10 000s	1000s	100s	10s	Units

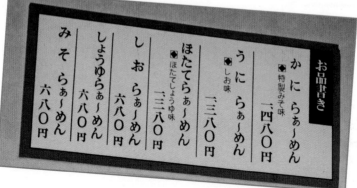

たん生日のプレゼント

ISBN 9780170198271

The idea that numbers are grouped together in threes is a characteristic of the English number system. In Japanese, the numbers are grouped in fours. Find more information on how to make large numbers in Japanese in the *Obento Supreme Workbook*.

iStockphoto/Ursula Alter

Shutterstock/AISPIX by Image Source

Alamy/Japan Stock

弁当
1,600 円

上にぎり1合折
1,650 円

Why *yen*?

Languages are dynamic, changing over time. For example, the way numbers are written in Japanese has changed, although the pronunciation hasn't. We can investigate another example of how language changes over time by finding out where the *ye* in *yen* might have come from.

There is no symbol for *ye* in *hiragana* and we write the reading for 円 as えん. Yet the word used in English for the Japanese currency is *yen*.

Hints
How and when did the word `yen' come into English?
Why is there a space for *ye* in the *hiragana* chart, but no symbol?
Is the name of the *hiragana* chart 五十音図 significant?

七十九

ISBN 9780170198271

たん生日のプレゼント

1 Asking and saying how much something is

DVDは　いくらですか。	DVDは　三千円です。
How much is the DVD?	The DVD is 3000 yen.
ざっしは　いくらですか。	ざっしは　十二ドルです。
How much is the magazine?	The magazine is 12 dollars.

2 Asking for an item

どれが　いいですか。	これを　ください。
Which one would you like?	I will have this one, please.
これを　みたいですか。	いいえ、　あれを　みたいです。
Do you want to see this one?	No, I would like to see that one over there.

3 Asking and saying which one

どの　くつを　かいましたか。	この　くつを　かいました。
Which shoes did you buy?	I bought these shoes.
その　ざっしは　おもしろいですか。	はい、　この　ざっしは　おもしろいです。
Is that magazine interesting?	Yes, this magazine is interesting.

4 Asking someone to do something

えんぴつを　かしてください。
Please lend me a pencil.
その　しゃしんを　みせてください。
Please show me that photo.

Photos by Getty Images/Petri Artturi
Asikainen, Alamy/Momel, Alamy/Picture
Contact BV, Shutterstock.com/Garsya

たん生日のプレゼント

ISBN 9780170198271

Group 1 verbs

ます form	て form	English
あいます	あって	meet
いいます	いって	say/call
かいます	かって	buy
つかいます	つかって	use
ききます	きいて	listen
かきます	かいて	write
およぎます	およいで	swim
はなします	はなして	speak/talk
かします	かして	lend
だします	だして	take out/put out
たちます	たって	stand up
まちます	まって	wait
もちます	もって	carry/hold
あそびます	あそんで	play
よみます	よんで	read
すわります	すわって	sit
つくります	つくって	make
はいります	はいって	enter
かえります	かえって	return

Group 2 verbs

ます form	て form	English
あけます	あけて	open
でかけます	でかけて	go out
つけます	つけて	turn on
みせます	みせて	show
でます	でて	leave
ねます	ねて	sleep
たべます	たべて	eat
しめます	しめて	close
いれます	いれて	put in
おきます	おきて	wake up
みます	みて	see

Group 3 (irregular) verbs

ます form	て form	English
きます	きて	come
します	して	do

Look at ぶんぽうプラス for more details about verb groups.

ISBN 9780170198271

たん生日のプレゼント

八十一

81

Large numbers

In English, commas or spaces are inserted into large numbers. When we see a large number such as 540,000, we know to say 'five hundred and forty thousand'.

In Japanese, a comma is inserted when the large number gets to 10,000. If you move the comma to the left by one digit (giving you four zeros), you can easily identify how many thousands to read. So, when we see 540,000, we know to say in Japanese '54 まん (ten thousand)'.

The word まん (万) means 10,000. To read large numbers, remember to shift the comma after four noughts instead of three.

Try these:

420,000	42 ten thousand	42万 (まん)
1,000,000	100 ten thousand	100万 (まん)

Verbs

Verbs are action words – 'hear', 'eat', 'go', etc. All verbs in Japanese have an *i* sound or an *e* sound straight before the ます. Check this rule by looking at the list of verbs in the たんご section of this unit.

Verb groups

Verbs in Japanese can be divided into three. You need to know which group a verb belongs to when using it. In this unit, we use the basic ます form and adapt it to say ～てください, meaning 'please do'. Instead of learning each verb one by one, it is easier to remember the pattern for each group and that will tell you how to change the verb to the て form. The verb groups are: group 1 verbs (also known as *i*–ます verbs), group 2 verbs (also known as *e*–ます verbs) and group 3 (irregular) verbs.

The pattern – how to make the て form

*	W	R	Y	M	H	N	T	S	K		
ん	わ	ら	や	ま	は	な	た	さ	か	あ	A
		り		み	(び)ひ	に	ち	し	き	い	I
		る	ゆ	む	ふ	ぬ	つ	す	く	う	U
		れ		め	(べ)へ	ね	て	せ	け	え	E
	を	ろ	よ	も	ほ	の	と	そ	こ	お	O

Many students use songs or rhythm to help them remember this pattern. Can you think of a tune that helps you?

い, ち and り become って
に, び and み become んで
き takes いて
ぎ takes いで
All the rest just take て.

たん生日のプレゼント

ISBN 9780170198271

The letters of the pattern refer to the い syllable of the group 1 (*i*–ます) verbs. If you look at the ひらがな chart, you will see that the possible い syllables are:

い　き(ぎ)　し　ち　に　ひ(び)　み　り

Take away this syllable and the ます ending. Add the correct て form. For example:

かいます	かって
ききます	きいて
およぎます	およいで
はなします	はなして
まちます	まって
しにます	しんで
あそびます	あそんで
よみます	よんで
はいります	はいって

iStockphoto/Photo Talk

> However, there is an exception:
> いきます　→　いって (*to go*)

This last line (all the rest just take て) refers to group 2 (*e*–ます) verbs. The pattern is simple for this group. Take away the ます and add て. You can identify these verbs easily because they all have an *e* syllable in front of the ます. According to the ひらがな chart, the possibilities are:

え　け　せ　て　ね　へ(べ)　め　れ

Some examples are:

あけます	あけて
みせます	みせて
ねます	ねて
たべます	たべて
しめます	しめて
いれます	いれて

> However, there are exceptions:
> おきます　→　おきて (*to wake up*)
> みます　→　みて (*to look*)
> きます　→　きて (*to wear*)

Group 3 verbs are irregular, but the list is short. Take away the ます and add て. For example:

きます	きて
します	して

> Remember here that
> きます　→　きて (*to come*)

05

八十三

ISBN 9780170198271

たん生日のプレゼント

Which one?

There are two sets of words to choose from in Japanese.

There are two patterns here. There is a pattern in the letters that the words begin with: d, k, s, a. The other pattern is that one set of words ends in れ, and one set ends in の.

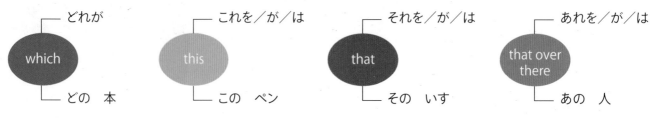

What pattern can you see this time? The words ending in れ are followed by a particle. The words ending in の are followed by a noun. Below are some whole-sentence examples of how you might see these words used.

Situation 1: You might be offered a choice of cakes.

どれが　すきですか。	これが　すきです。	これを　かいます。
Which one do you like?	I like this one.	I will buy this one.
どの　ケーキを　かいますか。	この　ケーキが　すきです。	この　ケーキを　かいます。
Which cake will you buy?	I like this cake.	I will buy this cake.

Situation 2: You might be looking for a pen that belongs to you.

どれが　わたしのですか。	それが　わたしのです。
Which one is mine?	That one is mine.
どの　ペンが　わたしのですか。	その　ペンが　わたしのです。
Which pen is mine?	That pen is mine.

Situation 3: You might be asking which magazine is interesting.

どれが　おもしろいですか。	あれが　おもしろいです。
Which one is interesting?	That one over there is interesting.
どの　ざっしが　おもしろいですか。	あの　ざっしが　おもしろいです。
Which magazine is interesting?	That magazine over there is interesting.

たん生日のプレゼント

ISBN 9780170198271

どんな人？

In this unit, you will learn to:

- describe someone's physical appearance
- describe someone's personality
- join い-adjectives in extended descriptions
- join な-adjectives in extended descriptions
- contrast characteristics using 'but'
- describe what someone is wearing
- write a personal letter
- recognise and write the *kanji* characters 手, 目, 耳 and 口

In this unit, you will learn about:

- Japanese culture: different Japanese fashion tribes and clothing statements
- intercultural understanding: differences in colour between English and Japanese, and how this can affect describing the world
- text types: letters

Photo by Alamy /Giovanni Mereghetti

かよとまきのかいわ

Maki: ねえ、 きいてください。 わたしは らい月から
オーストラリア人を ホストします。

Kayo: へえ、 どんな 人ですか。

M: ロジャーくんです。

K: へえ、 みせてください。 どれが ロジャーくんですか。

M: この 人です。 あかい シャツを きています。
ロジャーくんは せが たかくて、 かみが ちゃいろです。

K: へえ、 そうですか。 ロジャーくんは 目が
おおきくて、 やさしそうですね。 かっこいいですね。

M: そうですね。 ええと、 ロジャーくんは スキーが
すきです。 だから、 わたしは 冬休みが たのしみです。

K: いいですね。 この人は ロジャーくんに にていますね。
はいいろの Tシャツを きて、 ジーンズを
はいています。 せが たかくて、 かみが ちゃいろですね。
だれですか。

M: ええと、 この 人は ロジャーくんの おにいさんです。
なまえは ケンくんです。 この 人は ロジャーくんの
おとうさんです。 おとうさんも せが たかいですね。
これは おかあさんです。 ピンクの ワンピースを
きています。 おかあさんは 金ぱつですね。

K: それから、 これは だれですか。

M: ええと、 それは ロジャーくんの ともだちです。
アンドリューくんと ローレンさんと マイケルくんです。
それから、 ペットの いぬと ねこです。

K: へえ、 かわいい いぬですね。 ロジャーくんの うちは
おおきいですか。

M: はい、 ロジャーくんの うちは おおきくて、 しろいです。
うちの そとに おおきい にわと プールが あります。
わたしは いまから ロジャーくんに 手がみを
かきます。 かよさん、 手つだってください。

host

looks kind

attractive / cool

look forward to

looks alike

please give
me a hand /
please help me

06

八十六

86

どんな人?

ISBN 9780170198271

ロジャーくんへの手がみ

ロジャーくんへ、

おげんきですか。手がみを　ありがとう。わたしは　この手がみで　わたしと
わたしの　かぞくに　<u>ついて</u>　かきます。

about

わたしの　かぞくは　四人です。ちちと　ははと　おとうとと　わたしです。
ちちは　ちょっと　<u>ふとっています</u>が、　スポーツが　すきです。まい日　ご前
七時半から　ごご　八時ごろまで　<u>しごと</u>に　いきます。

fat

work

ははは　かいものが　すきです。ははは　<u>やせていて</u>、せが　あまり　たかくないです。
いつも　<ruby>耳<rt>みみ</rt></ruby>に　すてきな　イヤリングを　しています。りょうりが　<ruby>上手<rt>じょうず</rt></ruby>で、
いつも　いそがしいです。

skinny

おとうとは　十二さいです。しょう学　六年生です。サッカーと
コンピューターゲームが　すきです。<ruby>口<rt>くち</rt></ruby>が　おおきくて、はなが
ちいさいです。いつも　うるさいです。

わたしは　十五さいです。中学　三年生です。しゅみは　まんがと
バレーボールです。よく　ともだちと　<u>でんわ</u>で　はなします。

telephone

I am looking forward to seeing

ロジャーくんに　<u>あえるのを　たのしみに　しています</u>。
らい月の　二日に　かぞく　みんなで　<u>くうこうに　むかえに　いきます</u>。

go to meet you at the airport

じゃ、さようなら

十一月九日

まきより

Questions

1 Who is in the photos Kayo and Maki are looking at?
2 What is Roger wearing? How about Ken? What is he wearing?
3 What do Roger and Ken have in common?
4 How many people are in Maki's family and who are they? Describe each of them.

06

八十七

87

どんな人？

れんしゅう

1 Describing someone's physical appearance

A:	たかこさんは どんな 人ですか。
B:	Personは body partが adjectiveです。
B:	たかこさんは かみが ながいです。

2 Describing someone's personality

A:	ベンくんは どんな 人ですか。
B:	Personは adjectiveです。
B:	ベンくんは げんきです。

3 Joining い-adjectives in extended descriptions

Personは body partが い-adjective1くて、 adjectiveです。

たかこさんは かみが ながくて、 めが ちゃいろい です。

たんご

ながい	まじめ（な）	あおい
たかい	げんき（な）	くろい
みじかい	のんき（な）	ちゃいろい
ひくい	しずか（な）	

4 Joining な-adjectives in extended descriptions

Personは な-adjective 1で、 adjectiveです。

ベンくんは のんきで、 かっこいいです。

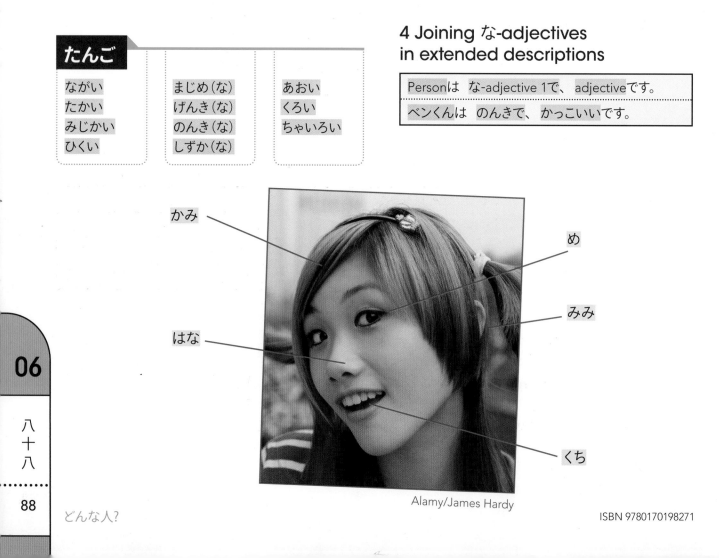

かみ

め

はな

みみ

くち

Alamy/James Hardy

5 Describing someone with contrasting characteristics

6.3, 6.4

Personは adjectiveですが、 adjectiveです。
かいくんは こわいですが、 やさしいです。
ココちゃんは ちいさくて、 かわいいですが、 うるさいです。

Getty Images/Yoshikazu Tsuno

Alamy /Jamie Marshall

Getty Images /Jerry Driendl

6 Describing what someone is wearing

A: かいくんは 何を きていますか。
B: Personは clothing itemを きています。 clothing itemを はいています。
B: かいくんは くろいジャケットを きています。 ジーンズを はいています。
B: ココちゃんは セーターを きています。 ぼうしを かぶっています。

たんご

きびしい	ぼうし	かぶっています
やさしい	くつ	はいています
まじめ	ジャケット	きています
こわい	めがね	かけています
おもしろい	ゆびわ	しています

八
十
九

....

ISBN 9780170198271

どんな人？

漢字
かんじ

These are the *kanji* and their readings introduced in this unit.

て hand

手

a hand with a pen

ノ	二	三	手			

手がみ → てがみ → letter
下手 → へた → not skilled
上手 → じょうず → skilled
手まきずし → てまきずし → hand-rolled sushi
みぎ手 → みぎて → right hand

め eye

目

an eyeball in an eye socket

丨	冂	冃	目	目		

ひだり目 → ひだりめ → left eye
目を　あけてください。 → めを　あけてください。 → Please open your eyes.
目の　前 → めの　まえ → right in front of you
目が　おおきいです。 → めが　おおきいです。 → His/her eyes are big.
二日目 → ふつかめ → the second day

みみ ear

耳

an ear

一	丆	干	干	耳	耳	

耳が　ちいさいです。 → みみが　ちいさいです。 → His/her ears are small.
耳が　とおいです。 → みみが　とおいです。 → He/she has bad hearing.

くち／コウ mouth

口

a square mouth

丨	冂	口				

口の　中 → くちの　なか → inside the mouth
口が　おおきいです。 → くちが　おおきいです。 → His/her mouth is big.
人口 → じんこう → population
口を　あけてください。 → くちを　あけてください。 → Please open your mouth.

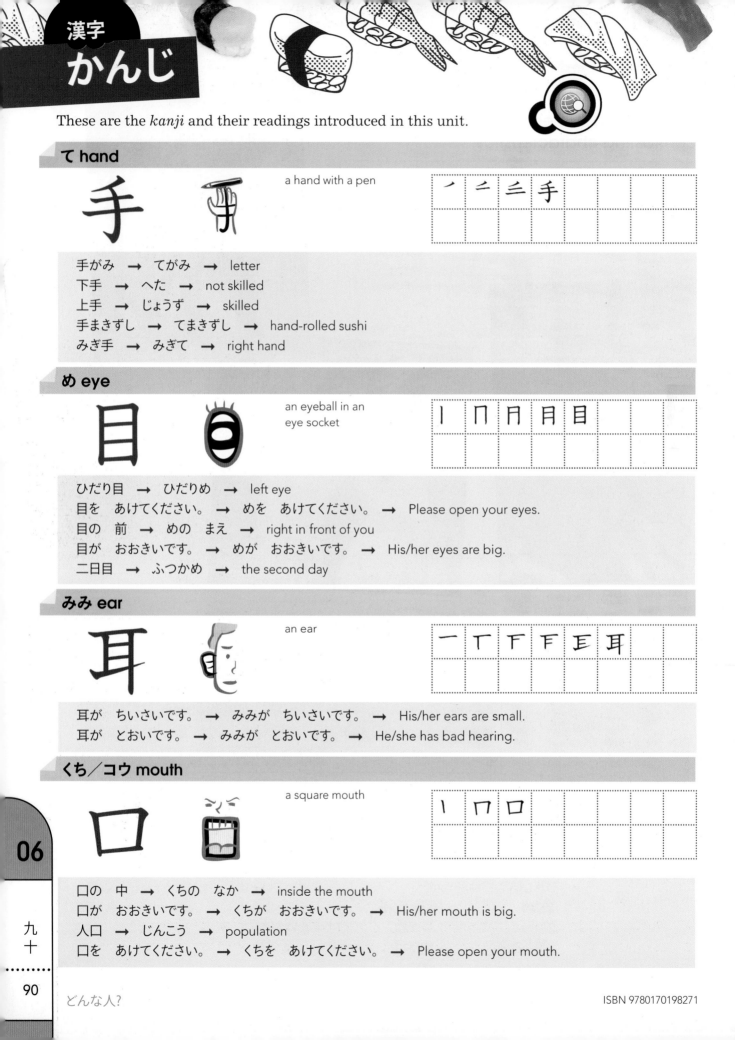

どんな人？

ISBN 9780170198271

日本文化
にほんぶんか

どんな人？

Consider the following Japanese fashion tribes.

ニックネーム： あゆみ
しゅみ： ジャズダンス
おんがく： Jポップ
すきなこと： メイク、ピンク、ディズニー

コスプレ： まんがや　アニメの　キャラクターに　なりたい

はらじゅく　ガール

Corbis/Demotix/Scilla

Alamy /Salvo Severino

ニックネーム： ゆう
しゅみ： ユーチューブ、アニメ
おんがく： ポップ
すきなこと： かいもの、ゲーム、
ぼくの　いぬ

ニックネーム： クー
しゅみ： バスケットボール、どくしょ
おんがく： インディー
すきなこと： サーフィン、ともだち

ロックンロール

おたく

Corbis/Blend Images/Take A Pix

ニックネーム： たさきくん
しゅみ： トランペット
おんがく： ジャズ、　AKB48
すきなこと： くるま、
ヒップホップ

Corbis/Laura Morton

ニックネーム： やざわ
しゅみ： やきゅう、カラオケ
おんがく： ロック
すきなかもく： か学、すう学

Questions

1   How can the way we dress express our personalities?
2   What are the possible consequences of judging people by their hairstyles or clothing?
3   Did your opinion of these people change after reading their profiles? Why?

ISBN 9780170198271

Different colours

Where does blue finish and green start? Where does あお finish and みどり start?

The concept of あお is quite different from the concept of 'blue' in English. Although the colour みどり matches the colour and English word for 'green', the word みどり is not used for all greens in Japanese.

It is helpful to remember that words don't always have a direct equivalent in another language. Understanding the differences in meaning between あお and 'blue', and みどり and 'green', will help you use them correctly in Japanese.

On these pages are things whose colour is あお in Japanese. Can you guess what they mean?

あおりんご

あおむし

あおしんごう

あおたけ

Photos by Shutterstock.com/Mahesh Patil, Shutterstock.com/MariusdeGraf, Shutterstock.com/Ziga Camernik, Alamy/MIXA, Shutterstock/Maceofoto

ISBN 9780170198271

どんな人?

あおのり

あおた

あおば

ISBN 9780170198271

Questions

1   What colour would you describe the objects pictured in English?
2   Can you find other examples of things that are described as あお?
3   Look for items that might be described as あか and think about the colour we use to describe them in English.

Remember that there may be some variation between speakers, just as there is in English. (Ask English speakers to point to something aqua and see how many different responses you get.)

Have a think ○○○○○○○○○○○○○○○○○○○○○

1   What do you think might be a consequence if you didn't know that English 'blue' wasn't an exact equivalent of Japanese あお?
2   Why is it important to understand the subtle difference between colour words in Japanese?

Have a go ○○○○○○○○○○○○○○○○○○○○○○

1   You can test the difference between あお and blue, あか and red, and other colour words by pairing up with a friend and pointing to different shades in the colour wheel on the previous page. Ask your friend (in Japanese) to identify the colour you're pointing to. When they answer, pause to consider these questions:
    • Did they use the correct Japanese word in context?
    • How would you identify that colour in English?
2   Swap roles, and try out different colours.

Photos by Shutterstock.com/Judy Kennamer, Shutterstock.com/Tomo, Shutterstock/Reika, Shutterstock/J Reika,

06

九十三

どんな人?

Getty Images/
Image Source

1 Describing someone's physical appearance

Describing physical appearance is done in a three-part sentence.

Personは body partが descriptionです。
たかこさんは かみが ながいです。 Takako has long hair.
ベンくんは 目が ちゃいろです。 Ben has brown eyes.

2 Describing someone's personality

Getty images.com

Personは adjectiveです。
せん生は きびしいです。 The teacher is strict.
あきらくんは やさしいです。 Akira is gentle.
ゆうこさんは げんきです。 Yuuko is full of energy.

Shutterstock.com
/AISPIX by Image Source

3 Joining adjectives in extended descriptions

When you want to describe someone, you can join two descriptions.
It is important to recognise the type of adjective in the first sentence.
If, as is most likely, the first adjective is an い-adjective, drop the
い and add くて. For example:

かみが ながいです。せが たかいです。 ↓ Drop **いです**. → add **くて、**. かみが ながくて、せが たかいです。 Her hair is long and she is tall.
かみが ながいです。きれいです。 → かみが ながくて、きれいです。 Her hair is long and she is pretty.

If the description in the first sentence is a な-adjective or a noun,
drop the す off です, leaving the で behind. For example:

Getty Images/
Katsutoshi Hatsuzawa

まじめです。しずかです。 ↓ Remove **す**。 → leave the **で** → add a comma. まじめで、しずかです。 He is serious and quiet.
きれいです。かみが くろいです。 → きれいで、かみが くろいです。 She is pretty and has black hair.
ちゃいろです → ちゃいろで、
金ぱつです → 金ぱつで、

どんな人?

ISBN 9780170198271

4 Describing someone with contrasting characteristics

When you want to describe someone with contrasting characteristics, use が (meaning 'but'). For example:

Shutterstock.com/gengirl

シュレックは　こわいです**が**、やさしいです。
Shrek is scary but gentle.
わたしの　いぬは　ちいさく**て**、かわいいです**が**、うるさいです。
My dog is small and cute but noisy.

5 Describing what someone is wearing

Japanese has many verbs meaning 'to wear'. The verb used depends on where and how you wear the item. For example, wearing a hat and wearing shoes use different verbs. The illustration below shows you which word to use for a particular item of clothing.

しています

かぶっています

かけています

はいています

きています

See ぶんぽうプラス on page 98 for an explanation on how to use these verbs.

ベンくんは　コートを　きています。
Ben is wearing a coat.
ようこさんは　ジーンズを　はいています。
Yooko is wearing jeans.
ベンくんは　めがねを　かけています。
Ben is wearing glasses.
ようこさんは　ゆびわを　しています。ぼうしを　かぶっています。
Yooko is wearing a ring. She is wearing a hat.

06

九
十
五

95

ISBN 9780170198271

どんな人？

6.8

Shutterstock.com/
Linda Bucklin

Getty Images/Muntz

istockphoto/
Yasuno Sakata

Getty Images/
Jun Takahashi

Glow Images

Body

あし	legs/feet
あたま	head
うで	arms
おしり	bottom
おなか	stomach
かた	shoulders
かみ（のけ）	hair
からだ	body
くび	neck
せなか	upper back
手	hands
ひざ	knees
ひじ	elbows
ゆび	fingers

Face

口	mouth
はな	nose
ひげ	beard/moustache
耳	ears
目	eyes

Physical appearance

かっこいい	attractive/trendy/cool
せが　たかい	tall
せが　ひくい	short (height)
ながい	long
ハンサム（な）	handsome
ほそい	skinny/thin
みじかい	short (length)
ふとっています	fat
やせています	skinny/thin

Personality

きびしい	strict
げんき（な）	lively/spirited
こわい	scary
わがまま（な）	spoilt/selfish
やさしい	kind/gentle
あかるい	bright
のんき（な）	easy-going
へん（な）	strange
まじめ（な）	serious
しずか（な）	quiet
あたまが　いい	intelligent
せいかくが　いい	nice-natured

Clothes

Tシャツ	T-shirt
セーター	sweater/woollen jumper
シャツ	shirt
ジャケット	jacket
ワンピース	(day) dress
水ぎ	bathers/swimsuit
くつ	shoes
ぞうり	thongs/traditional footwear
ジーンズ	jeans
スカート	skirt
スニーカー	sneakers/runners
ズボン	trousers
パジャマ	pyjamas
ブーツ	boots
ながぐつ	gumboots

どんな人？

Accessories

アクセサリー	accessories
イヤリング	earrings
ゆびわ	ring
ネクタイ	tie
時けい	watch
めがね	glasses
サングラス	sunglasses
ぼうし	hat

Getty Images/Emmanuel Faure

Colours

あか(い)	red
あお(い)	blue
きいろ(い/の)	yellow
くろ(い)	black
しろ(い)	white
みどり(の)	green
ちゃいろ(い/の)	brown
はいいろ(の)	grey
むらさき(の)	purple
ピンク(の)	pink
オレンジ(の)	orange
金ぱつ(の)	blond (hair)
ももいろ(の)	peach

Alamy/Jeremy Sutton-Hibbert

Colours aren't always what they seem! To find out more, look at the ぶんぽうプラス page.

Verbs

To put on	Wear/is wearing	Use with
きます	きています	Tシャツ／ドレス
はきます	はいています	ズボン／くつ
つけます	つけています	アクセサリー
かけます	かけています	めがね
かぶります	かぶっています	ぼうし
します	しています	ネクタイ／とけい

06

九十七

ISBN 9780170198271

どんな人？

6.1

Shutterstock.com /spline_x

い colours

あかい
あおい
くろい
しろい
きいろい
ちゃいろい

の colours

みどりの
はいいろの
むらさきの
ピンクの
オレンジの
ももいろの
きいろの
ちゃいろの

Nouns versus adjectives

Look at these examples:

I like red shoes. (Here 'red' is an adjective describing the shoes.)

I like red. (Here 'red' is a noun as in 'I like pasta'.)

In English 'red' (adjective) is the same as 'red' (noun), but in Japanese there is a difference:

I like red shoes. (adjective)
あかい くつが　すきです。

I like red. (noun)
あかが　すきです。

Alamy/J Marshall

ちゅうい!

Remember, きいろ and ちゃいろ can be used as きいろの and ちゃいろの OR きいろい and ちゃいろい.

金いろ is the colour 'gold' but 金ぱつ is only used to describe blond hair. Strange but true.

な-adjectives

Look at these examples:
あきらくんは **しずかな** 人です。
(Akira is a quiet person.)

あきらくんは **しずか**です。
(Akira is quiet.)

Both sentences are correct, but you need to remember that when you add a noun, in this case 人 (person), you need to add な. If you don't have a noun, you don't need な.

Alamy/Ron Yue

しています and つけています

Two verbs are used when talking about wearing accessories.
しています is for general accessories like a watch, necklace or ring.
つけています is for things you attach, such as a brooch.

ISBN 9780170198271

いただきます!

In this unit, you will learn to:

- ask what someone is doing at the moment and respond
- ask and say how many general items you want
- ask and say how many items (in glasses or cups) you want
- recognise and use common expressions at restaurants
- use the て form of verbs in new ways
- use counters for common items
- recognise and write the *kanji* characters 食, 飲, 行, 買, 安, 高, 大 and 小

In this unit, you will learn about:

- Japanese culture: Japanese table manners and a sushi recipe
- intercultural understanding: learn about Japanese culture and your own by comparing cuisine and food people eat every day
- text types: conversation, menu, recipe

Alamy/Giovanni Mereghetti

Akane, Roger and Tetsuya
are going to a restaurant.

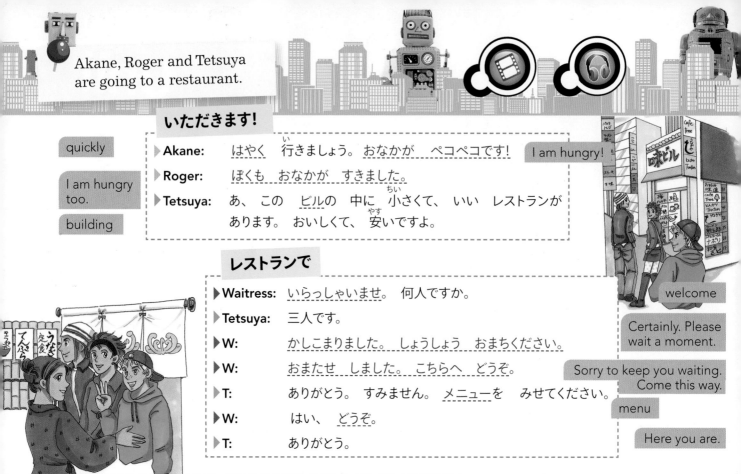

いただきます!

quickly

I am hungry
too.

building

▶ Akane: はやく 行きましょう。 おなかが ペコペコです!　　I am hungry!

▶ Roger: ぼくも おなかが すきました。

▶ Tetsuya: あ、 この ビルの 中に 小さくて、 いい レストランが
あります。 おいしくて、 安いですよ。

レストランで

▶ Waitress: いらっしゃいませ。 何人ですか。　　welcome

▶ Tetsuya: 三人です。

▶ W: かしこまりました。 しょうしょう おまちください。　　Certainly. Please wait a moment.

▶ W: おまたせ しました。 こちらへ どうぞ。　　Sorry to keep you waiting. Come this way.

▶ T: ありがとう。 すみません。 メニューを みせてください。　　menu

▶ W: はい、 どうぞ。　　Here you are.

▶ T: ありがとう。

くいしんぼうレストランメニュー

うどん＊そば	おすすめ		飲みもの	デザート
カレー うどん＊そば 580円	さしみ 980円	ハンバーガー 600円	コーラ 200円	アイスクリーム 550円
なべやき うどん 750円	ぎょうざ 480円	コロッケ 500円	ジュース 250円	チョコレートパフェ 780円
つきみ うどん＊そば 580円	とんかつ 680円	てんぷら 1080円	ビール 450円	プリン 650円
てんぷら うどん＊そば 800円	すのもの 380円	うなぎ 980円	コーヒー 350円	サンデー 650円
	やきとり 480円		こうちゃ 350円	あんみつ 650円
なべもの	とりのてりやき 580円	すし		フルーツパフェ 880円
すきやき 1870円	とうふ ステーキ 580円	まきずし 各 500円 ちらしずし 880円		each
しゃぶしゃぶ 2060円		おにぎり 250円		

おちゃ usually comes free with a meal.

いただきます!

ISBN 9780170198271

udon noodles with curry sauce	

Akane: ロジャーくんは　何に　しますか。

Roger: ええと、　ぼくは　<u>カレーうどん</u>に　します。　あかねさんは　何に　しますか。

A: わたしは　すしを　食^たべたいです。

chicken skewers	

Tetsuya: すみません、<u>やきとり</u>を　一^{ひと}つと　カレーうどんを　一つと　ちらしずしを　二^{ふた}つください。　飲^のみものは　ええと、　コーラを　ください。　**one**　**drinks**

How many glasses?	

Waitress: <u>何ばい</u>ですか。

three glasses	

R: ええと、　三ばいです。

W: かしこまりました。

Cheers!	

All: <u>かんぱい！</u>　<u>いただきます！</u>　**Let's eat.**

A: あれ、　ロジャーくん、　何を　していますか。

chopsticks	

R: ええと、　うどんを　食べています。　<u>おはし</u>を　<u>つかう</u>のは　むずかしいですね。　**using**

T: ねえ、　ロジャーくん、　きょう 何を　しましたか。

bookshop	

R: 買^かいものを　しました。　<u>本や</u>で　じしょを　買いました。　安くて、　いい　じしょが　ありましたよ。

I have finished eating.	

All: <u>ごちそうさま。</u>

I am full.	

T: <u>おなかが　いっぱいです。</u>

A: すみません。　いくらですか。

W: はい、　四千円です。　ありがとう　ございます。

A: ロジャーくん、　何を　していますか。

counting	

R: ええと、　お金^{かね}を　<u>かぞえています。</u>　百円、　百十円、　百二十円…

Questions ○○○○○○○○○○○○

1 Where was the restaurant they went to?
2 What kind of and how many drinks did they order?
3 What kind of food and drink did Tetsuya order for himself?
4 How many different counting systems were used?
5 How much was the total bill? What could you order for this amount in your own currency?

07

百
一

ISBN 9780170198271　　　　　　　　　　　　　　　　　　　　*いただきます！*

れんしゅう

1 Talking about what someone is doing now

A:	何を　していますか。
B:	Nounを　verbています。
一	何を　していますか。
	本を　よんでいます。

2 Asking for what you want

A:	Nounを　ください。
B:	かしこまりました。
一	すみません。　水を　ください。
	かしこまりました。

3 Saying how many general items

A:	いくつですか。
B:	Counter　です。
一	いくつですか。
	三つです。

たんご

おんがくを　ききます	メニュー	フォーク	一つ
テレビを　みます	おちゃ	すし	二つ
かんじを　れんしゅうします	おはし	ハンバーガー	四つ

いただきます！

ISBN 9780170198271

4 Saying how many items (in glasses, cups, bowls)

A:	何ばいですか。
B:	Counterです。
―	はい、何ばいですか。
	二はいです。

5 Telling your friend what you have decided on

A:	何に　しますか。
B:	Nounに　します。
―	ロジャーくんは　何に　しますか。
	ぼくは　カレーうどんに　します。

たんご

うどん	一ぱい	さしみ
コーヒー	三ばい	あかい　ジャケット
水	五はい	バスケットボール

いただきます!

These are the *kanji* and their readings introduced in this unit.

た(べます) to eat

食　食

The roof of a restaurant with a cake.

ノ	人	入	今	今	今	食	食
食							

カンガルーは　くさを　食べます。　→　カンガルーは　くさを　たべます。　→　Kangaroos eat grass.
食べたいです。　→　たべたいです。　→　I want to eat.
食べもの　→　たべもの　→　food
ケーキを　食べましょう。　→　ケーキを　たべましょう。　→　Let's eat a cake.

の(みます) to drink

飲

A waiter in a restaurant serves the drinks.

ノ	人	入	今	今	今	食	食
飠	飲	飲	飲				

おちゃを　飲みたいです。　→　おちゃを　のみたいです。　→　I want to drink tea.
飲みもの　→　のみもの　→　drinks
コーラを　飲みませんか。　→　コーラを　のみませんか。　→　Won't you drink a cola?
飲んでください。　→　のんでください。　→　Please drink it.

い(きます) to go

行　行

Three roads intersect.

ノ	ク	彳	行	行	行		

行きましょう。　→　いきましょう。　→　Let's go.
パーティーに　行きたいです。　→　パーティーに　いきたいです。　→　I want to go to a party.
いっしょに　行きましょう。　→　いっしょに　いきましょう。　→　Let's go together.
バスで　行きます。　→　バスで　いきます。　→　I will go by bus.

か(います) to buy

買　買

A person carries many boxes after shopping – three boxes on top and three underneath.

丶	冂	罒	罒	罒	罒	罒	買
買	買	買	買				

買いもの　→　かいもの　→　shopping
買いたいです。　→　かいたいです。　→　I want to buy (it).
買いました。　→　かいました。　→　I bought (it).
買ってください　→　かってください。　→　Please buy (it).

ISBN 9780170198271

やす(い) cheap

安

A woman calls people to a bargain shop.

`	` `	宀	宀	安	安		

安い ホテル → やすい ホテル → cheap hotel
これは 安いです。 → これは やすいです。 → This is cheap.
安いですか。 → やすいですか。 → Is it cheap?
安かったです。 → やすかったです。 → It was cheap.

たか(い)／コウ high/tall/expensive

高

A tall building is expensive.

`	亠	亠	古	古	古	高	高
高	高						

高い レストラン → たかい レストラン → expensive restaurant
それは 高いです。 → それは たかいです。 → That is expensive.
高かったですか。 → たかかったですか。 → Was it expensive?
せが 高い → せが たかい → tall
高校 → こうこう → senior high school

おお(きい)／ダイ big

大

The fish I caught was *this* big.

一	ナ	大					

大きい → おおきい → big/large
大あめ → おおあめ → heavy rain
大ゆき → おおゆき → heavy snow
大学 → だいがく → university
大人 → おとな → adult

ちい(さい)／ショウ small

小

The fish I caught was *this* small.

亅	小	小					

小さい いす → ちいさい いす → small chair
手が 小さいです。 → てが ちいさいです。 → S/he has small hands.
小学校 → しょうがっこう → primary school

ISBN 9780170198271 いただきます!

サラダまきのすしをつくろう

ざいりょう（4人分）

のり	2まい
こめ	2カップ
す	$\frac{1}{2}$カップ
さとう	（大きい スプーン） 4はい
しお	（大きい スプーン） 1ぱい
アボカド	一つ
きゅうり	一本
かにかまぼこ	100グラム
マヨネーズ	すこし
しょうゆ	すこし
わさび	すこし

1 あたたかい　ごはんに　すと　さとうと
   しおを　まぜます。　ちょっと　まちます。（10分）
2 アボカドと　きゅうりを　きります。
3 すしマットの　上に　のりを　のせます。
4 のりの　上に　ごはんと　アボカドと　きゅうりと
   かにかまぼこと　マヨネーズを　のせます。
5 まきましょう。
6 きりましょう。
できました！

Some people think that Japanese people always eat sushi and sashimi, but Japanese cuisine is more diverse than that! Research some foods that Japanese people eat every day or that are popular in Japan. Can you find a recipe for a dish that interests you and have a go at cooking it? Share your recipe with the class and write a review of the dish you made.

iStockpho

いただきます！

ISBN 9780170198271

マナー

おはしのもちかた
Holding your chopsticks

Hold your chopsticks towards the thicker end. Rest the bottom chopstick on your third finger and in the crook of your thumb. Place the top chopstick between your second finger and your forefinger. Place your thumb across both chopsticks.

おはしのうごかしかた
Moving your chopsticks

To move the top chopstick upwards, hold the bottom chopstick still and push your middle finger up. To move the chopstick downwards, push the top chopstick down with your forefinger. Make sure there is a reasonable angle between the chopsticks at the thick end. You can pick up small items using this technique.

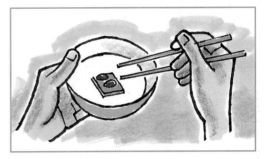

おわんのもちかた
Holding your bowl

When drinking soup or eating rice, it is an important point of etiquette to pick up your bowl. In Japan, it is not considered rude if you slurp your food.

わるいマナー
Poor manners

まよいばし

When you can't decide what you want to eat, don't wave your chopsticks around over the food. It is considered rude.

さしばし

Don't stab food with your chopsticks.

よせばし

Don't pull the dishes towards you using your chopsticks. Always pick up the dish.

Don't pass food from one person to another with your chopsticks.

Don't leave your chopsticks stuck in your rice.

ISBN 9780170198271

いただきます!

Let's get hungry

One of life's simple pleasures is trying the food of other cultures and discovering the differences between their tastes and yours. So, what foods are popular in Japan? What do students eat for lunch? (Hint: some of the answers to these questions can be found in the だいはっけん section of Unit 3).

By looking at recipes, Japanese restaurant menus, television advertisements and brochures, you might be able to discover some interesting things about food, diet, eating habits, customs and food preparation in Japan.

Getty Images/Robert Gilhooly

Alamy/Eye Ubiquitous

Have a think

How would you answer the questions: 'What is Japanese cuisine?' and 'What is Australian cuisine?' Why do you think these might be challenging questions to answer? Is one question more difficult to answer than the other? Do you think a Japanese person would answer the same way as you have?

Have a go

1 Go into one of the many Japanese restaurants in Australia and get a copy of its menu, or look up the restaurant's menu online. Drawing on your research about Japanese food, how well does the menu represent the range of foods that people in Japan eat on a daily basis?

2 With a partner, use a menu as a prompt and pretend that you are in a restaurant in Japan, ready to order your meal.

いただきます!

ISBN 9780170198271

文法
ぶんぽう

1 Talking about what someone is doing now

A:	何を　していますか。
B:	Nounを　verbています。
A:	ロジャーくんは　何を　していますか。 What are you doing/playing, Roger?
B:	本を　よんでいます。 I am reading a book.
A:	ともだちは　何を　みていますか。 What is your friend watching?
B:	ともだちは　テレビを　みています。 My friend is watching TV.

Getty Images/Peter Dazeley

2 Asking for what you want

A:	メニューを　ください。
A:	Noun を　ください。

> You can ask about drinks using いくつですか. You can also use the general counting words 一つ, 二つ, etc. to talk about drinks as well.

3 Saying how many general items

A:	いくつですか。 How many (do you want)?
B:	Counterです。
B:	一つです。 One.

Getty Images/BLOOM Image

4 Saying how many items (in glasses, cups, bowls)

A:	何ばいですか。
B:	Counterです。
B:	四はいです。

5 Telling a friend what you have decided

A:	何に　しますか。 (What will you have?)
B:	すしと　おちゃに　します。 I will have sushi and tea.

Getty Images/Dex

ISBN 9780170198271 いただきます！

Restaurant phrases

いらっしゃいませ。	Welcome.
かしこまりました。	Certainly.
しょうしょう　おまちください。	Please wait one moment.
おまたせ　しました。	Sorry to keep you waiting.
メニュー	menu
おつり	change
おなかが　ペコペコです。	I am hungry.
おなかが　すきました。	I am hungry.
かんぱい!	Cheers!
いただきます。	Let's eat!
ごちそうさま（でした）。	I have finished eating.
おなかが　いっぱいです。	I am full.
いくらですか。	How much is it?
大きい	large
小さい	small
高い	expensive/dear
安い	cheap

Counting long, cylindrical items

いっぽん 一本	ごほん 五本	きゅうほん 九本
にほん 二本	ろっぽん 六本	じゅっぽん 十本
さんぼん 三本	ななほん 七本	なんぼん 何本?
よんほん 四本	はっぽん 八本	

Counting small animals

いっぴき 一匹	ななひき 七匹
にひき 二匹	はっぴき 八匹
さんびき 三匹	きゅうひき 九匹
よんひき 四匹	じゅっぴき 十匹
ごひき 五匹	なんびき 何匹?
ろっぴき 六匹	

Counting general items

ひと 一つ	1	いつ 五つ	5	ここの 九つ	9
ふた 二つ	2	むっ 六つ	6	とお 十	10
みっ 三つ	3	なな 七つ	7	じゅういち 十一	11
よっ 四つ	4	やっ 八つ	8	じゅうに 十二	12

Counting glasses, cups and bowls

いっ 一ぱい	1 glass/cup	ろっ 六ぱい	6 glasses/cups
に 二はい	2 glasses/cups	なな 七はい	7 glasses/cups
さん 三ばい	3 glasses/cups	はっ 八ぱい	8 glasses/cups
よん 四はい	4 glasses/cups	きゅう 九はい	9 glasses/cups
ご 五はい	5 glasses/cups	じゅっ 十ぱい	10 glasses/cups

Did you notice the way items are counted up to 10? This way of counting uses *kun-yomi*, Japanese pronunciations, dating from before the Chinese influence on the Japanese language. They all end in a つ sound, except for 10. After 10, the counters are pronounced in the familiar way: 11 (じゅういち), 12 (じゅうに), etc.

いくつ is used to ask how many general items you want. 何ばい is used to ask how many items in glasses or cups.

ISBN 9780170198271

Photos by iStockphoto

Counting large animals

いっとう 一頭	ななとう 七頭
にとう 二頭	はっとう 八頭
さんとう 三頭	きゅうとう 九頭
よんとう 四頭	じゅっとう 十頭
ごとう 五頭	なんとう 何頭?
ろくとう 六頭	

Counting books and magazines

いっさつ 一冊	きゅうさつ 九冊
にさつ 二冊	じゅっさつ 十冊
さんさつ 三冊	なんさつ 何冊?
よんさつ 四冊	
ごさつ 五冊	
ろくさつ 六冊	
ななさつ 七冊	
はっさつ 八冊	

Counting floors in buildings

いっかい 一階	きゅうかい 九階
にかい 二階	じゅっかい 十階
さんがい 三階	なんがい 何階?
よんかい 四階	
ごかい 五階	
ろっかい 六階	
ななかい 七階	
はちかい 八階	

Counting houses and shops

いっけん 一軒	ななけん 七軒
にけん 二軒	はっけん 八軒
さんげん 三軒	きゅうけん 九軒
よんけん 四軒	じゅっけん 十軒
ごけん 五軒	なんげん 何軒?
ろっけん 六軒	

Counting thin, flat items

いちまい 一枚	ななまい 七枚
にまい 二枚	はちまい 八枚
さんまい 三枚	きゅうまい 九枚
よんまい 四枚	じゅうまい 十枚
ごまい 五枚	なんまい 何枚?
ろくまい 六枚	

Counting machinery

いちだい 一台	ななだい 七台
にだい 二台	はちだい 八台
さんだい 三台	きゅうだい 九台
よんだい 四台	じゅうだい 十台
ごだい 五台	なんだい 何台?
ろくだい 六台	

Questions

Which counters should be used when counting the following things:

1 うし (cows)?
2 パンや (bakeries)?
3 きんぎょ (goldfish)?
4 Tシャツ (T-shirts)?
5 ペン (pens)?
6 じしょ (dictionaries)?
7 コンピューター (computers)?

Japanese has many special words for counting items. Different counters are used depending on the characteristics of the items, such as their shape or size.

07

百十一

ISBN 9780170198271

いただきます!

Counters

Both English and Japanese use counting words. For example, in English, we say, 'six people' or '10 glasses of water'. In Japanese, you need to use different counting words depending on what you are talking about. You already know the counter for people (人). So 'six people' is 六人.

In this unit, counters that can be used in general situations were introduced. However, there are a number of other counters as well. はい is one example. It is the counter for liquids served in glasses or cups, and also for bowls of noodles.

You need to be careful with the pronunciation of counters because when they are written in *kanji*, you can't always tell how they should be said. The numbers with unexpected pronunciations are:

一　いっぱい
三　さんばい
六　ろっぱい
八　はっぱい
十　じゅっぱい

Getty Images/Indeed

Particle panic!

何に しますか。(What have you decided?)

This phrase is used when people are deciding what they will order to eat. Make sure you use に and not を because the meaning of the sentence changes.

に

A:	何に　しますか。What will you have?
B:	すしに　します。I've decided on sushi.

を

A:	何を　しますか。What do you do? / What will you do?
B:	すしを　食べます。I eat sushi. / I will eat sushi.

Shutterstock/bikeriderlondon

いただきます!

ISBN 9780170198271

ホームステイ

In this unit, you will learn to:

- ask for and give permission to do something
- refuse permission to do something
- ask someone to do something for you and respond when asked
- ask the reason why and respond when asked
- recognise and write the *kanji* characters 私, 男, 女, 書, 見, 聞, 父 and 母

In this unit, you will learn about:

- Japanese culture: Japanese etiquette and social customs, and cultural features of living in a Japanese home
- intercultural understanding: similarities and differences between school rules in Japan and Australia
- text types: email, conversation, speech

Jessica has just arrived in Japan on a short-term exchange program. She is sending emails to her friends back home, letting them know what her stay in Japan is like.

ジェシカのEメール

To: karen@hitmail.com; sarah@hitmail.com; tony@hitmail.com

Subject: こんにちは!

みなさん、 こんにちは。 私(わたし)は 日本に います。 日本は すばらしいです。 **amazing**

私の ホストファミリーは 三人 かぞくです。 とても しんせつです。

お父(とう)さんは とても いそがしいです。 でも、 水(すい)えいが 大(だい)すきですから、

この しゅうまつに いっしょに うみに 行きます。

お母(かあ)さんは やさしい です。

おねえさんも 高校(こうこう)生ですから、 あした いっしょに 学校に 行きます。

たのしみに しています。

じゃ、 また あした。 学校の あとで、 Eメールを 書(か)きます。

おやすみなさい。

ジェシカ

Questions ○ ○ ○ ○ ○ ○ ○ ○ ○ ○ ○

1 Who is in Jessica's host family?

2 What does she plan to do with each of them?

---

entrance	**Mother:**	ジェシカさん、 げんかんで くつを ぬいでください。
shoe box		それから、 くつを げたばこに いれて、 スリッパを はいてください。 **slippers**
	Jessica:	はい、 わかりました。
	M:	ジェシカさん、 この へやは わしつです。 たたみの へやです。 **quietly**
paper door		スリッパを ぬいでください。 これは しょうじです。 しずかに あけてください。
	J:	はい、 わかりました。 お母さん、 ともだちに Eメールを 書きたいです。 コンピューターを つかっても いいですか。
	M:	はい、 どうぞ。 ジェシカさんの へやに コンピューターが ありますよ。
	M:	ジェシカさん、 この へやは ジェシカさんの へやです。 おふろばは **bathroom**
any time		となりに あります。 いつでも シャワーを あびて ください。
window	**J:**	ありがとう。 わあ、 まどから こうえんが 見(み)えます。 **visible/can see**
		行っても いいですか。
	M:	はい、 ばんごはんの あとで、 いっしょに 行きましょう。

ホームステイ

ISBN 9780170198271

1 What places around the house does Jessica's host mother show her?
2 What is Jessica allowed to do?
3 What activities does she have planned for the rest of the day?

To : karen@hitmail.com; sarah@hitmail.com; tony@hitmail.com

Subject : もう一ど　こんにちは!

the first time

みなさん、　きょうは　<u>はじめて</u>　学校に　行きました。　じてんしゃで
行きました。　<u>ほんとうに　ドキドキしました</u>。 — I was really nervous.

私の　クラスメートは　みんな　やさしいですから、　うれしいです。

as well as — <u>男</u>（おとこ）<u>のこ</u>も　<u>女</u>（おんな）<u>のこ</u>も　います。　みんな　すこし　えいごが　<u>はなせます</u>。 — can talk

school rules — 学校の　<u>校そく</u>は　ちょっと　きびしいです。　<u>たとえば</u>、　きょうしつの　中で — for example
おんがくを　<u>聞</u>（き）<u>いては</u>　だめです。　けいたいでんわを　つかっては

gum — だめです。　<u>ガムを　かんで</u>は　だめです。　それから、　じゅぎょう<u>中</u>（ちゅう）に — chew

of course — ともだちと　<u>しゃべっては</u>　だめです。　<u>もちろん</u>、　ちこくを　しては　だめです。

schoolyard — それから、　<u>校ていで</u>　ひるごはんを　<u>食べては　だめです</u>。　へんですね。 — cannot eat
みんな　きょうしつで　ひるごはんを　食べます。

tired — じゃ、　<u>つかれています</u>から、　<u>もう</u>　ねます。 — already

reply — <u>へんじ</u>を　書いてくださいね。

ジェシカ

ISBN 9780170198271

ホームステイ

ジェシカの一日

Questions

1 How is Jessica's host mother taking care of her?

2 When does Jessica use set phrases?

ISBN 9780170198271

1 Asking permission to do something

A:	Verbても　いいですか。
B:	はい、　いいです。
—	でんわを　つかっても　いいですか。
	はい、　いいです。

2 Refusing someone permission

8.2, 8.5

| A: | Verb ては　だめです。 |
| — | このにわに　はいっては　だめです。 |

3 Giving a reason

B:	Reasonから。
—	どうして、　そとに　行っては　だめですか。
	あぶないですから。

4 Explaining an action

| A: | Reasonから、　outcome。 |
| — | たたみの　へやですから、　スリッパを　ぬいでください。 |

たんご

手を　あらいます
シャワーを　あびます
イヤリングを　します
パーティーに　行きます

じゅぎょう中に　はなします
学校で　おかしを　食べます
うちに　きます

あめが　ふっています。
さむいです。
じゅぎょう中です。

てんきが　わるいです。
らい年、日本に　行きます。
ひるごはんを　食べました。

テニスを　しません。
日本ごの　べんきょうを　しています。
おなかが　いっぱいです。

See the ぶんぽうプラス section of Unit 5 for more on the て form.

08

百十七

117

ISBN 9780170198271

ホームステイ

かんじ

These are the *kanji* and their readings introduced in this unit.

わたし（わたくし）／シ I/me

私 私

Japanese people point to their noses to indicate 'me'.

ノ	二	千	禾	禾	私	私	

私の → わたしの → my/mine
私たち → わたしたち → we
私立学校 → しりつがっこう → private school

Where would you point to indicate 'me' or 'mine'?

おとこ male/man

男 男

A man is working in a rice field.

一	口	冂	田	用	田	男	男	

男の人 → おとこの ひと → man
男の子 → おとこの こ → boy

おんな female/woman

女 女

A woman is wearing a kimono.

く	女	女				

女の人 → おんなの ひと → woman
女の子 → おんなのこ → girl

か（きます）／ショ to write

書 書

A hand is holding a brush writing the *kanji* にち.

⁊	⁊	⁊	글	글	聿	聿	書
書	書						

本を 書きます。 → ほんを かきます。 → I will write a book.
書いています。 → かいています。 → I am writing.
書道 → しょどう → calligraphy
図書館 → としょかん → library
辞書 → じしょ → dictionary

ISBN 9780170198271

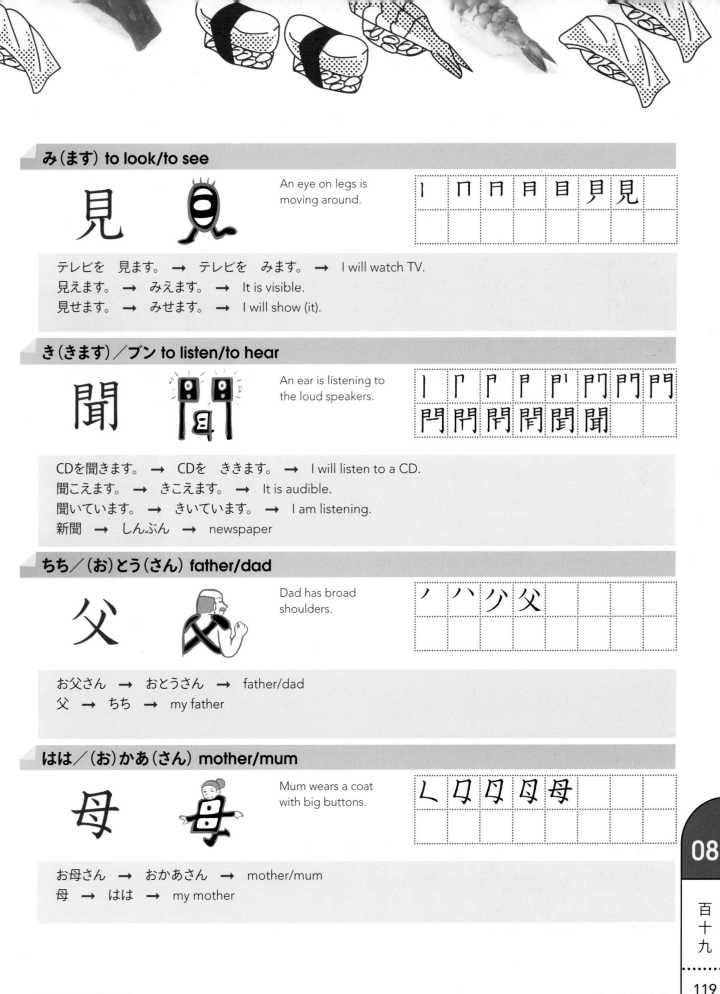

み（ます）to look/to see

見

An eye on legs is moving around.

一	冂	冃	月	目	貝	見	

テレビを　見ます。　→　テレビを　みます。　→　I will watch TV.
見えます。　→　みえます。　→　It is visible.
見せます。　→　みせます。　→　I will show (it).

き（きます）／ブン to listen/to hear

聞

An ear is listening to the loud speakers.

一	厂	F	F	門	門	門	門
門	門	門	間	聞	聞		

CDを聞きます。　→　CDを　ききます。　→　I will listen to a CD.
聞こえます。　→　きこえます。　→　It is audible.
聞いています。　→　きいています。　→　I am listening.
新聞　→　しんぶん　→　newspaper

ちち／（お）とう（さん）father/dad

父

Dad has broad shoulders.

ノ	ハ	ク	父				

お父さん　→　おとうさん　→　father/dad
父　→　ちち　→　my father

はは／（お）かあ（さん）mother/mum

母

Mum wears a coat with big buttons.

し	乫	毋	毋	母			

お母さん　→　おかあさん　→　mother/mum
母　→　はは　→　my mother

ISBN 9780170198271

ホームステイ

Here is a list of rules Jessica saw on a poster on the classroom wall in her host school. In what ways are the rules the same as or different from your school rules?

校そく

word

rubbish

wall

scribble

make-up

1 わるい　ことばを　つかっては　だめです。
2 学校で　ガムを　かんでは　だめです。
3 ごみを　ごみばこに　いれてください。
4 つくえと　かべに　らくがきを　しては　だめです。
5 きょうしつで　ひるごはんを　食べても　いいです。
6 きょうしつで　けいたいでんわを　つかっては　だめです。
7 まい日　しゅくだいを　してください。
8 けしょう、　マニキュア、　アクセサリーを　しては　だめです。
9 ちこくを　しては　だめです。

Getty Images/Mimi Haddon

Prepare a list of your school's rules to help a visiting exchange student.

The Japanese home Jessica is staying in has a わしつ – a Japanese-style room. Her host mother explained the rules of living in a Japanese home. What has she learnt about her host family and their lifestyle?

げんかんで　くつを　ぬいでください。

しょうじは　かみですから、　しずかに　あけてください。

とこのまに　あがっては　だめです。

to go up

ざぶとんの　上に　たっては　だめです。

こたつは　とても　あついですから、　きを　つけてください。

トイレでは　トイレの　スリッパを　はいてください。

Questions

○○○○○○○○○○○○○○○○○○○○○○○○○○○

Imagine you have a Japanese student staying in your home.
Talk to them about the rules in place in your house – things you are allowed to do and not allowed to do, and requests your parents might make of you. These might be about using the computer or TV, and about cleaning. Make a list for them.

ホームステイ

ISBN 9780170198271

Jessica has prepared a speech for her homeroom class. She will tell them a little about herself.

Jessica's speech

はじめまして。　私は　ジェシカ　テイラーです。　オーストラリア人です。
せん月　日本に　きました。　私は　ブリスベンに　すんでいます。　かぞくは
五人です。　父と　母と　あにが　二人　です。

私は　十年生です。　すきな　かもくは　ちりと　すう学と　日本ごです。
しゅうまつに　ともだちと　うみに　行きます。　私の　うちは　うみに
ちかいですから、　よく　うみで　水えいを　します。　みなさん、　日本では
わかい　人は　しゅうまつに　何を　しますか。　おしえてください。

日本の　食べものは　とても　おいしいです。　日本の　食べものが
すきですから、　母と　よく　日本りょうりを　つくります。　一ばん
すきな　りょうりは　手まきずしです。　いっしょに　つくりましょう。
私の　ホストの　お母さんは　りょうりが　上手ですから、　まい日
ばんごはんが　たのしみです。　私の　ホストファミリーは　とても
しんせつです。

日本の　学校の　きそくは　きびしいです。　この　学校は
大きくて、　生とが　たくさん　います。　さいしょは　ちょっと
ドキドキ　しました。　でも、　みなさん　とても　やさしいです。
ともだちが　たくさん　できましたから、　うれしいです。

日本ごと　日本の　ぶんかを　いっしょうけんめい
べんきょう　します。

close
teach/tell
hand-rolled sushi
rules
at first
nervous
culture
as hard as I can

Shutterstock/Kheng Guan Toh

Have a go ○○○○○○○○○○○○○○○○○

What kind of information does Jessica give about herself?
In preparation for introducing yourself to Japanese people you might meet, write a profile detailing who you are, your likes, your dislikes and your other characteristics.

08

百二十一

121

ISBN 9780170198271

ホームステイ

大発見
だいはっけん

Being yourself

The things that are the most important to you might not be the most important to a Japanese student, or to other people for that matter. Following rules and guidelines is often a balancing act between respecting your surroundings and being true to yourself. However, understanding the importance of rules and being aware of how your actions can affect others are very important skills for adapting to new situations, particularly if you want to avoid giving the wrong impression about yourself.

Have a think ○○○○○○○○○○○

Walking in someone else's slippers

Imagine you are on exchange at a school in Japan:

1   Which school rules in Japan would you find the most difficult to stick to? Why?
2   Would you be more careful about finding out the rules and sticking to them than you would be if you moved to another school in your own state? Why?
3   To test for different perspectives, explain your views to your teacher or to a Japanese speaker. What do they think would be most important in this scenario? What advice can they give you on how to speak or act in Japan?

Corbis/Kevin R. Morris

Getty Images/Annie Griffiths Belt

ホームステイ

ISBN 9780170198271

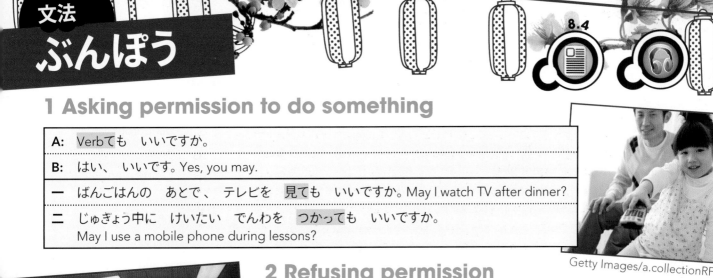

8.4

1 Asking permission to do something

A:	Verbても　いいですか。
B:	はい、　いいです。Yes, you may.
一	ばんごはんの　あとで、　テレビを　見ても　いいですか。May I watch TV after dinner?
二	じゅぎょう中に　けいたい　でんわを　つかっても　いいですか。 May I use a mobile phone during lessons?

Getty Images/a.collectionRF

Glow Images

2 Refusing permission

A:	Verbて は　だめです。
一	じゅぎょう中に　けいたい　でんわを　つかっては　だめです。 You must not use a mobile phone during lessons.

3 Asking for a reason

A:	どうして〜か。
一	うちの　中で　くつを　はいては　だめです。　どうしてですか。 We must not wear shoes in the house. Why is that?
二	どうして、　ほうかご　買いものに　行きますか。 Why are you going shopping after school?

4 Explaining an action

A:	Reasonから、　outcome。
A:	きたないですから、　うち　の　中で　くつを　はいては　だめです。 We must not wear shoes in the home because they are dirty.
A:	あたらしい　せいふくを　買いたいですから、　買いものに　行きます。 I will go shopping because I want to buy a new uniform.

There are other ways to use から, but these are the ways you have learnt to use it in this unit to mean 'because':

After です

私は　日本ごが　すきですから、　日本に　行きたいです。 I want to go to Japan because I like Japanese.
高いですから、　買いません。 I will not buy it because it is expensive.
きょうは　いい　てんきですから、　こうえんに　行きましょう。 Let's go to the park because the weather is good today.

Getty Images/hana

After ます／ました verbs

しゅくだいを　しましたから、　テレビを　見ても　いいですか。 May I watch TV because I have done my homework?

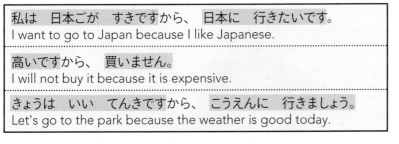

ISBN 9780170198271

ホームステイ

08

単語 たんご

Places

きょうしつ	classroom
げんかん	entrance
校てい	schoolyard
たたみの　へや	tatami room

Verbs

あらいます	wash
いれます	put in
おきます	get up (おきます is a group 2 verb.)
おしえます	teach
おふろに　はいります	have a bath
かみます	chew
さわります	touch
しゃべります	chat
シャワーを　あびます	have a shower (あびます is a group 2 verb.)
そうじ（を）します	clean
ちこく（を）します	be late
つかいます	use
つかれます	get tired
ドキドキします	be nervous/excited
ぬぎます	take off (clothing)
ねます	sleep
はいります	enter
かえます	change

Adjectives

あぶない	dangerous
うるさい	noisy
うれしい	happy/glad
きたない	dirty
しんせつ（な）	kind
すばらしい	amazing
わかい	young
あたらしい	new

Phrases

いただきます	(Appreciation given before eating.)
いってきます。	I will be back.
いってらっしゃい	See you when you get back.
おかえりなさい。	Welcome home.
ごちそうさま。	Thank you for the meal/drink (after eating).
ごめんなさい。	I am sorry.
しつれいします。	Excuse me/ Goodbye.
すみません。	I am sorry/Excuse me/Thank you.
ただいま。	I am home.
もちろん	of course

Corbis/AID

ISBN 9780170198271

School-related words

じゅぎょう	lessons
じゅぎょう中	during lessons
ほうかご	after school

Alamy

Nouns

かばん	bag
きそく	rules
けいたいでんわ	mobile phone
けしょう	make-up
げたばこ/くつばこ	shoe box
校そく	school rules
ごみ	rubbish
ごみばこ	rubbish bin
せいふく	uniform
マニキュア	manicure/nail polish
らくがき	graffiti

Refer to the verb lists on page 81 for more verbs in the て form.

The て form

Group 1 verbs

ます form	て form	English
あそびます	あそんで	play
行きます	行って (exception)	go
およぎます	およいで	swim
買います	買って	buy
聞きます	聞いて	listen
飲みます	飲んで	drink
はしります	はしって	run
まちます	まって	wait

Group 2 verbs

ます form	て form	English
でかけます	でかけて	go out
見ます	見て	see

Group 3 (irregular) verbs

ます form	て form	English
きます	きて	come
します	して	do/play sport

Getty Images/Atsushi Sakai

08

百二十五

125

ISBN 9780170198271

ホームステイ

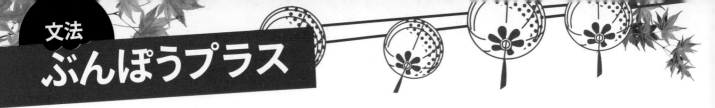

ぶんぽうプラス

Ways to use the て form

Have you noticed in this unit that the て form can be used in many ways?
Look at your choices:

食べて、…	(I eat and … (do something else))
食べています。	(We are eating.)
食べても　いいです。	(You are allowed to eat.)
食べては　だめです。	(I am not allowed to eat.)
食べてください。	(Please eat.)

Once you have made the て form, you just choose the ending you need to express what you want to say.

Alamy/MIXA

Before and after

You have learnt the words 前 (before) and あと (after). These are very useful. For example:

あさごはんの　前に	(before breakfast)
ばんごはんの　あとで	(after dinner)

How many other examples can you think of?

> A special word for `after school' is
> ほうかご, so you don't have to say
> 学校の　あとで.

Both … and …

You have seen this sentence:

男のこも　女のこも　います。 (There are both boys and girls.)

'〜も〜も' means 'both … and …' or '… as well as …'. You can use it to mean 'neither … nor …'.

男のこも　女のこも　いません。 (There are neither boys nor girls.)

Corbis/doable

08

百二十六

126

ホームステイ

ISBN 9780170198271

ともだちのプロフィール

Develop a profile of a Japanese student by asking the questions listed below. Think of some situations where this type of profile might be useful. Ask a friend these questions and write their answers in your exercise book.

1　おな前は？
2　何時に　おきますか。
3　学校の　前に　何を　しますか。
4　学校の　あとで　ともだちと　何を　しますか。
5　何で　学校に　行きますか。
6　学校で　何を　べんきょうしていますか。
7　一ばん　すきな　おんがくは　何ですか。
8　しゅうまつに　何を　しますか。
9　うちの　中で　くつを　はいていますか。
10　うちで　よく　コンピューターを　つかいますか。

だれでしょうか。Draw up a table of five or six questions to ask a class member. Report back to the class without saying who you are talking about and see if the rest of the class can identify who it is.

Getty Images/ULTRA.F

ISBN 9780170198271

ホームステイ

役所
City Office
250m

280m

西武新宿駅
Seibu-Shinjuku Sta.

現在地
Address
新宿区新宿3丁目38番
3-38, Shinjuku,
Shinjuku City

■ 広域図 / Key Map

新宿区
Shinjuku City

まっすぐ行きます

In this unit, you will learn to:

- ask where something is
- give directions (going straight ahead, crossing, turning, getting there)
- say when/if you do something and what happens next
- join two or more sets of actions
- show the order of actions
- ask how long it takes to go somewhere or do something, and respond
- recognise and write the *kanji* characters 右, 左, 入, 出, 東, 西, 南 and 北

In this unit, you will learn about:

- Japanese culture: differences between Japanese and Australian addresses
- intercultural understanding: Japanese addresses off the map – how history, culture and social networks play a part in how people think of place and location
- text types: manga, map directions, games

Alamy/Jochen Tack

3430
7604

Shintaro invited Sarah and Shoko to come to a festival at Yasaka Shrine near his house. Sarah is very excited, but Shoko is a little bit worried they might get lost. Shintaro gave them instructions on how to get there. Can they find Yasaka Shrine?

セーラとしょうこ

To: sarah@hitmail.com
Subject: おまつりに 行きましょう。

セーラさん、 らいしゅうの 土曜日に やさかじんじゃで
おまつりが あります。 いっしょに 行きませんか。
ホストシスターの しょうこさんと きてください。
ごご三時に やさかじんじゃで あいましょう。
しんたろうより

じんじゃで おまつり！たのしみ！

きょうと、
きょうと、
きょうとです。
ドアが しまります。

The door will close.

大きい えき！

セーラさん、
しんたろうくんの
Eメールを
見せてください。

きょうとえきの 西口を 出てから、
右に まがってください。 そうすると、
バスていが あります。 205ばんの
バスに のって しじょうかわらまち まで
行きます。 えきから 「しじょうかわらまち」
まで バスで 十分ぐらいです。

タクシーのりば
おおさか
バスてい
トイレ
ゆうびんきょく
デパート
グランドホテル
グランドホテル
グランドホテル
東京→
しんかんせん 西口
しんかんせん 中央口
トイレ

えーと。 西口を
出てから、
右に まがって…

すみません。
西口は どこですか。

西口ですか。
あのかいだんの
上です。

まっすぐ行きます

ISBN 9780170198271

Questions

1 What is the relationship between Shoko and Sarah?
2 When is the festival? What time and where are they meeting?
3 Where did Sarah want to go as well as to the shrine?
4 From the exit, how does she get to the Yasaka Shrine?
5 What other information would you give in English that has not been used here?

れんしゅう

1 Asking where something is

A:	えきは　どこですか。
A:	このへんに　トイレが　ありますか。
B:	すみません。　バスていに　行きたいんですが…

2 Giving directions

Going straight ahead
Nounを　まっすぐ　行きます。
この　みちを　まっすぐ　行きます。
Crossing
Nounを　わたります。
はしを　わたります。
Turning
Noun(place)を　directionに　まがります。
二つめの　かどを　左に　まがります。
Getting there
そうすると、　directionがわに　nounが　あります。
そうすると、　左がわに　ゆうびんきょくが　あります。

POST OFFICE

たんご

ぎん行 こうえん きっさてん	しんごう あの　みち	こうさてん ふみきり	ぎん行の　かど、南（みなみ） つぎの　しんごう、左	右がわ、コンビニ 目の前、バスてい

　　　ISBN 9780170198271

3 Joining two or more sets of actions

A:	Direction A verbて、direction B verbてください。
B:	まっすぐ　行って、　しんごうを　右に　まがってください。
一	あの　こうさてんを　まっすぐ　行って、　一つ目の しんごうを　右に　まがります。
二	あの　しんごうを　わたって、　まっすぐ　行ってください。
三	あの　かどを　右に　まがって、　まっすぐ　行って、 コンビニの　かどを　左に　まがります。　そうすると、 大きい　こうえんが　あります。

4 Showing the order of actions

Direction A　verbて から、direction B verbてください。
あのかどを　左に　まがってから、　はしを　わたってください。

5 Asking and telling how long it takes

A:	どの　ぐらい　かかりますか。
B:	Duration ぐらい　かかります or です。。
一	どの　ぐらい　かかりますか。
	バスで　四十分ぐらい　かかります。

たんご

右に　まがってください、　はしを　わたってください。
まっすぐ　行ってください、　ふみきりを　わたります。
こうさてんを　右に　まがってください、　まっすぐ　いきます。

でんしゃで、　五十分
ひこうきで、　十三時かん半
あるいて、　十五分

09

百
三
十
三

133

ISBN 9780170198271

まっすぐ行きます

かんじ

These are the *kanji* and their readings introduced in this unit.

みぎ／ユウ right

右

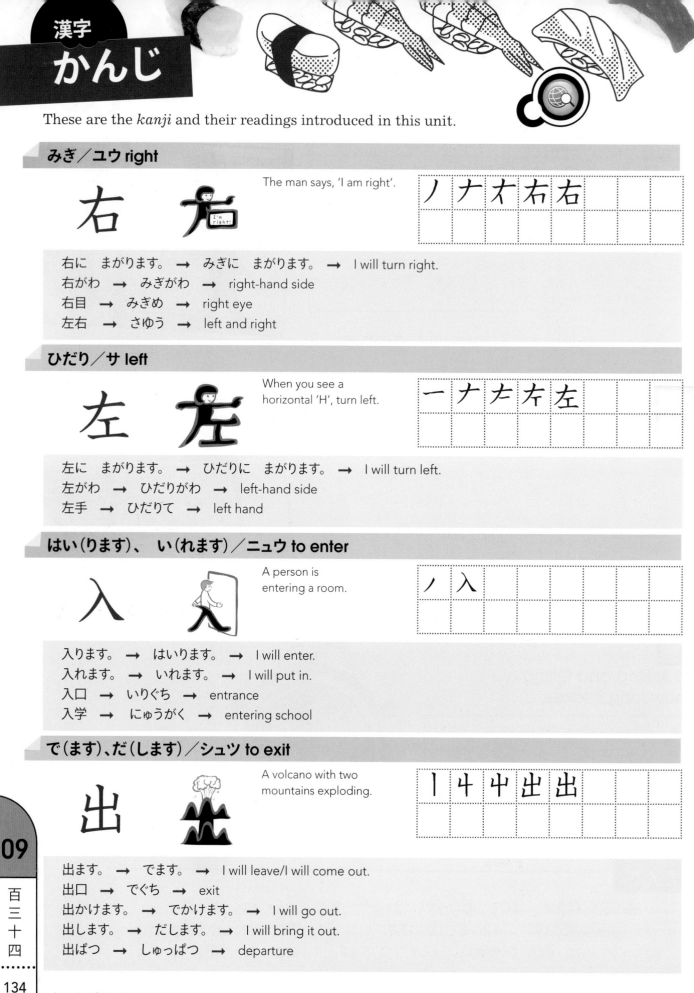

The man says, 'I am right'.

ノ ナ ナ 右 右

右に　まがります。　→　みぎに　まがります。　→　I will turn right.
右がわ　→　みぎがわ　→　right-hand side
右目　→　みぎめ　→　right eye
左右　→　さゆう　→　left and right

ひだり／サ left

左

When you see a horizontal 'H', turn left.

一 ナ ナ 七 左

左に　まがります。　→　ひだりに　まがります。　→　I will turn left.
左がわ　→　ひだりがわ　→　left-hand side
左手　→　ひだりて　→　left hand

はい（ります）、 い（れます）／ニュウ to enter

入

A person is entering a room.

ノ 入

入ります。　→　はいります。　→　I will enter.
入れます。　→　いれます。　→　I will put in.
入口　→　いりぐち　→　entrance
入学　→　にゅうがく　→　entering school

で（ます）、だ（します）／シュツ to exit

出

A volcano with two mountains exploding.

｜ 屮 屮 出 出

出ます。　→　でます。　→　I will leave/I will come out.
出口　→　でぐち　→　exit
出かけます。　→　でかけます。　→　I will go out.
出します。　→　だします。　→　I will bring it out.
出ぱつ　→　しゅっぱつ　→　departure

まっすぐ行きます

ISBN 9780170198271

ひがし／トウ east

東

The sun rises from behind a tree in the east.

一 丆 亓 亓 亘 車 東 東

東 → ひがし → east
東がわ → ひがしがわ → eastern side
東口 → ひがしぐち → eastern entrance
東北 → とうほく → north-eastern district of Japan

にし／セイ west

西

Four wise men in the west invented pi.

一 丆 亓 丙 西 西

西 → にし → west
西がわ → にしがわ → western side
西口 → にしぐち → western entrance
南西 → なんせい → south-west

The English order for compass points is North, South, East, West but the Japanese order is 東西南北.

みなみ／ナン south

南

Criminals bury some money under a hill.

一 十 广 广 内 内 南 南
南

南 → みなみ → south
南がわ → みなみがわ → south side
南口 → みなみぐち → south entrance
南東 → なんとう → south-east

きた／ホク north

北

Which way is north? One says this way, one says that way.

一 十 土 北 北

北 → きた → north
北がわ → きたがわ → north side
北口 → きたぐち → north entrance
北西 → ほくせい → north-west

ISBN 9780170198271

まっすぐ行きます

にほんぶんか

On the streets

One of the most striking differences you might notice in any new country is the look and feel of the street signs in a different language.

Getty Images/Pan Tang

iStockphoto/winhorse

百三十六

136

まっすぐ行きます

On the map

Yusuke has written down how to get to places from his house for his host brother, Alex. Read Yusuke's directions, and find his school and subway station.

学校

うちを　出て　右に　行きます。　そうすると、　しんごうが　あります。　その、　しんごうを
右に　まがります。　そして、　つぎの　しんごうを　左に　まがって、　まっすぐ
行ってください。　右がわに　中学校が　あります。　うちから　学校まで
あるいて　五分です。
こまった　ときは　でんわしてください。

when you have a problem

けいたいでんわ：０７０１—８１９—４０３

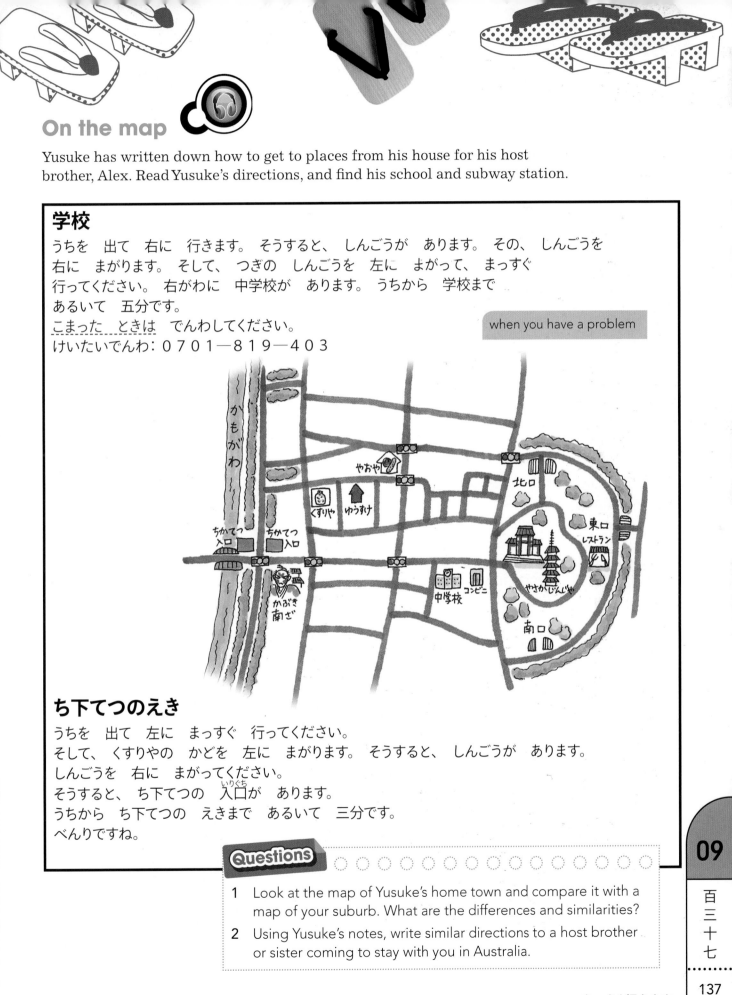

ち下てつのえき

うちを　出て　左に　まっすぐ　行ってください。
そして、　くすりやの　かどを　左に　まがります。　そうすると、　しんごうが　あります。
しんごうを　右に　まがってください。
そうすると、　ち下てつの　入口が　あります。
うちから　ち下てつの　えきまで　あるいて　三分です。
べんりですね。

Questions

1　Look at the map of Yusuke's home town and compare it with a map of your suburb. What are the differences and similarities?

2　Using Yusuke's notes, write similar directions to a host brother or sister coming to stay with you in Australia.

百三十七

ISBN 9780170198271

まっすぐ行きます

9.4

Alamy/Peter Horee

Getty Images/Melissa Tse

Japanese addresses off the map

It is very easy to assume that everyone uses the same method to find an address as you do. However, a person's sense of place and location is influenced by factors such as history, culture and even technology, all of which differ between countries. In Japan, an address is more about what else is nearby than about street names.

In Australia, the names of streets are the main way of finding directions to a house or other location. Each building in a street has a number. But what if not all streets had names?

In Japan, large streets, roads and highways may be named, but small streets often do not have names. Houses may be numbered by block, not street. The block a Japanese person lives on will have a reference number and be a part of a local precinct.

Questions

○○○○○○○○○○○○○○○○○○○○○○○

1 Find a large-scale map of part of a town or suburb in a city in Japan. What do you notice about the map's features and layout? How would these features affect giving directions in Japan?

2 Compare the map to a large-scale map of a town or suburb in Australia. What differences can you find in the Australian map's features and layout compared with a Japanese map?

Directions

North (北), south (南), east (東) and west (西) are the four compass points. Between these points are north-east (北東), north-west (北西), south-east (南東) and south-west (南西). Note that the characters and words for these compass points are written and said in the same order as in English.

However, you may also see words like 東南アジア (South-East Asia). Note that this is written as 'East-South-Asia' in Japanese, but the meaning is the same as saying 'South-East Asia' in English. This is a good example of how you cannot simply translate word-for-word from English to Japanese.

Shutterstock/
Martin Mette

Have a go

○○○○○○○○○○

A Japanese speaker asks you for directions. They speak very little English, so you must use your language and cultural knowledge to give directions in Japanese. Create a list of useful phrases that you may need to know.

Corbis/Nobuaki Sumida

iStockphoto/Andrejs Zemdega

1 Asking where something is

A: Placeは　どこですか。
A: このへんに　place が　ありますか。
A: すみません。　Place に　行きたいんですが。
一　すみません。　えいがかんは　どこですか。 Excuse me. Where is the movie theatre?
二　この　へんに　トイレが　ありますか。 Is there a toilet around here?
三　すみません。　ゆうびんきょくに　行きたいんですが。 Excuse me. I want to go to the post office.

Use んです to give a reason.

2 Giving directions

Going straight ahead

Nounを　まっすぐ　行きます。
この　みちを　まっすぐ　行きます。 Go straight along this road.

を indicates what you go along, turn, cross or pass through (like a road or intersection). Use を with 行きます, わたります, まがります and 出ます.

Crossing

Nounを　わたります。
しんごうを　わたります。 Cross at the traffic light.

Turning

Noun(place)を　direction に　まがります。
一　ぎん行の　かどを　右に　まがります。 Turn right at the corner where the bank is.
二　二つめの　かどを　左に　まがります。 Turn left at the second corner.

Getty Images/Kohei Hara

Getting there

そうすると、　direction がわに　noun が　あります。
一　そうすると、　左がわに　パンやが　あります。 When you do that, the bakery is on the left-hand side.
二　えいがかんは　えきの　前に　あります。 The movie theatre is in front of the station.

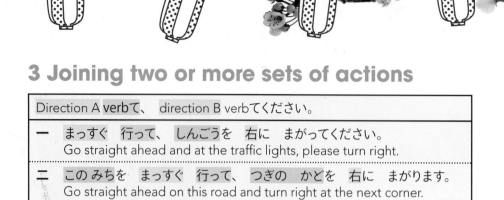

3 Joining two or more sets of actions

Direction A **verb**て、 direction B **verb**てください。
一　まっすぐ　行って、　しんごうを　右に　まがってください。 Go straight ahead and at the traffic lights, please turn right.
二　このみちを　まっすぐ　行って、　つぎの　かどを　右に　まがります。 Go straight ahead on this road and turn right at the next corner.

4 Showing the order of actions

Direction A **verb**てから、direction B。
えきを　出てから、　しんごうを　わたります。 Go out of the station and (after that) cross at the traffic lights.

5 Asking and telling how long it takes

A:	どの　ぐらい　かかりますか。
B:	Duration　ぐらい　かかりますor です。
一	うちから　学校まで　どの　ぐらい　かかりますか。 How long does it take from home to school?
	うちから　学校まで　あるいて　十五分ぐらい　です。 From home to school, it takes about 15 minutes on foot.

iStockphoto/Rich Legg

まっすぐ行きます

ISBN 9780170198271

たんご

9.5

Place names

えいがかん	movie theatre
きっさてん	coffee shop/cafe
と書かん	library
びじゅつかん	art gallery
ふみきり	railway crossing
りょかん	Japanese-style inn
はなや	flower shop
にくや	butcher
本や	bookshop
やおや	greengrocer
くすりや	pharmacy
くつや	shoe shop
こうえん	park/playground
えき	train station
パンや	bakery
ぎん行	bank
ゆうびんきょく	post office
びょういん	hospital
おてら	Buddhist temple
スーパー	supermarket
じんじゃ	Shinto shrine
コンビニ	convenience store
デパート	department store
バスてい	bus stop
ホテル	hotel
タクシーのりば	taxi stand
ち下てつ	subway
プラットフォーム	platform

Landmarks

入口	entrance
かど	corner
こうさてん	intersection
しんごう	traffic signal/lights
出口	exit
はし	bridge
みち	road

Other direction words

一つめ or 一ばんめ	first
二つめ or 二ばんめ	second
三つめ or 三ばんめ	third
つぎ	next
右	right
左	left
右がわ	right-hand side
左がわ	left-hand side
東	east
西	west
南	south
北	north
そうすると	when you do that

Getty Images/MIXA

こ/そ/あ/ど

ここ	here (near the speaker)
そこ	there (near the listener)
あそこ	over there (away from both the speaker and listener)
どこ	where
このへん	around here

Shutterstock/Blend Images

Verbs

かかります	to take time
出ます	to exit/leave
入ります	to enter
まっすぐ　行きます	to go straight
(右に)　まがります	to turn (right)
(みちを)　わたります	to cross (the road)

Adjectives

ちかい	nearby/close
とおい	far

09

百四十一

ISBN 9780170198271

まっすぐ行きます

9.1, 9.2

Do you remember この, その, あの and これ, それ, あれ in Unit 5? In this unit, ここ, そこ, あそこ and どこ have been introduced. Study the summary below.

Near the speaker

When an object is near the speaker, use こ.

この + noun → この人 (this person)

これ + particle → これを　ください。(I'll have this one please.)

ここ → ここに　あります。(It is here.)

Getty Images/DAJ

Near the listener

When an object is near the listener, use そ.

その + noun → その人 (that person)

それ + particle → それは　きれいです。(That one is pretty.)

そこ → そこに　あります。(It is there.)

Far away from the speaker and listener

When an object is far away from the speaker and the listener, use あ.

あの + noun → あの人 (that person over there)

あれ + particle → あれが　食べたいです。(I want to eat that one over there.)

あそこ → あそこです。(It is over there.)

Question words

When you ask a question, use ど.

どの + noun → どの人 (Which person?)

どれ + particle → どれが　すきですか。(Which one do you like?)

どこ → どこですか。(Where is it?)

iStockphoto/Christine Glade

Asking directions

We have learnt three different ways to ask directions.

1　きっさてんは　どこですか。(Where is the coffee shop?)
2　この　へんに　きっさてんが　ありますか。(Is there a coffee shop around here?)
3　きっさてんに　行きたいんですが… (I want to go to a coffee shop, but ...)

　　When you want to go to a coffee shop, you can say きっさてんに 行きたいです。But by inserting ん, you emphasise your reason for going. By adding が to the end of a sentence, you are inviting the listener to join the conversation.

まっすぐ行きます

ISBN 9780170198271

エクストラ

Stockphoto/Mark Massel

Getty Images/Senchy

ゲームをしましょう。

You can play this game with a partner or against another team.

- Take turns to nominate a category. For example, 「かんじの 五　おねがいします」 ('*Kanji* for 5 points, please').
- If you answer correctly, you receive the points allocated to the question.
- For はなしましょう, answer the questions in Japanese.
- You must answer within 30 seconds. じゃあ、　ゲームを　スタート!

Points	かんじ	たんご	ぶんぽう	はなしましょう
一	What does this *kanji* mean? 南	What does this word mean? ゆうびんきょく	Say 'From here to school'.	学校から　まちまで どのぐらい　かかりますか。
二	What do these *kanji* mean? 出口 and 入口	What is 'hospital' in Japanese?	Say 'Turn right at the corner where the bank is'.	このへんに トイレが　ありますか。 どこですか。
三	How do you read these *kanji*? 北 and 西	Say 'the first', 'the second' and 'the third' in Japanese.	Ask where the coffee shop is in three different ways.	このへんに コンビニが ありますか。 どこですか。
四	Write the *kanji* for 'east'.	Say four place names in Japanese.	Say 'Go straight and cross the bridge'.	うちから　学校まで どのぐらい　かかりますか。
五	Write the *kanji* for ひだりて.	What are じんじゃ, おてら, やおや, びじゅつかん and こうさてん?	Say 'Do homework and after that, watch TV'.	えきの　前に　何が ありますか。

スコア		
14–20	**9–13**	**0–8**
すごいですね! Congratulations! You are a champion!	もうちょっと… Nearly there! Go over the questions that you got wrong.	がんばって! Go over the ぶんぽう and たんご pages. Good luck!

09

百四十三

143

ISBN 9780170198271

まっすぐ行きます

Unit

10

スポーツヒーロー

In this unit, you will learn to:

- make the dictionary form of verbs
- say that you like or dislike doing things
- say that someone is good at or not good at doing something
- say that you can, cannot, could or could not do something
- conduct an interview in Japanese
- recognise and write the *kanji* characters 毎, 今, 週, 先, 来, 住, 好 and 名

In this unit, you will learn about:

- Japanese culture: the lifestyle of a trainee sumo wrestler, traditional and popular sports in Japan and Japanese Olympians
- intercultural understanding: how do you take a compliment?
An investigation into how Japanese and Australian people talk about their strengths
- text types: conversation, web page

Corbis/Bloomimage

Ayumi is writing an article about an athlete for next week's edition of her school newspaper. She is doing an interview via an Internet chat room for the article.

インタビュー

▶ **Ayumi:**	こんにちは。 お名前(なまえ)は何ですか。
▶ **Hideki:**	高見(たかみ)ひできです。
▶ A:	学校しん聞で、 スポーツせんしゅについてのきじを書きたいんですが、 インタビューをしてもいいですか。
▶ H:	はい、 いいですよ。
▶ A:	ひできさんはおいくつですか。
▶ H:	十七さいです。
▶ A:	ひできさんはどんなスポーツが好(す)きですか。
▶ H:	ぼくはすもうが大好(だいす)きです。
▶ A:	どこに住(す)んでいますか。
▶ H:	東京(とうきょう)のすもうべやに住んでいます。 今年(ことし)から、 すもうべやでれんしゅうをしています。
▶ A:	そうですか。 何年(なんねん)かんすもうをしていますか。
▶ H:	八年かんぐらいしています。 ぼくはこどもの時(とき)、テレビですもうを見ることが好きでした。 つよくて、ゆう名(めい)なりきしによくあこがれました。
▶ A:	れんしゅうはどうですか。 どのぐらいれんしゅうをしますか。
▶ H:	毎日(まいにち)六時かんぐらいれんしゅうをします。 れんしゅうはとてもきびしいですよ。 毎日ごぜん六時から十二時までれんしゅうをします。
▶ A:	じゃあ、 ごご、 何をしますか。
▶ H:	ひるねをします。 それから、 本をよんで、 テレビを見ます。六時ごろにばんごはんを食べます。

Margin glossary:

- an article about athletes
- How old are you?
- sumo
- sumo training stable
- How many years?
- When I was a child
- I often admired sumo wrestlers.
- nap

Photos by Shutterstock.com/J. Henning Buchholz, Corbis/Sol Neelman, Corbis/Sol Neelman

10

百四十五

ISBN 9780170198271

スポーツヒーロー

What kind of things?

sumo wrestlers	▶A: りきしは大きくて、 ふとっていますね。 いつもどんなものを食べますか。
chankonabe – Japanese dish	▶H: ちゃんこなべを食べます。 でも、 一日(いちにち)に二かいだけです。 ひるごはんとばんごはんです。
	▶A: 一日に二かいだけですか!
snacks	▶H: はい、 一日に二かいですが、 一かいにたくさん食べます。 そうすると、 ふとりますよ。 でも、 時(とき)どきおやつも食べます。 りきしはみんなちゃんこなべをつくるのがとても上手です。
	▶A: そうですか。 ひできさんのすもうべやにりきしが何人ぐらいいますか。
kilos	▶H: ええと、 十八人です。 私が一ばん小さいです。 大きい人のたいじゅうは 百八十キロぐらいですよ。 私のたいじゅうは九十四キロです。
competition	▶A: つぎのたいかいはいつですか。
not really	▶H: 来週(らいしゅう)です。 ぼくはあまりつよくないですから、 まだたいかいに 出(で)ることができません。
to participate in/appear in	▶A: あしたも六時かられんしゅうがありますか。
	▶H: はい、 あります。
Good luck!	▶A: 今日(きょう)はどうもありがとうございました。 れんしゅう、 がんばってください。
	▶H: はい、 ありがとう。 たのしかったです。 じゃあ、 また。

body weight (right margin)

yet (right margin)

Shutterstock.com/ J. Henning Buchholz

Questions ○○○○○○○○○○○○○○○○○

1 How old is Hideki?
2 Where does Hideki live?
3 Why do you think Hideki began sumo?
4 How many hours of training does Hideki do every day?
5 How do sumo wrestlers stay heavy?
6 Will Hideki appear in the next competition? Why?

10

百四十六

146

スポーツヒーロー

ISBN 9780170198271

練習
れんしゅう

1 Saying what you like and dislike doing

Verb (dictionary form) ことが好きです。
Verb (dictionary form) ことがきらいです。
およぐことが好きです。

2 Saying how skilled someone else is

Verb (dictionary form) ことが上手です。
Verb (dictionary form) ことが下手です。
先生はえをかくことが上手です。

3 Saying what you are able to do

Verb (dictionary form) ことができます。
ダニエルさんは、 じてんしゃにのることができます。

たんご

すう学をべんきょうします	しゃしんをとります	あした八時にいきます
フットボールを見ます	おはしをつかいます	さしみを食べます
へやをそうじします	りょうりをします	けんどうをします

ISBN 9780170198271

スポーツヒーロー

漢字
かんじ

These are the *kanji* and their readings introduced in this unit.

マイ every

毎　　母

Every day, Mum puts on her hat.

ノ　ケ　仁　勽　匂　毎

毎日　→　まいにち　→　every day
毎月　→　まいつき　→　every month
毎年　→　まいとし　→　every year
毎日しん聞をよみます。　→　まいにちしんぶんをよみます。　→　I read the newspaper every day.

いま／コン now/this

今　　今

Who wants to eat now?

ノ　人　今　今

今から　→　いまから　→　from now
今日　→　きょう　→　today
今月　→　こんげつ　→　this month
今年　→　ことし　→　this year

シュウ week

週　　週

Which shoes will you wear this week?

ノ　刀　月　円　円　円　周　周
㇉周　调　週

今週　→　こんしゅう　→　this week
毎週　→　まいしゅう　→　every week
週まつ　→　しゅうまつ　→　weekend
週に一かい　→　しゅうにいっかい　→　once a week

セン previous

先　　先

The teacher is holding a pen.

ノ　ゲ　屮　生　先　先

先生　→　せんせい　→　teacher
先週　→　せんしゅう　→　last week
先月　→　せんげつ　→　last month
先日　→　せんじつ　→　the other day

10

百四十八

148

スポーツヒーロー

ISBN 9780170198271

き（ます）／く／こ／ライ to come/next

来

Birds sit on a tree branch waiting for morning to come.

一 ー 匸 平 来 来

来てください。 → きてください。 → Please come.
来週 → らいしゅう → next week
来月 → らいげつ → next month
来年 → らいねん → next year

す（んでいます）／ジュウ to live

住

The people live in a three-storey building with an antenna.

ノ イ イ 仁 仹 住

住んでいます。 → すんでいます。 → I am living.
住んでいました。 → すんでいました。 → I was living.
京都に住んでいます。 → きょうとにすんでいます。 → I am living in Kyoto.
住所 → じゅうしょ → address

す（き） to like

好

The mother loves her child.

く 夕 女 好 好 好

好きな食べもの → すきなたべもの → the food I like
ケーキが好きです。 → ケーキがすきです。 → I like cake.
ゴルフが好きでした。 → ゴルフがすきでした。 → I used to like golf.
好きな人 → すきなひと → the person I like

な／メイ name

名

My name is タロ (Taro).

ノ ク タ タ 名 名

名前 → なまえ → name
名古屋 → なごや → Nagoya (name of Japanese city)
ゆう名な人 → ゆうめいなひと → famous person
名人 → めいじん → expert/master

ISBN 9780170198271

スポーツヒーロー

Kyudo (弓道), aikido (合気道), kendo (剣道), karate (空手) and judo (柔道) – could you identify them if you saw them? They are all Japanese martial arts. Every culture has sports, and Japan is no exception. Some popular international sports are also big in Japan, such as soccer and baseball.

からて

きゅうどう

けんどう

サッカー

Sumo is a popular, traditional Japanese sport. The sport is even mentioned in the myths and legends of the *Kojiki* and *Nihonshoki* (Japanese history books that date back as far as the eighth century). Sumo matches were originally held by the rich who dedicated the matches to the gods for a good harvest, or to raise money for towns. Today, many traditional aspects are still maintained in sumo – such as the outfits they wear, the topknots, the rituals and the rules of the game. Sumo is therefore more than just a sport; it is a living example of traditional Japanese culture, and it is a hugely popular spectator sport in Japan.

すもう

Photos by Alamy/Photo Japan, Getty Images Sport/Masashi Hara, Corbis/Michael S. Yamashita, Alamy/Darby Sawchuk

Questions

1 Investigate another traditional Japanese sport. Research its history, popularity in Japan and overseas, its rules and skills, and its famous players. Can you gather first-hand information by talking to Japanese speakers about it?

2 Most people like a variety of sports but may not play all or any of them. Research the types of sports that are popular as spectator sports and as participatory sports for people of different age groups in Japan. Create a presentation in Japanese, using graphs, charts and pictures with captions. Include information gained by interviewing people in Japanese whenever you can.

10

百五十

スポーツヒーロー

ISBN 9780170198271

Search:

Home　Contact　About

オリンピック

夏のオリンピック

30回目: ロンドンオリンピック（2012）　　イギリス
29回目: 北京オリンピック（2008）　　中国
28回目: アテネオリンピック（2004）　　ギリシャ

冬のオリンピック

22回目: ソチオリンピック（2014）　　ロシア
21回目: バンクーバーオリンピック（2010）　カナダ
20回目: トリノオリンピック（2006）　　イタリア

Related Pages

Sumo
Baseball
Soccer
Golf
Ski and Snowboard
Martial Arts
Fuji Speedway
Suzuka Circuit
Tokyo Marathon

日本でのオリンピック

1998　長野オリンピック（冬）
1972　札幌オリンピック（冬）
1964　東京オリンピック（夏）

Getty Images Sport/ Paul Gilham

Getty Images/ Jacques Demarthon

Getty Images/Lars Baron

日本の1998年の冬季オリンピック

長野県

人口: 2 133 000人

長野は東京の北西にあります。
長野県には山がたくさんあります。
冬（12月〜2月）の気温はれい下で、
ウィンタースポーツにとてもいいです。

北京	Beijing
中国	China
人口	population
長野県	Nagano Prefecture
れい下	below zero

👍 8,659

Likes

ISBN 9780170198271　　スポーツヒーロー

だいはっけん

Alamy/PCN Photography

Getty Images/
Doug Pensinger

ぜんりょくをつくす

If you are asked in English if you are good at something, how might you respond? It is acceptable for you to be at least generally honest about your abilities. However, this notion of showing your strengths and being truthful about your skills may not be the same as ぜんりょくをつくす, the concept of 'using all your strengths' in Japanese.

Let's investigate some everyday situations for giving and receiving compliments in Japanese. For example, is it worse in Japanese to undersell yourself or to seem self-promoting? This requires making some decisions about how you want to be seen by others and having some strategies to help you achieve this.

Examples of giving and receiving compliments

A journalist speaks to a tennis player who has won her match.

> ジャーナリスト:くみこさん、 今日はすごかったですね。
> Kumiko, you were fantastic today.
> くみこ:ええ、 そうですか。 ありがとうございます。
> 今日はたまたまうまくいきました。
> Oh really, thank you very much, I was just lucky today.

A friend of Hideyoshi's mother sees the picture he drew at school today.

> たかやま:ひでよしさん、えがお上手ですね。
> Hideyoshi, you are good at drawing, aren't you?
> ひでよし:ええ。 そうですか、 まだまだですよ。
> Oh really, do you think so? I am not very good yet.

A teacher speaks to a student.

> せんせい:このれきしのしゅくだい、 たいへんよくできました。
> Your history homework was very well done.
> けんじ:そうですか。 先生、 ありがとうございます。 先生のおかげです。
> Really? Thank you, Miss. It is all down to you.

Have a think

1 What patterns can you identify in the Japanese responses? What do they tell you is important to Japanese speakers?
2 How would you respond if you received each of the compliments above in English? What sort of impression do you think you would make in Japan if you answered a compliment in the same way as you would normally in Australia?
3 How would it make you feel to adopt the Japanese approach to receiving compliments?
4 How do you think a Japanese speaker might feel trying to sound natural in English in a similar situation?

Have a go

How would you respond to the following in Japanese?
- Your teacher tells you that your assignment was excellent.
- A friend says you are very good at swimming.

10

百五十二

スポーツヒーロー

ISBN 9780170198271

ぶんぽう

1 The dictionary form of verbs

You have seen several different verb forms so far: the polite (ます) form (e.g. うたいます) and the て form (e.g. うたって). In this unit you will learn another verb form, the plain present or dictionary form.

The plain form is used in a variety of ways such as:

* in dictionaries
* in forming other grammar patterns
* for less formal (friendly, casual) speech
* for diary entries, newspapers and academic reports.

You may have seen examples of verbs used in the plain form previously.

Group 1 verbs

うたいます	うたう (to sing)
よみます	よむ (to read)
かえります	かえる (to return)

> Delete ます and change the stem sound from *i* to *u*.

Group 2 verbs

あけます	あける (to open)
食べます	食べる (to eat)
見ます	見る (to see/watch)

> Delete ます and add る.

Getty Images/Holly Harris

Group 3 verbs (irregular)

来ます	来る (to come)
します	する (to do/play)

> Delete ます, change the stem sound from *i* to *u* and add る.

To work out the polite (ます) form from a verb in the plain present (dictionary) form, just reverse the above steps. For example:

聞く (group 1) → 聞き → 聞きます

Are these verbs group 1, 2 or 3?		
買います	します	ねます
飲みます	出かけます	あります

Check your answers with a partner. Then, find these verbs in a dictionary, remembering to put them into plain present form to look them up.

スポーツヒーロー

2 Saying what you like and dislike doing

You can already say 'I like basketball' in Japanese:

> バスケットボールが好きです。

Here you will learn how to say things like 'I like playing basketball' or 'I don't like watching basketball'.

Verb (dictionary form)ことが好きです。
Verb (dictionary form)のがきらいです。
すもうを見ることが好きです。　I like watching sumo.
まんがをよむのが好きでした。　I liked reading/to read comics.
カラオケバーでうたうのがきらいです。　I don't like singing at karaoke bars.

3 Saying how skilled someone else is

In general, this pattern is used to say someone is good at or not good at something.

Verb (dictionary form)ことが上手です。
Verb (dictionary form)ことが下手です。
ジェニーさんはピアノをひくことが下手です。 Jenny is not good at playing the piano.
たかはしさんは人の前ではなすことが上手です。 Mr Takahashi is good at speaking in front of people.
いもうとはかんじを書くことが下手です。 My little sister is not good at writing *kanji*.

You can't use this pattern for expressions like 'I am good at getting up in the morning'.

Getty Images/Shuji Kobayashi

4 Saying what you are able to do

To say you can do an action, use the plain present (dictionary) form and add the pattern ことができます。

Verb (dictionary form)ことができます。
Verb (dictionary form)ことができません。
日本のしんぶんをよむことができます。　I can read a Japanese newspaper.
キムさんはノートを見つけることができません。　Kim can't find her notebook.
ひろふみくんはカラオケパーティーに来ることができました。　Hirofumi was able to come to the karaoke party.
ひできさんはしあいにかつことができませんでした。　Hideki couldn't win the match.

スポーツヒーロー

ISBN 9780170198271

The dictionary form of verbs: talking about sports

Group 1 verbs

ます form	Dictionary form	English
およぎます	およぐ	swim
おわります	おわる	finish
かちます	かつ	win
がんばります	がんばる	try hard
けります	ける	kick
たちます	たつ	stand up
つかいます	つかう	use
のります	のる	ride
はしります	はしる	run
入ります	入る	enter
行きます	行く	go

Group 2 verbs

ます form	Dictionary form	English
うけます	うける	catch/receive
おきます	おきる	get up/wake up
おしえます	おしえる	teach
おぼえます	おぼえる	remember
つづけます	つづける	continue
出ます	出る	leave/participate/attend
なげます	なげる	throw
まけます	まける	lose
見つけます	見つける	find
見ます	見る	see
やめます	やめる	quit

Group 3 (irregular) verbs

ます form	Dictionary form	English
来ます	来る	to come
うんてんします	うんてんする	drive
さんかします	さんかする	participate
じゅんびします	じゅんびする	prepare
ジョギングします	ジョギングする	jog
そうじします	そうじする	clean
リラックスします	リラックスする	relax
れんしゅうします	れんしゅうする	practise

Getty Images/ChinaFotoPress

Did you notice how many verbs appear in group 3 irregular verbs? Check the endings and you will see that there are only really two variations.

You can use verbs you already know with the patterns from the ぶんぽう pages. Just remember that they have to be in the plain form. Be careful to use the correct particles! For more verbs and a quick reference to the plain forms, refer to page 201 at the back of the book.

Getty Images/Koji Watanabe

ISBN 9780170198271

スポーツヒーロー

10

百五十五

Getty Images/Manzo Niikura

Names of sports

あいきどう	aikido
からて	karate
きゅうどう	kyudo (archery)
クリケット	cricket
けんどう	kendo (fencing)
ゴルフ	golf
サッカー	soccer/football
じゅうどう	judo
じょうば	horseriding
水えい	swimming
スケート	skating
ソフトボール	softball
たいそう	gymnastics
テニス	tennis
とびこみ	diving
ネットボール	netball
フットボール	football
マラソン	marathon
ラグビー	rugby
ローイング	rowing

Nouns

位（一位、 二位）	place (1st place, 2nd place)
オリンピック	the Olympics
キャプテン	captain
きょうぎ	sporting discipline
金メダル	gold medal
銀メダル	silver medal
銅メダル	bronze medal
しあい	competition/game
じゅんびたいそう	warm-up
しんちょう	height
たいじゅう	body weight
チーム	team
チャンピオン	champion
てん	point/score

Getty Images/The Asahi Shimbun

Getty Images/Chung Sung-Jun

スポーツヒーロー

ISBN 9780170198271

Speaking or writing

Some of the patterns introduced in this unit offer more than one way of saying the same thing in Japanese. So is there a difference in their uses? Look at the following examples.

うたをうたうことが好きです。＝ うたをうたうのが好きです。

　こと and の are often interchangeable, but の is used less often in formal written Japanese.

私はえをかくのが下手でした。

(I was not good at drawing pictures.)

Getty Images/artparadigm

Corbis/AID

ISBN 9780170198271

10.3, 10.4

インタビューをしましょう!

Interviews are great because they give you the chance to use your Japanese. One of the keys to a successful interview is careful preparation. Try to use as many different patterns as you can. Often the person is doing a favour for you, so show your appreciation at the beginning and the end of the interview. You might like to record or film the interview. If so, you should seek permission from the interviewee before you start.

Preparation

Purpose

What do you want to find out? What can you do with the information you have gained?

Structure

Prepare your questions in Japanese before the interview. Prepare vocabulary you think may be used in the responses, and check that you are clear about the words' meaning.

Asking permission to conduct the interview

- すみません。すこし時かんがありますか。
  Excuse me, can you spare some time?
- すこしいいですか。
  Do you have a few spare moments?
- インタビューをしてもいいですか。
  May I interview you?
- Topic についてインタビューをしているんですが…
  I am conducting an interview about (topic).
- すみません。インタビューをろくおんしてもいいですか。
  Excuse me, may I record the interview?

Keeping the conversation flowing

あいづち (listener responses) are important features in a Japanese conversation because they keep the conversation flowing. They indicate that the listener is listening to the speaker. They also offer polite encouragement. Practise using あいづち when you talk in Japanese. Here are some you could use.

はい。	Yes.
うん。 ええ。	Yes. (casual)
そうですか。	I see.
へえ!	Wow! (casual)
ふうん。	I see. (casual)
わあ。	Wow! (casual)
ほんとうですか。	Really?
すごいですね。	Isn't it great?
そうですね。	I think so./Let me think.
ああ、 そうですか。	Oh, is that so?

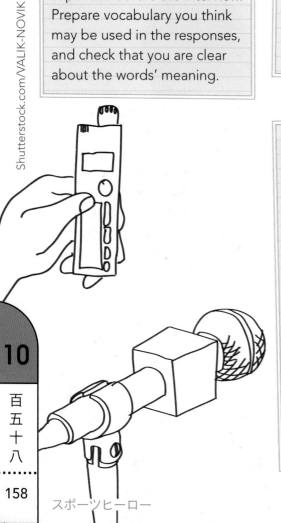

ISBN 9780170198271

Question words

おいくつですか。	How old are you?
何か	something/anything
何を	What?
どこで	Where?
いつから／何時に	When from/What time?
どうして	Why?
だれが／だれと	Who?/Who with?
どのぐらい	About how long?
どれが	Which one?
どんな	What kind of ...?

Showing your appreciation

- 今日はどうもありがとうございました。
  Thank you very much for today.
- いろいろ聞かせていただいてありがとうございました。
  Thank you for telling us about all these things.

When you need the information repeated

- もう一どおねがいします。
  Please say it again.
- もう一どいってください。
  Please say it again.
- もう一どゆっくりおねがいします。
  Please say it again more slowly.
- ゆっくりいってください。
  Please speak more slowly.

メモをとりましょう!

Although you may be able to record or film the interview, it is always handy to take notes. Note-taking helps you to keep track of the information, alter your questions depending on the answers and ask additional questions. It can also save time when you come to summarise the information. The key is to take down information quickly and briefly (but not too brief so that you can still understand what you have written when you read it later). Take notes in Japanese rather than English. Jot down words or phrases rather than whole sentences. But, most of all, relax and have fun!

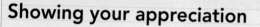

Have a go

Conduct an interview in Japanese with a person such as an exchange student, a visitor or a tourist. Think about the purpose of the interview and prepare your questions. Take notes while interviewing. Present an oral or written summary of the information you have gained from the interview.

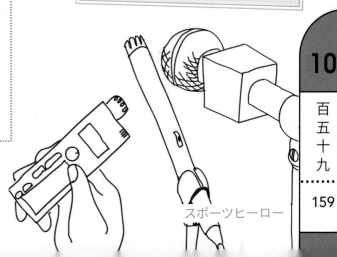

アルバイト

In this unit, you will learn to:

- describe things you do in non-sequential order
- say what you want to become
- compare two things and give your opinion
- read and write a modified curriculum vitae in Japanese
- prepare for a job interview in Japanese
- participate in a job interview
- read and write a job application letter in Japanese
- recognise and write the *kanji* characters 語, 英, 家, 友, 会, 社, 間 and 町

In this unit, you will learn about:

- Japanese culture: what to do during a job interview, working in Japan and jobs using Japanese, and counting years according to the Japanese system
- intercultural understanding: education and careers in Japan and Australia
- text types: interview, advertisement, Japanese curriculum vitae, personal history form

John is looking for a holiday job.
He has found a job advertisement in a local Japanese newspaper.

11.1

アルバイト

英語の家ていきょうし
えいご か

home tutor

中学一年生のむすめに英語をおしえてください。

daughter

一年前にオーストラリアに来ました。 英語が
まだ上手じゃないですから、 会わと
かい
ぶんぽうをおしえてください。
日本語がすこしはなせて、
あかるいせいかくの人がいいです。
でんわをください。

one year ago

(not) yet

grammar

conversation

can talk

person with a cheerful personality

西村
むら
でんわばんごう：8993 2459

けいたいでんわ：0909 133 256

Eメール：nishimura.k@hitmail.com

John has gone to Ms Nishimura's house for an interview.

John:	こんにちは、 ジョンです。 はじめまして。 どうぞよろしく。
Nishimura:	ジョンさんですか。 どうぞよろしく。 ええと、 ジョンさんはおいくつですか。
J:	私は十六さいです。 高校一年生です。
N:	ジョンさん、 日本語が上手ですね。 あのう、 ジョンさんは日本語を何年間べんきょうしていますか。 なんねんかん
J:	中学一年生の時から、 日本語のべんきょうを四年間しています。 それから、 きょ年の夏休みに日本に四週間行って、 ホームステイをしました。
N:	へえ、 そうですか。 ジョンさんはひまな時に何をしますか。
J:	ええと、 私はスポーツが好きですから、 よく週まつに友だちと とも テニスをしたり、 バスケットボールをしたりします。
N:	そうですか。 どんなかもくが好きですか。
J:	好きなかもくは日本語です。 日本に日本人の友だちがいますから、 日本語でEメールを書いたり、 でんわをしたりします。 それから、 英語やれきしが好きです。 よく日本のれきしの本をよみます。
N:	そうですか。 ええと、 ジョンさんはしょう来何をしたいですか。

how old (are you?)

11

百六十一

アルバイト

import/export company	▶J:	しょう来、 ぼうえき会社で はたらきたいです。 I want to work.
with all one's might		いっしょうけんめいはたらいて、 会社の社ちょうになりたいです。
	▶N:	へえ、 社ちょうですか。 すごいですね。
		ええと、 ジョンさんはどこに住んでいますか。
	▶J:	町のちかくに住んでいます。
	▶N:	そうですか、 じゃあ、 この家までどのぐらいかかりますか。
	▶J:	ええと、 二十分ぐらいです。
Do you have any questions?	▶N:	ああ、 それはいいですね。 じゃあ、 ジョンさん、 何かしつもんがありますか。
hourly rate	▶J:	はい、 ええと、 時きゅうはいくらですか。
	▶N:	ええと、 三十ドルですが、 いいですか。
	▶J:	はい、 わかりました。 何曜日ですか。
	▶N:	火曜日と木曜日とでは、 どちらのほうがいいですか。
	▶J:	ええと、そうですね。 木曜日はテニスのれんしゅうがありますから、火曜日のほうがいいです。
	▶N:	はい、 わかりました。 じゃ、 ジョンさん、 来週から来ることができますか。
	▶J:	はい、 できます。
	▶N:	じゃ、 来週の火曜日の四時半に来てください。
	▶J:	わかりました。 来週の火曜日の四時半ですね。
	▶N:	はい、 よろしくおねがいします。
	▶J:	よろしくおねがいします。 じゃ、 しつれいします。

Questions

1 What does the part-time job involve according to the advertisement?

2 What further details about the job does he learn from the interview?

3 What skills, experience or qualities does John have that make him suitable for the job?

4 What language does John use that reflects the more formal situation in an interview?

1 Saying things you do in any order

Verbたり、 verbたりします。
友だちとはなしたり、 スポーツをしたりします。

2 Saying what you want to become

Nounになりたいです。
ぼくはいしゃになりたいです。

Take the verb stem: なります → なり.
Add たいです: なりたいです.

3 Comparing two things (A and B)

A:	AとBとでは、 どちらのほうがadjectiveですか。
B:	A or Bのほうがadjectiveです。
—	冬と夏とでは、 どちらのほうが好きですか。
	冬のほうが好きです。

たんご

本をよみます、 Eメールを書きます	びようし	カタカナ、かんじ、むずかしい
えいがを見ます、 レストランに行きます	だいく	ウェイター、ひしょ、たいへん
ケーキをつくります、 さんぽします	じゅうい	テニス、ゴルフ、おもしろい

ISBN 9780170198271

アルバイト

These are the *kanji* and their readings introduced in this unit.

ゴ word/language

語　語

I can speak five languages.

丶	二	二	言	言	言	言	言
訂	詔	語	語	語	語		

フランス語　→　フランスご　→　French
ドイツ語　→　ドイツご　→　German
語学　→　ごがく　→　language study
日本語をはなすことができます。　→　にほんごをはなすことができます。　→　I can speak Japanese.

エイ England/wise

英　英

An English farmer with a top hat stands in front of the farm fence.

一	十	卄	丱	苎	苹	英	英

英語　→　えいご　→　English
英語の本　→　えいごのほん　→　English book
英語ではなします。　→　えいごではなします。　→　I speak in English.
好きなかもくは英語です。　→　すきなかもくはえいごです。　→　My favourite subject is English.

うち／いえ／カ house/home

家　家

A little pig is in a house. 'I will huff and puff and blow your house down.'

丶	丷	宀	宀	宇	宇	宇	家
家	家						

家の中　→　うちのなか　→　inside the house
家のちかくにうみがあります。　→　うちのちかくにうみがあります。　→　There is a beach near my house.
家ていか　→　かていか　→　home economics
家ぞく　→　かぞく　→　family
まんが家　→　まんがか　→　cartoonist

とも／ユウ friend/friendship

友　友

An odd couple – one is tall and one is short.

一	ナ	方	友				

友だち　→　ともだち　→　friend
友だちの家ぞく　→　ともだちのかぞく　→　friend's family
友人　→　ゆうじん　→　friend
友好　→　ゆうこう　→　friendship

アルバイト

ISBN 9780170198271

あ（います）／カイ to meet

会

Meet me at the restaurant.

ノ	人	ム	会	会	会		

友だちに会います。　→　ともだちにあいます。　→　I will meet my friend.

五時に会いましょう。　→　ごじにあいましょう。　→　Let's meet at 5 o'clock.

会話　→　かいわ　→　conversation

会ぎ　→　かいぎ　→　meeting/conference

シャ society

社

A society is made up of men and women.

`	ラ	ネ	ネ	ネー	ネ	社	

社会　→　しゃかい　→　society

会社　→　かいしゃ　→　company

じん社　→　じんじゃ　→　shrine

社会学　→　しゃかいがく　→　sociology

社ちょう　→　しゃちょう　→　company president

あいだ／カン between/duration

間

The sun is shining in between the loud speakers.

l	「	门	門	門	門	門
門	門	間	間			

ひる休みの間　→　ひるやすみのあいだ　→　during lunchtime

あさごはんとひるごはんの間　→　あさごはんとひるごはんのあいだ　→　between breakfast and lunch

ぎん行とえきの間　→　ぎんこうとえきのあいだ　→　between the bank and the station

時間　→　じかん　→　time

三日間　→　みっかかん　→　three days

一時間　→　いちじかん　→　one hour

まち town

町

An apartment block near a T-intersection.

l	口	田	田	田	町	町	

町の中心　→　まちのちゅうしん　→　town centre

一ばん大きい町　→　いちばんおおきいまち　→　the biggest town

私の町　→　わたしのまち　→　my town

みなと町　→　みなとまち　→　port town

11

百六十六

165

ISBN 9780170198271

アルバイト

にほんぶんか

11.2, 11.5

めんせつ

As you have already learnt, there are different levels of politeness in the
Japanese language. In a job interview the です／ます form is appropriate.
Here are some Japanese expressions to help you prepare.

Personal details

Name:
私／ぼくは name です。
Where/what you study:
School で subject をべんきょうしています。
School で subject のべんきょうをしています。

How long you have been studying:
Subject のべんきょうを years 年間ぐらい／years 年半し
ています。

The skills/experience/qualities that make you a
suitable employee:
Skill がすこし上手になりました。
あかるいせいかくです。
Noun が好きです。
Years 年前にアルバイトをしました。
日本語をすこしはなすことができます

Getty Images/AID/a.collectionR

Finding out about the job

When:
しごとは何曜日ですか。
Hours:
何時から何時までですか。
Hourly wages:
時きゅうはいくらですか。
Starting date:
いつからできますか。
Type of job:
しごとは何ですか。

Other strategies

Opening the interview:
おはようございます／こんにちは。
はじめまして。　どうぞよろしくおねがいします。

Closing the interview:
（どうも）ありがとうございました。
しつれいします。

Confirming that you have heard the
information correctly (use particle ね):
木曜日の四時半ですね。

If the job requirements are not suitable,
mentioning this politely:
（すみませんが、）木曜日はちょっと…

アルバイト

ISBN 9780170198271

りれきしょ

Here is a personal history form. This type of form is often used when applying for a job in a Japanese company.

履歴書（りれきしょ） 平成（へいせい）二十五年十月十八日現在（げんざい） ❶			
		男・女	
ふりがな	ジョン・プーロス		
氏名（しめい）	JOHN POULOS	印（いん） ❷ プーロス	
生年月日（せいねんがっぴ） ❸ 昭和（しょうわ） （平成（へいせい））	9年9月15日（16さい）		
本籍（ほんせき） ❹	オーストラリア		
ふりがな	37 スコット ストリート 、 エッセンドン、 ビクトリアしゅう、 オーストラリア〒3040		
住所（じゅしょ）	37 Skote Street, Essendon, Victoria, Australia 3040		
電話番号（でんわばんごう）	(03) 8331 2015		

学歴（がくれき） ❺		
年	月	
平成（へいせい）15	2	アベフェルディ小学校 入学
平成20	12	同校（どうこう）そつぎょう
平成21	1	バックリー・パーク高校 入学（にゅうがく）
好きな科目（かもく）		日本語、 れきし、 たいいく

職歴（しょくれき） ❻		
年	月	
平成23	5	せん車（しゃ）のアルバイト

健康状態（けんこうじょうたい） ❼	ぜんそく		
趣味（しゅみ）動機	スポーツ、 読書（どくしょ）、 えいが		
志望（しぼう）の動機（どうき） ❽	日本語をつかってしごとをしたいです。		
本人希望記入欄（ほんにんきぼうきにゅうらん） ❾	週まつきぼう		
通勤時間（つうきん） ❿ やく30分	扶養家族（ふようかぞく） ⓫ 0人	配偶者（はいぐうしゃ） ⓬ 有（う）・無（む）	

1 平成（へいせい）二十五年
   In Japan, the years are often written according to the Emperor's reign. For example, the Heisei reign began in 1989 so that year is written as Heisei 1. Therefore, this application is dated 2013.
2 name stamp
3 date of birth (John was born in Heisei 9 or 1997)
4 place of residency (place/country of origin)
5 education history
6 work history
7 medical conditions (serious conditions only)
8 reason for applying
9 special requests for the position
10 commuting time
11 number of dependants/ family members
12 spouse

11

百六十七

アルバイト

ISBN 9780170198271

だいはっけん

Comparing education and career opportunities

Most people think about what they want to be when they leave school.
Options for school leavers may depend on the society you live in.
For instance, will you continue your education? Get a job? Travel?
Do all of the above?

Comparing education and expectations in Japan and Australia may tell you quite a lot about the things that are important in each society.

Questions ○○○○○○○○○○

In the classroom and beyond

1   Find out the age at which students can leave school in Japan and Australia. Can you explain any differences?

2   Investigate university entrance requirements in Japan. When and how do students need to start preparing to get into their preferred university? What differences do you notice between the Japanese and the Australian education systems?

Getty Images/RunPhoto

アルバイト

ISBN 9780170198271

The language of education

Examining some different terms used in Japanese and English provides interesting comparisons, especially when they have no direct equivalent in the other language.

Think about these questions for each of the Japanese terms listed below:
- What does the term mean?
- Is there a common equivalent term in English?
- How would you explain the term to another English speaker?
- What does the term say about students or education in Japan?

あおたがり　(cut grass before ripe)

フリーター

ろうにん

しゅうしょくかつどう

きょういくママ

しょうがっこう
小学校

ちゅうがっこう
中学校

高校

大学

じゅけん

アルバイト

Alamy/John Lander

Think about these questions for each of the English terms listed below:
- What does the term mean?
- Is there an equivalent term in Japanese?
- How would you explain the term to a Japanese speaker?
- What does the term say about students or education in Australia?

gap year

school leaver

schoolies

primary school

high school

college

technical college/TAFE

VET

work experience

Getty Images/Campus Life

Have a go

Imagine that Yuki is a member of your Japanese host family and has applied for a student exchange to Australia. Before leaving Japan, she asks you to explain the important differences between school in Japan and Australia. What will you tell her? What are the most important differences she needs to understand to avoid confusion?

11

百六十九

169

ISBN 9780170198271

アルバイト

1 Making the た form of verbs

Group 1 verbs

い → った	き → いた	に → んだ
ち → った	ぎ → いだ	び → んだ
り → った	し → した	み → んだ

> Delete ます and, depending on the syllable before ます, change the ending. Or change the verb into the て form and then change the final て to た or で to だ.

Group 2 verbs

食べます → 食べた
見て → 見た

> Delete the ます and add た. Or, change the verb into the て form and change the final て to た.

Group 3 verbs (irregular)

します → した
来ます → 来た

> Delete the ます and add た. Or, change the verb into the て form and change the final て to た.

iStockphoto/Mie Ahmt

2 Saying things you do in any order

Verbたり、 verbたりします。
本をよんだり、 べんきょうしたりします。 I do things like reading books and studying.
一 こどもの時、 じてんしゃにのったり、 ローラーブレードをしたりしました。
When I was a child, I did things like bike riding and rollerblading.
二 夏休みに買いものをしたり、レストランでばんごはんを食べたりしたいです。
During the summer holidays, I want to do things like shopping and have dinner at restaurants.

Verbたり、verbたりします is used when you want to describe some of the different actions you do, or someone else does. Note: in this pattern, the same person does all of the activities.
I do things like ... and ... /I sometimes ... and sometimes ...

Use the た form and add り to make the たり form.

アルバイト

ISBN 9780170198271

3 Saying what you want to become

Nounになりたいです。
パイロットになりたいです。 I want to become a pilot.
しょう来、 何になりたいですか。 What do you want to be in the future?
しょう来、 カメラマンになりたいです。 I want to become a cameraman in the future.

4 Saying where someone works

どこ/placeではたらいていますか。 Where do you work? / Where are you working? / Do you work at …?
おみやげやではたらいています。 I work at a souvenir shop. / I am working at a souvenir shop.

5 Saying where you want to work

どこ/placeではたらきたいですか。 Where do you want to work? / Do you want to work at …?
きっさてんではたらきたいです。 I want to work in a café.

6 Comparing two things

A:	AとBとでは、 どちらのほうがadjective ですか。
B:	A or B のほうがadjective です。
一	すう学と日本語とでは、 どちらのほうがおもしろいですか。 Which is more interesting: maths or Japanese?
	すう学より日本語の ほうがおもしろいです。 Japanese is more interesting [than maths].
二	ひこうきとしんかんせんとでは、 どちらのほうがべんりですか。 Which are more convenient, aeroplanes or bullet trains?
	しんかんせんのほうがべんりです。 Bullet trains are more convenient.

Getty Images/Dex Image

Nounが一ばんadjectiveです。
春が一ばん好きです。 I like spring best.

11

百七十一

171

ISBN 9780170198271

アルバイト

たんご

Occupations

いしゃ	doctor
会けいし	accountant
会社いん	company worker
か手	singer
家ていきょうし	home tutor
カメラマン	photographer/camera operator
かんごふ	nurse
ぎし／エンジニア	engineer
きょうし／先生	teacher
ぎん行いん	banker
けいかん	police officer
げいじゅつか	artist
けんちく家	architect
コンピュータープログラマー	computer programmer
シェフ	chef
社ちょう	company president
じゅうい	veterinarian
しゅふ	housewife/husband
スポーツインストラクター	sports instructor
せいじ家	politician
せいびし／メカニック	mechanic
大学生	university student
タクシーのうんてん手	taxi driver
ツアーガイド	tour guide
てんいん	shop assistant
にわし	gardener
はいしゃ	dentist
はいゆう／女ゆう	actor/actress
パイロット	pilot
はなや	florist
ひ書	personal assistant
びようし	beautician/hairdresser
ぶちょう／せきにんしゃ	company manager
べんごし	lawyer
やくざいし	pharmacist

Getty Images/ULTRA.F

Places

おみやげや	souvenir shop
カジノ	casino
ガソリンスタンド	petrol station
どうぶつえん	zoo
はくぶつかん	museum
ぼうえき会社	international trading company
めんぜいてん	duty-free shop
りょ行会社	travel agent

Talking about occupations

アルバイトをします	do a part-time job
しごとをします	work at a job
はたらきます	work
めんせつをうけます	have an interview
いんたいしています。	S/he is retired.
アルバイト	part-time job
時きゅう	hourly rate
しごと	work

Refer to Unit 9 for more places.

アルバイト

ISBN 9780170198271

ぶんぽうプラス

11.8, 11.9

Comparing 〜たり, 〜たりします and the て form

て is used for listing the order of what you do in a particular situation.
For example:

毎あさ、 あさごはんを食べて、 学校に行きます。

(Every morning, I eat breakfast and go to school.)

〜たり, 〜たりします is used to say some of the things you might do, and they are in no particular order. The pattern is often translated as 'I sometimes do … and I sometimes do …' or 'I do things like … and …'
For example:

ご前中はジョギングをしたり、 テレビを見たりします。

(In the morning, I do things like jogging and watching television.)

Comparing two actions

In this unit we learnt to compare two nouns using the pattern
のほうがいいです.

木曜日と金曜日とでは、 どちらのほうがいいですか。

金曜日より木曜日のほうがいいです。

This pattern can also be used to compare two actions.

Noun (optional)	Verb (dictionary form) + のと	Verb (dictionary form) + のとでは	どちらのほうが	Adjective + ですか。
テニスを	見るのと	するのとでは、	どちらのほうが	好きですか。

(Which do you prefer, watching or playing tennis?)

Noun (optional)	Verb (dictionary form)	ほうが	Adjective + ですか。
テニスを	する	ほうが	好きです。

(I prefer playing tennis.)

The た form of verbs

The た form is actually the plain past form of a verb.
For example:

よみました → よんだ
ねました → ねた

It is used instead of the polite form in informal speech or for diary and journal entries. It is also used for other grammar patterns, as you have learnt in this unit.

iStockphoto/Robert Churchill

11

百七十三

173

ISBN 9780170198271

アルバイト

まんが

In this unit, you will learn to:

- ask and say what someone will try doing
- talk about someone doing two actions at the same time
- ask and say what you have or have not done
- recognise and use the plain negative form of present and past tense verbs
- revise the て form and the plain forms of verbs
- recognise casual speech
- recognise some ending particles
- recognise and write the *kanji* characters 新, 読, 電, 車, 外, 国, 話 and 々

In this unit, you will learn about:

- Japanese culture: manga, anime, Japanese television and using Japanese onomatopoeia
- intercultural understanding: a global phenomenon – Japanese manga and anime – how manga and anime no longer belong to the Japanese
- text types: manga, conversation

Andrew from Australia has come to a まんがきっさ (manga café). He meets Kenji at the café. Kenji is good at drawing manga, and he shows his manga to Andrew.

まんがきっさ

Andrew: すみません。　ここにすわってもいいですか。

Kenji: ええ、　いいですよ。　どうぞ。

A: どうも、　すみません。

K: 日本語が上手ですね。

No, not at all.

helps my learning

culture

A: いいえ、　まだまだです。　でも、　日本のまんがをよく読みます。
日本語のべんきょうになります。　まんがを読みながら、
日本のぶんかをべんきょうすることができます。
まんがはとてもすばらしいですね。

Excuse me, but …

K: そうですか。　しつれいですが、　お名前は。

A: ぼくはアンドリューです。

K: ぼくはまつだけんじです。　アンドリューくんは大学生ですか。

I'm an exchange student and

A: いいえ、　高校生です。　留学生で、　日本語をべんきょうしています。

K: ここに来たことがありますか。

the first time

A: いいえ、　ありません。　はじめてです。

K: ここはいいですよ。　ぼくは時々来ます。　おいしいコーヒーを
飲みながら、いろいろなまんがを読みます。　そうすると、
いろいろなまんがのアイデアが出ます。

various

have/appear

cartoonist

A: えっ。　じゃ、　まつださんはまんが家ですか。

K: いいえ、　まだ、　まんが家じゃないですよ。　でも、　まんが家に
なりたいです。

A: へえ、　そうですか。

ISBN 9780170198271

drawing

beginner

through manga

politics

love stories

science fiction
(エスエフ)

three months

▶K: ええ、 でも、 まんがを<u>かくこと</u>はむずかしいですよ。
ぼくはまだ<u>しょしんしゃ</u>ですから、 あまり上手じゃないです。

▶A: そうですか。

▶K: はい。 ぼくは外国(がいこく)のまんがより、 日本のまんがのほうが好き
です。 日本のまんがはすばらしいです。 <u>まんがでれきしや
せいじについてしる</u>ことができます。 日本ではまんがはこども
から大人まで<u>人気(にんき)があります</u>。

get to
know

to be popular

▶A: そうですね。 大人もよく、 電車(でんしゃ)の中でまんがを読んでいますね。
まつださんはどんなまんがをかきますか。

K: ぼくは<u>れんあい</u>や<u>ＳＦ</u>のまんがをかきます。 <u>四コマまんが</u>(よん)も
かきますよ。

four-frame
comic

▶A: へえ、 すごいですね。 一つのまんがにどのぐらいかかりますか。

▶K: ぼくはテレビを見ながら、 話(はなし)をかんがえたり、 おんがくを
聞きながら、 まんがをかいたりしますから、 時間がかかります。
一つの話に<u>三か月間</u>ぐらいかかりますよ。

story

▶A: へえ、 たいへんですね。

▶K: あ、 ここに私の一ばん新(あたら)しいまんががあります。 どうぞ、
読んでみてください。

▶A: わあ、 かっこいいですね。 ぼくもまんがをかいてみたいです。

*You can read Kenji's manga
on pages 177 and 178.*

Questions ○○○○○○○○○○

1　What benefits does Andrew believe he
gets from reading comics in Japanese?

2　Why does Kenji like the manga café?

3　What types of Japanese comics are
mentioned in the conversation?

4　While creating his comics, what else
does Kenji do?

12

百
七
十
六

まんが

ISBN 9780170198271

四コマまんが

ISBN 9780170198271

まんが

まんが

かおるとしんじ

Find extra vocabulary on page 187.

ISBN 9780170198271

練習

れんしゅう

1 Saying what someone will try doing

Verbてみます。

日本語でアニメを見てみます。

2 Talking about someone doing two actions at the same time

Verb (stem) ながら、verb

ジュースを飲みながら、まんがをかいています。

3 Saying that you have done something before

A: Verbたことがありますか。

B: はい、verbたことがあります。

B: いいえ、verbたことがありません。

— 日本のテレビドラマを見たことがありますか。

はい、見たことがあります。

たんご

カラオケでうたって	おんがくを聞き、しゅくだいをしています	日本に行った
外国に行って	あさごはんを食べ、新聞(しんぶん)を読みました	すもうを見た
一人で電車にのって	シャワーをあび、うたをうたっています	アルバイトをした

12

百七十九

ISBN 9780170198271

まんが

4 Saying what you won't do, using casual language

Verb ません。	→	Verb ない。
読みません。	→	読まない。

5 Saying what you didn't do, using casual language

Verb ませんでした。	→	Verb なかった。
聞きませんでした。	→	聞かなかった。

たんご

_{はな}
話しません、話さない
見ません、見ない
しません、しない

行きませんでした、行かなかった
食べませんでした、食べなかった
来ませんでした、来なかった

12

百八十

180

まんが

ISBN 9780170198271

漢字
かんじ

These are the *kanji* and their readings introduced in this unit.

あたら（しい）／シン new

新

A man is making a new workbench out of wood.

`	㇒	㇒	㇒	立	立	辛	辛
亲	新	新	新	新			

新しいテレビ → あたらしいテレビ → new television
新聞 → しんぶん → newspaper
新車 → しんしゃ → new car
新年 → しんねん → the New Year

よ（みます）／ドク to read

読

A teacher is reading a book.

`	㇒	言	言	言	言	言	言
計	詰	詰	詰	読	読		

まんがが読みたいです。 → まんががよみたいです。 → I want to read a comic.
読み書き → よみかき → reading and writing
読み方 →よみかた → the way of reading
読書 →どくしょ → reading

デン electricity

電

Rain, heat and lightning form electricity.

一	一	一	雨	雨	雨	雨	雨
雫	雷	雪	雪	電			

電車 → でんしゃ → train
電話をします。 → でんわをします。 → I will make a telephone call.
るすばん電話 → るすばんでんわ → answering machine
電気 → でんき → light/electricity

くるま／シャ car

車

A go-cart has wheels and an axle.

一	一	一	百	百	亘	車	

新しい車 → あたらしいくるま → new car
好きな車 → すきなくるま → the car that I like
じてん車 → じてんしゃ → bicycle
車いす → くるまいす → wheelchair

12

百八十一

181

ISBN 9780170198271

まんが

そと／ガイ outside/out

外　外

Taro (タロ) and Tom (トム) are playing outside.

ノ	ク	タ	タ	外			

外に行きます。 → そとにいきます。 → I will go outside.
外国人 → がいこくじん → foreigner
海外 → かいがい → overseas
外食します。 → がいしょくします。 → I will eat out.

くに／コク country

国　国

A country's jewels and national treasure is surrounded by a great wall.

丨	冂	冂	国	囯	国	国	

大きい国 → おおきいくに → big country
中国 → ちゅうごく → China
外国語 → がいこくご → foreign language
国語 → こくご → national language

はな（します）／はなし／ワ to speak/a talk/story

話　話

Speaking a thousand words all at once.

、	二	二	言	言	言	言	言
言	許	話	話	話			

しずかに話します。 → しずかにはなします。 → I will speak quietly.
話を聞きました。 → はなしをききました。 → I heard the story.
会話 → かいわ → conversation
手話 → しゅわ → sign language

kanji repetition sign

々　々

'R' is for 'repeat'.

ノ	夂	々					

時々 → ときどき → sometimes
人々 → ひとびと → people
日々 → ひび → day by day
年々 → ねんねん → year after year

ISBN 9780170198271

Onomatopoeia

Onomatopoeia is a word that is very similar to the sound it describes. Japanese, like English, has many onomatopoeic words. A simple example of onomatopoeia is ワンワン for 'woof woof', or ケロケロ for a frog's croak. These examples imitate sounds that are heard in nature, so why do they sound different? For instance, why is ワンワン not ウフウフ, or conversely, why is 'woof woof' not 'wan wan'? The simple answer is that how we interpret sounds is subjective, and can therefore differ from culture to culture.

Onomatopoeia is used extensively in Japanese manga. Below are some examples that you can use in your own manga or anime. Listen to the audio and repeat.

1 eating greedily/craving something
2 something soft and soggy/something in awful disarray/grumbling
3 to become irritated/nervous
4 to be excited/thrilled
5 to lie around/loaf about
6 to dawdle/hang around
7 to be slow at/laze around
8 to feel excited/nervous
9 to smile radiantly
10 to sob/whimper
11 to speak fluently
12 to write fluently
13 to be very hungry/starving
14 a jumble/a mess
15 to be sopping wet

1 がつがつ

2 ぐちゃぐちゃ

3 いらいら（する）

4 わくわく（する）

5 ごろごろ（する）

6 ぶらぶら（する）

7 だらだら（する）

8 どきどき（する）

9 にこにこ（する）

10 めそめそ（する）

11 ぺらぺら（話す）

12 すらすら（書く）

13 ぺこぺこ

14 ごちゃごちゃ

15 びしょびしょ

Find more onomatopoeic words on page 66 in Unit 4.

12

百八十三

ISBN 9780170198271

まんが

メディア and テクノロジー

Japanese manga and anime – global phenomena

Manga and anime reflect aspects of Japanese art, culture and popular literature. They each have a long history in Japan; however, today many manga and anime have gained global popularity and their style influences artists all over the world. Both manga and anime have become part of popular culture in Australia too.

Traditional Japanese manga

The order in which you read traditional manga frames can be different from what you might be used to in other comics. (For more on this, read *Obento Deluxe Student Book*, pages 14–15.) Find some examples of Japanese action or adventure manga and record what you notice about them. Compare them with another comic book such as *Superman* or *Emily the Strange*. Can you identify the key differences in the cartoon plots? What about in the drawing styles? What is it about the manga that presents such a Japanese look and feel?

Art and design

When it comes to manga characters, you might notice, for example, that they are often drawn with large eyes and small noses and mouths. What are some other characteristic design features and drawing and perspective techniques used in manga?

Language and genre

How easy is it to follow a Japanese manga by looking at the illustrations and guessing the language? How is onomatopoeia used? In what direction is the text written? What other aspects of writing style make manga different from traditional English-language comics? What genres of manga can you identify? Are there more genres and types of manga than there are English-language comics?

Alamy/FocusCulture

Alamy/Photos 12

ISBN 9780170198271

Purpose

Investigate who manga are designed for. Who buys them? How old are they? Where can they be bought? Where can they be accessed? How much do they cost?

Characters

'Cosplay' describes a subculture of people who dress up like their favourite characters from manga, anime, comic books, video games, and so on. It began in Japan in the 1990s and has grown exponentially since then. How does cosplay influence Japanese street fashion and popular culture? How popular are the manga characters? Are cartoon characters popular in Australia in the same way?

OEL manga

OEL (original English-language) manga are essentially manga-style comics written in the English language. They replicate the design, style and expression of traditional Japanese manga. Research some OEL manga. While they are influenced by the look and feel of Japanese manga, can you spot any significant differences?

Anime in Japan

Popular anime include *Astro Boy*, *Pokemon*, or more recently, *Howl's Moving Castle*. Anime is often referred to as an art form; like manga, anime has its own distinct characteristics and features. Anime sometimes also borrows elements from manga, such as panel layouts and background text.

Which anime or Japanese animated films have you seen? Who was the intended audience? What similarities and differences did they have with American, Australian or other cartoons or animated feature films?

Have a go

Design your own manga or anime that includes some distinctive Japanese features.

Alamy/Photos 12

Photo Japan/Kenneth Hamm

ISBN 9780170198271

Getty Images/MIXA

1 Saying what someone will try doing

This pattern literally means that you will do it and see what it is like.
In other words, you will try doing it.

Verbてみます。
ぼくは日本のまんがを読んでみます。I will try to read a Japanese comic.
食べてみてください。Please taste/try it.

2 Talking about someone doing two actions at the same time

Use this pattern to describe two actions a person is doing – the main
thing they are doing, while doing something else at the same time.

Verb(stem) ながら、action。
わたしはコーヒーを飲みながら、 インターネットで チャットをします。
I chat on the Internet while drinking coffee.
きみこさんはJポップを聞きながら、 しゅくだいをしました。
Kimiko did homework while listening to J-pop

ながら is used to show
two actions are occurring
simultaneously. The
verb directly followed
by ながら is always
secondary to the action
that follows.

3 Saying that you have done something before

This pattern allows us to express what we have experienced
or ask someone what they have experienced.

A:	Verbたことがありますか。
B1:	はい、verbたことがあります。
B2:	いいえ、verbたことがありません。
—	日本のアニメを見たことがありますか。 Have you ever seen a Japanese animated cartoon?
	はい、 見たことがあります。 Yes, I have seen one.
	いいえ、 見たことがありません。 No, I've never seen one/I haven't seen one.

Corbis/Franck Robichon

See pages 201–2 for how to make all the verb and
adjective forms needed for these patterns.

ISBN 9780170198271

Media

アニメ	animation/cartoons
イーメール/Eメール	email
インターネット	Internet
うたばんぐみ	singing show
えいが	movie
けいじばん	bulletin board
こうこく	advertisement/publicity
コマーシャル	commercial
コメディー	comedy
ざっし	magazine
時だいげき	period drama/film
じまく	subtitles
Jポップ	J-pop (Japanese popular music)
新聞	newspaper
チャット	chat
テレビ	television
テレビきょく	television station
ドラマ	drama shows
ニュース	news
バラエティーショー	variety show
ばんぐみ	TV or radio program
ひるメロ	soap opera (midday melodrama)
ふきかえ	dubbing
ほうがく	Japanese music
ほうそう	broadcast
本	book
まんが	comics
メディア	media
メルマガ	mail magazine
ようがく	Western music
ラジオ	radio

まんが vocabulary

モグモグ	sound of chewing
ニャーニャー	meow (cat)
スースー	sound of sleeping
ギャーギャー	sound of screaming loudly
シーン	silence
みらい	the future
ヒューマノイドロボット	humanoid robot
かくしていて（かくす）	hide
ごめん。	Sorry.
シクシク	sound of weeping
でも	even
ガバッ	sound of a sudden movement
ワーワー	sound of bawling
うそ	a lie
ワハハハ	sound of laughing
ばか	idiot
ゲラゲラ	a cackling laugh
バシッ	a bang

Refer to manga on pages 177 and 178.

エクストラ vocabulary

しめきり	deadline
おきた	got up
すぐに	immediately
しごとづくえ	work desk
はじめた	started
かんがえた	thought/considered
下書き	sketch/draft
げんこう	manuscript
とりに行きます	go and collect
がんばります	do my best
出版社	publishing company
できるかな	I wonder if I can ...
ラーメン	hot noodle soup
今度	this time
つかれた	got tired
しまった!	Oops!
ねてしまった	fell asleep
でかい	huge

Refer to manga on page 190.

ISBN 9780170198271

Getty Images/ Koki Nagahama

まんが

12

百八十七

Why not try using てみます?

This is a really handy language pattern to learn, but be careful to remember the following points when using it.

- てみます is used for something you or someone else will try doing to see what it is like. It is often used when trying something that may be considered a challenge, but is also used for trying to do something that you haven't done before.
- てみます is written in *hiragana*, not *kanji*. It is always used with a verb and is just seen as an extension of the main verb. Patterns that are used in this way in Japanese are often not written in *kanji*.
- In English, the verb is often omitted when you say you are trying to do something. However, in Japanese the verb must be included. For example: 食べてみます (I will try eating it/I will try it).

There are lots of ways to use this pattern because we can change the tense of てみます, as in the examples below:

～てみました	(I tried ...)	～てみましょう	(Let's try ...)
～てみませんでした	(I did not try ...)	～てみてもいいですか	(May I try ...)
～てみてください	(Please try ...)	～てみたいです	(I want to try ...)
～てみませんか	(Won't you try ...?)		

Using ながら correctly

Here are some of the rules for using ながら:

- This pattern can only be used to talk about the actions of one person.
- The main action you are doing goes at the end of the sentence.
- The activities should occur simultaneously.
- To change the tense of the sentence, change the final verb. This tense then applies to the whole sentence.

For example:

おやつを食べながら、まんがを**かきました**。

(I **drew** comics while I was **eating** a snack.)

Have you ever ...?

The たことがあります pattern is used to talk about what you have done. Can you see how this grammar is formed?

日本に行った → ことが → あります。(I have been to Japan.)

日本に行きました。(I went to Japan.)

For this pattern, the verb before ことがあります is always in the plain past positive form (verb た). The verb at the end of the sentence must be in the present tense (i.e. あります or ありません).

Corbis/Uwe Anspach

Making negatives

Do you want to write something in a more casual style? The dictionary form can be used, but how do you make negatives? Here are some simple steps that will help.

Group 1 verbs

話す → 話さない

読む → 読まない

会う → 会わない

> Change the *u* sound to *a* and add ない.

Group 2 verbs

食べる → 食べない

見る → 見ない

> Delete る and add ない.

Group 3 verbs

する → しない

来る → 来ない

iStockphoto/mbbirdy

> You will notice that manga often use the casual style. Find out more on page 196, すらすらじしょけい.

Final particles – boys versus girls

There are a variety of final particles in Japanese. Which ones you use depends on whether you are male or female. You will often hear females use a combination of particles to show empathy or sympathy. Here are some examples:

むずかしいわよね。	(It is really difficult.)
きれいだわ。	(She is really pretty.)
私はしらないわ。	(I have no idea.)

Male speakers occasionally use some of the above final particles but often use more masculine-sounding particles, like the ones below:

これ、 うまいな。	(This is delicious.)
あれはそうおもわないな。	(I don't think that's right.)
行くぞ。	(I am going!)
このぼうし、 かっこいいぜ。	(This hat is really cool.)

> Language use is always changing and young people often bend informal rules such as these. Listen to young Japanese speakers to keep up-to-date.

ISBN 9780170198271

まんが

Grammar

Here is a list of the grammar patterns introduced in *Obento Supreme*. The list is arranged according to the grammar patterns you can use with verbs, adjectives and nouns. Refer to pages 197 and 199 for the verb conjugation rules.

Verbs

〜ます form

Group 1	飲<ruby>の</ruby>みます	drink
Group 2	食<ruby>た</ruby>べます	eat
Group 3 (irregular)	します 来<ruby>き</ruby>ます	do/play come

Do
一週間<ruby>いっしゅうかん</ruby>に五時間<ruby>ごじかん</ruby>ぐらいインターネットをつかいます。
I use the Internet for about five hours a week.

Don't
新聞<ruby>しんぶん</ruby>をあまり読<ruby>よ</ruby>みません。
I don't often read newspapers.

Won't you?
いっしょにえいがを見<ruby>み</ruby>ませんか。
Won't you come to the movies with me?

Did
メリッサさんは先週<ruby>せんしゅう</ruby>の金曜日に日本につきました。
Melissa arrived in Japan on Friday last week.

Didn't
きのう、 しゅくだいをしませんでした。
I didn't do my homework yesterday.

Because
家<ruby>うち</ruby>のちかくにありますから、 車<ruby>くるま</ruby>がありません。
I don't have a car because the station is near my house.

> These patterns use the ます stem (the ます form with ます deleted).

Go to do
こうえんにはな火<ruby>び</ruby>を見<ruby>み</ruby>に行<ruby>い</ruby>きました。
I went to the park to see the fireworks.

I want to do
週<ruby>しゅう</ruby>まつに友<ruby>とも</ruby>だちとあそびたいです。
I want to play with my friends on the weekend.

Do while doing
私<ruby>わたし</ruby>はおんがくを聞<ruby>き</ruby>きながら、 しゅくだいをします。
I do my homework while listening to music.

〜て form

Group 1	飲<ruby>の</ruby>んで	drinking
Group 2	食<ruby>た</ruby>べて	eating
Group 3 (irregular)	して 来<ruby>き</ruby>て	doing/playing coming

Doing
今<ruby>いま</ruby>、 えきでかなえさんをまっています。
I am waiting for Kanae at the station now.

Continue to do (habitual action)
三年間<ruby>さんねんかん</ruby>ぐらい日本語<ruby>ご</ruby>をべんきょうしています。
I have been studying Japanese for about three years.

The verbs listed below are generally written in the て form to show a state of being or a habitual action.	
しっています	はたらいています
べんきょうしています	住<ruby>す</ruby>んでいます
入<ruby>はい</ruby>っています	

... and
友<ruby>とも</ruby>だちとえいがを見<ruby>み</ruby>て、 買<ruby>か</ruby>いものに行<ruby>い</ruby>きました。
I watched movies with my friends and went shopping.

Please do
ドアをしめてください。
Please close the door.

May I?
お父<ruby>とう</ruby>さん、 車<ruby>くるま</ruby>をうんてんしてもいいですか。
Dad, may I drive your car?

ISBN 9780170198271

Mustn't

アクセサリーをつけてはだめです。
You mustn't wear accessories.

Try doing

今ばん、 すしを食べてみます。
I will try eating sushi tonight.

After …

えきを出てから、 みちをわたってください。
After leaving the station, please cross the road.

Plain (dictionary) form

Group 1	飲む	drink
Group 2	食べる	eat
Group 3 (irregular)	する 来る	do/play come

I do (casual speech)

週まつに友だちとあそぶ。
On the weekend I play with my friends.

Can do

日本語で手がみを書くことができます。
I can write letters in Japanese.

Like/Don't like to do

まんがをかくことが好き／きらいです。
I like/don't like drawing comics.

Good at/Not good at

山中さんは人々の前で話すことが上手／下手です。
Mr Yamanaka is good at/not good at speaking in front of people.

Plain negative（〜ない）form

Group 1	飲まない	don't drink
Group 2	食べない	don't eat
Group 3 (irregular)	しない 来ない	don't do/play don't come

I don't (casual speech)

今日、 ぼくは行かない。
I won't go today.

Plain past（〜た）form

Group 1	飲んだ	drank
Group 2	食べた	ate
Group 3 (irregular)	した 来た	did do/played came

I did (casual speech)

三時半に京都えきでまさよさんに会った。
I met Masayo at 3.30 at Kyoto Station.

I sometimes … and sometimes …

日曜日に読んだり、 べんきょうしたりします。
On Sunday, I sometimes read and sometimes study.

I have …/I haven't …

日本のアニメを見たことがあります。
I have seen a Japanese animated cartoon.
まだ日本に行ったことがありません。
I haven't been to Japan yet.

Plain past negative（〜なかった）form

Group 1	飲まなかった	didn't drink
Group 2	食べなかった	didn't eat
Group 3 (irregular)	しなかった 来なかった	didn't do/ didn't play didn't come

I didn't (casual speech)

おなかがいっぱいだったから、
ひるごはんを食べなかった。
I didn't eat lunch because I felt full.

ISBN 9780170198271

Adjectives

Refer to the adjective list on pages 202 and 203 for how to change adjective tenses.

い-adjective	おいしい
な-adjective	しずかな

And

Eメールははやくて、べんりです。
Email is fast and convenient.

Doing ... is ...

かんじを書くことはたのしいです。
Writing *kanji* is fun.

Which is better/~er?

東京と大阪とでは、どちらのほうが大きいですか。
Which is bigger, Tokyo or Osaka?
としょかんとこうえんとでは、
どちらのほうがしずかですか。
Which is quieter, the library or the park?

The best/-est

しんかんせんは一ばんはやい電車でした。
The bullet train was the fastest train.
一ばんすきなか目は日本語です。
My favourite subject is Japanese.

Nouns

Places	東京 (Tokyo)
People	夏子 (Natsuko)
Times	三時 (three o'clock)
Things	つくえ (desk)
Animals	ねこ (cat)
Activities	買いもの (shopping)

And (joining nouns)

テーブルの上にふでばことノートがあります。
There is a pencil case and a notebook on the table.

... and ... etc.

たいいくのじゅぎょうでじゅうどうやたいそうなどを
します。
In physical education class we do judo and gymnastics, etc.

It is ... and ...

ニコルキッドマンはオーストラリア人で、
ゆうめいな女ゆうです。
Nicole Kidman is an Australian and is a famous actress.

Which is better ... or ...?

おはしとフォークとでは、どちらのほうがいいですか。
Which is better, chopsticks or a fork?

It takes ... (time)

オーストラリアから日本まで九時間ぐらいかかります。
It takes about nine hours from Australia to Japan.

Want to become

しょう来、いしゃになりたいです。
In the future, I want to become a doctor.

ISBN 9780170198271

Particle chart

か	question marker	どこから来ましたか。	Where did you come from?
が	あります	手がみがあります。	There is a letter.
	います	ねこがいます。	There is a cat/I have a cat.
	上手／下手	えみこさんはおりがみが上手です。	Emi is good at origami.
	好き、きらい	サッカーが好きです。	I like soccer.
	can do	テニスができます。	I can play tennis.
	but	ふるい車ですが、とてもはやいです。	It is an old car, **but** it is very fast.
	分かります	「日本語が分かりますか。」「はい、すこし分かります。」	Do you understand Japanese? Yes, I understand a little.
から	after	しゅくだいをしてから、テレビを見ます。	I will watch TV **after** I do my homework.
から	because	買いものに行きましたから、お金がありません。	I haven't got any money **because** I went shopping.
から	from	日本から来ました。	I came **from** Japan.
で	at (place of action)	家でテレビを見ます。	I watch TV **at** home.
	by (transport)	電車で行きました。	I went **by** train.
	in (using)	日本語で書きます。	I will write it **in** Japanese.
	with everyone/by myself	みんな／一人で行きます。	I will go with everyone/by myself.
	because	びょうきでパーティーに行くことができません。	I can't go to the party **because** I am sick.
	in total	ぜんぶで六人です。	There are six people **in all**.
と	and (nouns)	ケリーさんとドナさんです。	It is Kerry **and** Donna.
	with (people/animals)	友だちと出かけます。	I am going out **with** my friends.
と～とでは	which one?	英語とれきしとでは、どちらのほうがむずかしいですか。	Which is harder, English **or** history?
に	at (specific time)	三時に行きました。	I went **at** 3 o'clock.
	going to a place/direction	町に行きます。	I am going **to** town.
	going to a place to do an activity	やまにスキーに行きます。	I am going **to** the mountains **to** ski.
		プールにおよぎに行きます。	I am going **to** the pool **to** swim
	direction of movement	左にまがってください。	Please turn left.
	for	あさごはんに何を食べますか。	What do you eat **for** breakfast?

ISBN 9780170198271

	in	休み**に**うみに行きました。	I went to the beach **in** the holidays.
	in/at (location)	いぬはにわ**に**います。	The dog is **in** the garden.
	direction	友だち**に**電話します。	I am going to telephone **[to]** my friend.
	会います	ミックジャガー**に**会いました。	I met Mick Jagger.
	かよいます	高校**に**かよいます。	She attends senior high school.
	します (to decide on)	すきやき**に**します。	I will have sukiyaki.
	なります	先生**に**なりました。	He became a teacher.
	のります	ローラーコースター**に**のりました。	I rode on a rollercoaster.
	入ります	ピンポンのクラブ**に**入っています。	She is in the table tennis club.
には	in/at	家**には**ペットがいますか。	Do you have a pet **at** your home?
ね	isn't it?/wasn't it?	それはいいです**ね**。	That is good, **isn't it**?
の〜	of (possession)	私**の**ケーキはどこ？	Where is my cake?
〜の〜に	in a position	テーブル**の**上**に**あります。	It is on the table.
〜のが	making the verb act like a noun	ねる**のが**すきです。	I like sleeping
は	topic marker	私**は**春こです。	I am Haruko.
は〜が	topic/subject	あね**は**まんが**が**大好きです。	My older sister loves comics.
		ベンくん**は**目**が**あおいです。	Ben has blue eyes.
		私**は**たいいく**が**に**が**手です。	PE is my weak point.
まで	to/until	しあいは七時**まで**です。	The game goes **until** 7 o'clock.
も	also/too	ぼく**も**十五さいです。	I am **also** 15 years old.
や〜など	and/etc.	ペン**や**ノート**など**があります。	There are pens **and** notebooks, **etc.**
よ	emphasis	おもしろいです**よ**。	It is interesting, you know!
を	object marker	ドア**を**あけてください。	Please open the door.
	within	日本**を**りょ行したいです。	I want to travel **within** Japan.
	at (passing through)	かど**を**まがってください。	Please turn **at** the corner.
	saying what you want	コーヒー**を**ください。	Some coffee, please.
な	isn't it?/it is! (usually male speakers)	うまい**な**。	It is delicious!
よね	showing sympathy/empathy (usually female speakers)	むずかしい**よね**。	It is really difficult.
わ	showing emphasis (used by females)	私はしらない**わ**。	I am not sure.
		きれいだ**わ**。	She is really pretty.

ISBN 9780170198271

すらすらじしょけい
The plain (dictionary) form

Japanese can be spoken or written in the plain (dictionary) form, or the polite (です/ます) form. You may have heard dialogues in the plain form on the audio tracks, or you may have read them in previous units.

The plain forms cover all the same tenses as the polite forms: do, don't, did, didn't, is, isn't, was, wasn't, etc. The difference is when you use them. The plain form is commonly used in:

- dictionaries, manga, newspapers or advertisements
- grammatical patterns
- informal speech: among close friends or younger people
- informal writing: a diary excerpt, an itinerary or note-taking.

The level of politeness in Japanese speech reveals the type of relationship between the speakers. As in English, formal language creates respect and distance between speakers. You will hear Japanese people speaking in the polite form to their superiors and their superior sometimes replying in the plain form.

The context in which you are speaking or writing can also affect the type of language used. If you are uncertain about the appropriate level of politeness, use the polite form. It might sound too formal, distant, or even cold in some situations, but it is generally better to be more formal than informal in Japanese.

Adjectives

い-adjectives

To make the plain form of い-adjectives from the polite form, remove the です.

Polite form	安^{やす}いです。	安^{やす}くないです。	安^{やす}かったです。	安^{やす}くなかったです。
English	It is cheap.	It is not cheap.	It was cheap.	It wasn't cheap.
Plain form	安^{やす}い	安^{やす}くない	安^{やす}かった	安^{やす}くなかった

な-adjectives

Follow the rules for the different tenses to make the plain forms of な-adjectives.

Polite form	しずかです。	しずかじゃないです。	しずかでした。	しずかじゃなかったです。
English	It is quiet.	It is not quiet.	It was quiet.	It wasn't quiet.
Plain form	しずかだ Delete です and add だ.	しずかじゃない* Delete です.	しずかだった。 Delete でした and add だった.	しずかじゃなかった Delete です.

*Note how ない acts like an い-adjective!

The ~な ending is only used when the な-adjective comes straight before a noun.

ISBN 9780170198271

Nouns

Nouns + です

です means 'to be' and is translated in many ways depending on the context and tense – it is/we are/they are/she is/etc. It is attached to い-adjectives to make the polite forms, but when it follows a な-adjective or a noun, it follows its own rules.

The tenses of です with nouns and な-adjectives are the same!

Polite form	本です。	本じゃないです。	本でした。	本じゃなかったです。
English	It is a book.	It is not a book.	It was a book.	It wasn't a book.
Plain form	本だ	本じゃない	本だった	本じゃなかった

Verbs

Group 1 verbs

Group 1 verbs have different endings in the plain form and the て form depending on the syllable before ます. Below is a summary of the changes for each ending. All group 1 verbs with the same ending change accordingly, so it is helpful if you can memorise these endings. 行きます is the only exception. The verb chart on pages 200–1 is arranged in a similar way to this table.

Verb	Syllable before ますchanges to the following for the plain form endings				て form
	Present	Present negative	Past	Past negative	
会います	う	わない	った	わなかった	って
書きます	く	かない	いた	かなかった	いて
およぎます	ぐ	がない	いだ	がなかった	いで
話します	す	さない	した	さなかった	して
まちます	つ	たない	った	たなかった	って
しにます	ぬ	なない	んだ	ななかった	んで
あそびます	ぶ	ばない	んだ	ばなかった	んで
読みます	む	まない	んだ	まなかった	んで
すわります	る	らない	った	らなかった	って

The て form of 行きます is 行って and the plain past is 行った.

The て verb forms can be found on pages 200–1.

See the rules for group 1 verbs on page 198.

ISBN 9780170198271

Present

I listen　聞きます → 聞く
plain positive (dictionary form)
Delete ます and change the final syllable from an *i* sound to an *u* sound using your *hiragana* chart.
い → う　　　き → く　　　ぎ → ぐ　　　し → す
ち → つ　　　に → ぬ　　　び → ぶ　　　み → む　　　り → る

Present negative

I don't listen　聞きません → 聞かない
plain negative (ない form)
Delete ません, change the syllable before ます from an *i* sound to an *a* sound using your *hiragana* chart and add ない.
い → わ　　　き → か　　　ぎ → が　　　し → さ
ち → た　　　に → な　　　び → ば　　　み → ま　　　り → ら

> ～う verbs change to わ for negatives.
> For example, 買う → 買わない.

Past

I did listen/I listened　聞きました → 聞いた
plain past (た form)
Delete ました and depending on the syllable before ます, change the ending as follows:
い → った　　　き → いた　　　に → んだ
ち → った　　　ぎ → いだ　　　び → んだ
り → った　　　し → した　　　み → んだ
Or change the verb into the て form and then change the final て to た.

Past negative

I didn't listen　聞きませんでした → 聞かなかった
plain past negative (なかった form)
Change the verb to plain (ない form), delete the final い and add かった.

Summary of the polite and plain forms for Group 1 verbs

Polite form (ます)	書きます	書きません	書きました	書きませんでした
English	I write	I don't write	I wrote	I didn't write
Plain form	書く	書かない	書いた	書かなかった

ISBN 9780170198271

Group 2 verbs

Present

I eat　食^たべます → 食^たべる plain positive (dictionary form)
Delete ます and add る.

Present negative

I don't eat　食^たべません → 食^たべない plain negative (ない form)
Delete ません and add ない.

Past

I did eat/I ate　食^たべました → 食^たべた plain past (た form)
Delete ました and add た, or change the verb into て form and change the final てto た.

Past negative

I didn't eat　食^たべませんでした → 食^たべなかった plain past negative (なかった form)
Change the verb to plain negative (ない form), delete the final い and add かった.

Summary of the polite and plain forms for group 2 verbs

Polite form (ます)	見^みます	見^みません	見^みました	見^みませんでした
English	I see	I don't see	I saw	I didn't see
Plain form	見^みる	見^みない	見^みた	見^みなかった

Group 3 verbs (irregular)

Polite form (ます)	します	しません	しました	しませんでした
English	I do	I don't	I did	I didn't
Plain form	する	しない	した	しなかった

Polite form (ます)	来^きます	来^きません	来^きました	来^きませんでした
English	I come	I don't come	I came	I didn't come
Plain form	来^くる	来^こない	来^きた	来^こなかった

ISBN 9780170198271

Verb chart

Here is a list of all the verbs in *Obento Deluxe* and *Obento Supreme*, and an example of how to change verbs with the same ending to make the tenses you want.

Group 1 verbs

〜ます form	English	ます do/will do	て doing
〜います	to meet	会います	会って
〜きます	to write	書きます	書いて
〜ぎます	to swim	およぎます	およいで
〜します	to speak	話します	話して
〜ちます	to wait	まちます	まって
〜にます	to die	しにます	しんで
〜びます	to play	あそびます	あそんで
〜みます	to read	読みます	読んで
〜ります	to sit	すわります	すわって

あらいます to wash うたいます to sing 買います to buy かよいます to commute つかいます to use もらいます to receive いいます to say	行きます to go *Note the て form of 行きます is 行って, and the plain past is 行った. かきます to draw 聞きます to listen/hear/ask さきます to bloom つきます to arrive ぬぎます to take off はきます to wear (lower body) はたらきます to work ひきます to play (stringed instruments) まきます to roll	おします to push おろします to lower down かくします to hide かします to lend けします to turn off 出します to bring out/post ためします to attempt/try もどします to restore/turn back	かちます to win たちます to stand たちます to pass (time) もちます to hold/carry

Group 2 verbs

〜ます form	English	ます do/will do	て doing
〜い sound + ます	to get up	おきます	おきて
〜え sound + ます	to eat	食べます	食べて

あびます to take a shower います to exist おります to get off きます to wear (upper body)	あけます to open あこがれます to be attracted to できます to be able to	入れます to put/let it in うけます to catch/receive おしえます to teach おぼえます to remember	かぞえます to count かんがえます to think 聞こえます to be audible/can hear しめます to close

Group 3 verbs (irregular)

English	ます do/will do	て doing	Plain present do/will do
come	来ます	来て	来る
do/play	します	して	する

あんしんします to be relieved あんないします to guide いらいらします to become irritated/nervous うんてんします to drive 外食します to eat out きんちょうします to be nervous けしょうします to wear make-up	ごろごろします to lie around/to loaf about さんかします to participate さんぽします to stroll/walk じこしょうかいします to give a self-introduction します to wear (an accessory)/decide on/have to eat or drink じゅんびします to prepare/get ready ジョギングします to jog

二百

200

ISBN 9780170198271

Plain present	Plain present negative	Plain past	Plain past negative
do/will do	don't/will not do	did	did not do
会う	会わない	会った	会わなかった
書く	書かない	書いた	書かなかった
およぐ	およがない	およいだ	およがなかった
話す	話さない	話した	話さなかった
まつ	またない	まった	またなかった
しぬ	しなない	しんだ	しななかった
あそぶ	あそばない	あそんだ	あそばなかった
読む	読まない	読んだ	読まなかった
すわる	すわらない	すわった	すわらなかった

よびます to call	かみます to chew	あります to exist	つくります to make
	住みます to live	おどります to dance	とおります to pass through
	飲みます to drink	おわります to finish	とまります to stop
	休みます to rest	かえります to return	とります to take
		かかります to take time	なります to become
		かぶります to wear (head)	のりかえます to change (transport)
		がんばります to try hard	のります to ride
		きります to cut	入ります to enter
		けります to kick	はじまります begin/start
		さわります to touch	はしります to run
		しゃべります to chat	ふとります to get fat
		しります to know	ふります to fall (rain/snow)
		分かります to understand	まがります to turn
		わたります to cross	まもります to protect

There are a few group 1 verbs that end in an **i** sound plus る, or an **e** sound plus る. It is a good idea to learn these so you don't confuse them with Group 2 verbs, which all have one of these sounds, plus る.

Plain present	Plain present negative	Plain past	Plain past negative
do/will do	don't/will not do	did	did not do
おきる	おきない	おきた	おきなかった
食べる	食べない	食べた	食べなかった

つかれます to become tired	出かけます to go out	見ます to watch/look at	見せます to show
つけます to switch on	出ます to attend/participate	はじめます (I) begin	見つけます to find
つけます to wear (accessories)	なげます to throw	まけます to lose	やせます to lose weight
つづけます to continue	ねます to sleep	まぜます to mix	やめます to quit/give up

Plain present negative	Plain past	Plain past negative
don't\will not do	did	did not do
来ない	来た	来なかった
しない	した	しなかった

電話します to telephone	めそめそします to sob/whimper
どきどきします to feel excited/nervous	れんしゅうします to practise
にこにこします to smile radiantly/beaming	りょ行します to travel
ひっこしします to move house	リラックスします to relax
ぶらぶらします to dawdle/hang around	ろくおんします to record
べんきょうします to study	わくわくします to be nervous/excited/thrilled
ホストします to host	

Adjective chart

Here is a complete list of the い- and な-adjectives introduced in *Obento Deluxe* and *Obento Supreme*.

い-adjectives

	Positive	Negative
Present	高^{たか}いです。It is expensive.	高くないです。It is not expensive.
Past	高かったです。It was expensive.	高くなかったです。It was not expensive.

Before a noun: 高**い**きものです。It is an expensive kimono.
And: 高**くて**、 ふるいです。It is expensive and old.

あおい	blue		
あかい	red	すずしい	cool (weather)
あかるい	light/bright	すばらしい	wonderful/amazing
あたたかい	warm	せまい	narrow
新^{あたら}しい	new	高い	tall/expensive
あつい	hot/thick (from front to back)	たのしい	enjoyable/fun
あぶない	dangerous	小^{ちい}さい	little/small
いい *	good	ちかい	near
いそがしい	busy	つまらない	boring
いっぱい	full	つめたい	cold (objects)
うすい	thin (from front to back)	つよい	strong
うつくしい	beautiful	とおい	far/distant
うるさい	noisy	ながい	long
うれしい	happy	ねむい	sleepy
おいしい	delicious	はずかしい	embarrassing
おおい	many/much	はやい	fast/quick
大^{おお}きい	big/large	ひくい	low
おかしい	funny/strange	ひどい	awful
おそい	slow	ひろい	wide/spacious
おもい	heavy	ふとい	thick
おもしろい	interesting/fun	ふるい	old
かっこいい	cool	ほそい	thin/slender/small (diameter)
かっこわるい	ugly/idiotic	まずい	(tastes) awful
かなしい	sad	まるい	round
かわいい	cute	みじかい	short
きいろい	yellow	むしあつい	humid
きたない	dirty	むずかしい	difficult
きびしい	strict	めずらしい	rare/unusual
くさい	smelly	やさしい	easy/kind/gentle
くらい	dark/gloomy	安^{やす}い	cheap
くろい	black	わかい	young
こわい	scary	わるい	bad
さびしい	sad/lonely		
さむい	cold (weather)		
しろい	white		
すくない	few		
すごい	amazing		

Note: いい *becomes* よくない *in the negative,* よかった *in the past and* よくなかった *in the past negative.*

ISBN 9780170198271

な-adjectives

	Positive	Negative
Present	とくべつです。It is special.	とくべつじゃないです。It is not special.
Past	とくべつでした。It was special.	とくべつじゃなかったです。It was not special.

Before a noun: とくべつ**な**きものです。It is a special kimono.
And: とくべつ**で**、　すてきです。It is special and wonderful.

いや（な）	unpleasant		すてき（な）	wonderful
いろいろ（な）	various		でんとうてき（な）	traditional
かわいそう（な）	pitiable		とくい（な）	good at/proud
きらい（な）	dislike		とくべつ（な）	special
きれい（な）	pretty/clean		にが手（な）	not good at
げんき（な）	lively/spirited		にぎやか（な）	lively/crowded
ざんねん（な）	pitiful		のんき（な）	easy-going
しずか（な）	quiet		ばか（な）	silly
しぜん（な）	natural		ハンサム（な）	handsome
しつれい（な）	impolite		ひま（な）	free/idle
上手（な）	skilful/good at		下手（な）	unskilful/no good at
しんせつ（な）	kind		へん（な）	strange
好き（な）	like		べんり（な）	convenient
すてき（な）	nice/wonderful		まじめ（な）	serious
大きらい（な）	dislike a lot/hate		ゆう名（な）	famous
大じょうぶ（な）	all right		らんぼう（な）	rough/violent
大好き（な）	like a lot/love		りっぱ（な）	great
大せつ（な）	important		わがまま（な）	spoilt/selfish
大へん（な）	difficult			

ISBN 9780170198271

かな rules

てんてん and まる

The rules for the five sound changes in ひらがな and かたかな are the same.

K sounds change to G   T sounds change to D
S sounds change to Z   H sounds change to B or P

K	か	き	く	け	こ	カ	キ	ク	ケ	コ
G	が	ぎ	ぐ	げ	ご	ガ	ギ	グ	ゲ	ゴ
S	さ	し	す	せ	そ	サ	シ	ス	セ	ソ
Z	ざ	じ	ず	ぜ	ぞ	ザ	ジ	ズ	ゼ	ゾ
じ and ジ sound like ji not zi										
T	た	ち	つ	て	と	タ	チ	ツ	テ	ト
D	だ	ぢ	づ	で	ど	ダ	ヂ	ヅ	デ	ド
H	は	ひ	ふ	へ	ほ	ハ	ヒ	フ	ヘ	ホ
B	ば	び	ぶ	べ	ぼ	バ	ビ	ブ	ベ	ボ
P	ぱ	ぴ	ぷ	ぺ	ぽ	パ	ピ	プ	ペ	ポ

Sound combinations

If two かな are the same size (e.g. き and よ), they are said as two separate sounds. If や, ゆ, or よ are small, then the two sounds run together (e.g. きょ).

や	ゆ	よ	ヤ	ユ	ヨ
きゃ	きゅ	きょ	キャ	キュ	キョ
ぎゃ	ぎゅ	ぎょ	ギャ	ギュ	ギョ
しゃ	しゅ	しょ	シャ	シュ	ショ
じゃ	じゅ	じょ	ジャ	ジュ	ジョ
ちゃ	ちゅ	ちょ	チャ	チュ	チョ
にゃ	にゅ	にょ	ニャ	ニュ	ニョ
ひゃ	ひゅ	ひょ	ヒャ	ヒュ	ヒョ
びゃ	びゅ	びょ	ビャ	ビュ	ビョ
ぴゃ	ぴゅ	ぴょ.	ピャ	ピュ	ピョ
みゃ	みゅ	みょ	ミャ	ミュ	ミョ
りゃ	りゅ	りょ	リャ	リュ	リョ

Small つ/ツ

Often you see a word with small つ or ツ. For example, when you listen to the pronunciation of がっこう or ペット, you cannot hear the sound of small つ／ツ. However, there is a pause between the two sounds you do hear.

Listen carefully to the pause indicating the small つ/ツ in the following words and repeat.

がっこう   ちょっと   じゅっぷん
ペット   レッスン   サッカー

Long vowels

A long vowel in ひらがな is written as two sounds. Listen and repeat.

おかあさん   おじいさん   すうがく
おねえさん   おとうさん

However, in カタカナ, the double vowel is written as a line (ー) either horizontally as in コーラ, or vertically as in コ
ー
ラ.

クイズ タイム!

First, listen to the pairs of words and repeat. Next, listen to one of each pair and, with a partner, predict which word will be said next. The person who predicts correctly gets a point.

1	おかし	おかしい
2	きて	きって
3	すてき	ステーキ
4	おばさん	おばあさん
5	おじいさん	おじさん
6	きて	きいて
7	しゅじん	しゅうじん
8	して	しって
9	とり	とおり
10	びょういん	びよういん
11	すうじ	しゅうじ
12	くさい	きゅうさい

Special カタカナ sounds

カタカナ is used for foreign words. Yet, there are some sound combinations that cannot be written just using ヤ, ユ or ヨ. (In addition, small ア, イ, エ or オ are also used.)

(ティ)	パーティー	party
(ディ)	ディズニーランド	Disneyland
(ウィ)	ウィリアム	William
(ウェ)	ウェリントン	Wellington
(ファ)	ファッション	fashion
(フィ)	サーフィン	surfing
(フォ)	フォーク	fork
(ジェ)	ジェット	jet

ISBN 9780170198271

Using げんこうようし

The four rules for well-balanced writing are:
1 correct strokes
2 correct stroke order
3 correct placement for each stroke
4 allowing the correct space between characters.

When Japanese students practise writing characters or draft a written piece such as an essay or a magazine article, they use squared writing paper called げんこうようし (see below). The squares help in the:
- writing of balanced and even-sized characters
- accurate positioning of characters, which allows for correcting and adding ふりがな to difficult かんじ.

Traditionally, Japanese was written vertically. To do this using げんこうようし, turn the paper around so that you start at the top right-hand corner and write down the column and then continue to the next left-hand column.

Today, Japanese is written vertically or horizontally on げんこうようし. To write horizontally, you start from the top left-hand corner, like in English, and write across the page. Study both styles on the following page. What differences can you find?

げんこうようし rules

Looking at the examples on the following page, there are similarities and differences in the two written styles. Some of the rules for using げんこうようし are slightly different in each case.

General rules

1 Leave three blank squares for the title.
2 Leave a blank square at the start of a new line for each paragraph.
3 Don't leave spacing between words. (Words can run onto the next line.)
4 Write commas (、) full stops (。), and quotation marks (「 」) in their own square. However, when a full stop is used with a closing quotation mark, they are written together in the same square.
If 、。「 or 」 are at the end of a line, they are written in the last square with the final character.

ISBN 9780170198271

Rules for よこがき (horizontal writing)

1 、and 。 or small や, ゆ, よ and つ are written in the bottom left-hand corner of the square.
2 The カタカナ long sound dash is written horizontally.
3 Opening quotation marks are written in the top right-hand corner and closing marks are written in the bottom left-hand corner of the square.
4 Use ⌄ between characters to insert a missing character above.
5 ふりがな is written above the かんじ.

			し	ん	か	ん	せ	ん									
日	本	に	、	は	や	い	で	ん	し	ゃ	が	あ	り	ま	す	。	「し
ん	か	ん	せ	ん	」	で	す	。									

しんかんせんのスピードはへいきん二百四十キロ^でぐらいす。九^{しゅう}州から本^{しゅう}州のきたまで行きます。

きっぷはたかいです。でも、べんりですね。

Rules for たてがき (vertical writing)

1 、and 。 or small や, ゆ, よ and つ are written in the top right-hand corner of the square.
2 The カタカナ long sound dash is written vertically.
3 Opening quotation marks are written in the bottom right-hand corner and closing marks are written in the top left-hand corner of the square. Note their shape.
4 Use く between characters to insert a missing character.
5 ふりがな is written to the right of the かんじ.

きっぷはたかいです。でも、べんりですね。

十キロぐらいす。九州から本州のきたまで行

しんかんせんのスピードはへいきん二百四

かんせん」です。

日本に、はやいでんしゃがあります。「し

ISBN 9780170198271

Vocabulary list
日本語ー英語

あ

ああ、 そうですか。	Oh, really is that so?
あいきどう	aikido
あいだ、 間	duration/between
あいたいです。 会いたいです。	I want to meet you.
あいます、 会います	meet
あえるのをたのしみ にしています	looking forward to seeing
あお（い）	blue
あおしんごう	green traffic light
あおた	green paddy/rice field
あおたけ	green bamboo
あおのり	green seaweed
あおば	green leaves/foliage
あおむし	green caterpillar
あおりんご	green apple
あか（い）	red
あがります	go up
あかるい	bright/light
あかるいせいかくの人	person with a cheerful personality
あき、 秋	autumn
アキバ	abbreviation for Akihabara
あきはばら	Akihabara
あきまつり、 秋まつり	autumn festival
アクセサリー	accessory/jewellery
あけましておめでとう	Happy New Year!
あけます	open
あこがれます	long for
あし	leg/foot
あした	tomorrow
あそこ	over there (away from both the speaker and listener)
あそびにきてください。 あそびに来てください。	Please come and play.
あそびにきませんか。 あそびに来ませんか。	Won't you come and play?
あそびます	play

あたたかい／ぽかぽか	warm
あたま	head
あたまがいい	intelligent
あたらしい、 新しい	new
あつい	hot
あとで	after/later
アドレス	address
あなた	you
あに	older brother (*humble*)
アニメ	animation/cartoons
あね	older sister (*humble*)
あの	that …
アパート	apartment
あびます	take (a shower)
あぶない	dangerous
アボカド	avocado
あまり（あんまり）	not really/not very often/ not well
あめ	rain
あらいます	wash
あらし	storm
あります	have/be/there is … (for inanimate objects)
あるいて（いきます）	on foot
アルバイト	part-time job
あれ	that one

い

い（三い）	place (e.g. 3rd place)
いい	good
いいます、 言います	say/call (a name)
イーメール、 Eメール	email
いえ、 家	house/home
いきます、 行きます	go
いくら（ですか。）	How much?
いけばな	flower arranging
いしゃ	doctor
いす	chair
いそがしい	busy

ISBN 9780170198271

いただきます	Let's eat. I accept the meal/drink. (said before eating)
イタリアご、 イタリア語	Italian language
いちじかんめ、一時間目	first period
いちにちめ、一日目	the first day
いちねんせい、一年生	Year 1/Grade 1
いちばん、一ばん	number one/the most ...
いちばんめ、一ばん目	first (one)
いつ／いつから	when/from when
いっしょうけんめい	with all one's might
いっしょに	together
いつつ、五つ	five
いってきます。	I will be back. (said when leaving home)
いつでも	anytime
いってらっしゃい。	Farewell. Take care. (said when going out)
いつも	always
いとこ	cousin (*humble*)
いとこさん	cousin (*polite*)
いま	living room
いま、今	now
いまから、今から	from now
います	have/be/there is ... (for animals and people)
いもうと	younger sister (*humble*)
いもうとさん	younger sister (*polite*)
いや(な)	unpleasant
イヤリング	earrings
いらいらします	irritated/nervous
いらっしゃいませ	Welcome/May I help you?
いりぐち、 入り口	entrance
いります	need
いれます、 入れます	put in
いろ	colours
いろいろ(な)	various
インストラクター	instructor
インターネット	Internet
インターネットサイト	Internet site
いんたいしています	retired
インタビュー	interview

う

うえ、 上	on/above
ウェイター	waiter
ウェイトレス	waitress
うけます	catch/receive
うごかしかた	way of moving
うし	cow
うしろ	behind
うそ	lie/fib
うた	song
うたいます	sing
うたばんぐみ	singing show
うち、 家	house/home
うちわ	fans
うつくしい	beautiful
うで	arm
うどん	udon noodles
うまい	delicious
うみ	sea
うるさい	noisy
うれしい	happy/glad
うん。	Yes. (*casual*)
うんてんします	drive
うんどう	exercise
うんどうかい	sports day

え

え	picture
エアコン	air conditioner
えいが	movie
えいかいわ、 英会話	English conversation
えいがかん	cinema/movie theatre
えいご、 英語	English language
えーと、 ええと	umm
えき	train station
エスエフ (SF)	science fiction
えん、 円	yen
えんがわ	verandah
エンジニア	engineer
えんぴつ	pencil

ISBN 9780170198271

お

おいくつですか。	How old are you?
おいしい	delicious
おいで	come here
おおあめ、 大あめ	heavy rain
おおきい、 大きい	big/large
おかあさん、 お母さん	mother (*polite*)
おかえりなさい。	Welcome home.
おかげ	it is all down to you/ thanks to you
おかし	sweets
おかしい	funny/amusing
おかね	money
おからだにきをつけて。	Take care of yourself.
おきます	get up
おげんきですか	How are you?
おしえます	teach/tell
おします	push
おしょうがつ、おしょう月	New Year
おじ	uncle (*humble*)
おしり	bottom
おじいさん	grandfather (*polite*)
おじさん	uncle (*polite*)
おすすめ	recommendation
おせちりょうり	New Year's food
おちゃ	tea
おちゃわん	tea cup/bowl
おつきみ、 お月見	moon viewing
おつり	change
おてあらい、お手あらい	toilet
おてら	Buddhist temple
おとうさん、 お父さん	father (*polite*)
おとうと	younger brother (*humble*)
おとうとさん	younger brother (*polite*)
おとこのこ、 男のこ	boy
おとこのひと、 男の人	man
おとな、 大人	adult
おどります	dance
おなか	tummy/stomach
おなかがいっぱいです。	I am full.
おなかがすきました。	I am hungry.
おなかがペコペコです。	I am starving. (*casual*)
おにいさん	older brother (*polite*)
おにぎり	rice cake
おねえさん	older sister (*polite*)
おねがいします	Would you do me the favour? Please …
おはし	chopsticks
おはなみ、 おはな見	flower viewing
おば	aunt (*humble*)
おばあさん	grandmother (*polite*)
おばさん	aunt (*polite*)
おふろ	bath/bathroom
おふろにはいります	have a bath
おふろば	bathroom
おへんじをたのしみにしています。	I am looking forward to your reply.
おべんとうばこ	lunch box
おぼえます	remember
おまたせしました。	Thank you for waiting.
おまつり	festival
おみやげ	souvenir
おみやげや	souvenir shop
おもいます	think/consider
おもしろい	interesting
おもち	rice cakes for New Year
おやすみなさい。	Good night.
おやつ	snack
およぎます	swim
おりがみ	origami
おります	get off
オリンピック	the Olympics
オレンジ（の）	orange
おろします	drop off
おわります	finish
おわん	bowl
おんがく	music
おんせん	natural hot springs
おんなのこ、 女のこ	girl
おんなのひと、 女の人	woman

か

～かい	counter for floors
かいがい、 海外	overseas
かいぎ、 会ぎ	meeting
かいけいし	accountant
がいこく, 外国	overseas
がいこくご、 外国語	foreign language

ISBN 9780170198271

がいこくじん、 外国人	foreigner	かていか、 家ていか	Home Economics
かいしゃ、 会社	company	かていきょうし、家ていきょうし	home tutor
かいしゃいん、会社いん	company employee		
がいしょくします、外食します	eat out	かど	corner
		かならず	certainly
かいだん	stairs	かにかまぼこ	crab fish cake
かいます、 買います	buy	ガバッ	sound of a sudden movement
かいもの、 買いもの	shopping		
かいわ、 会話	conversation	かばん	bag
かえります	go home/return	かぶります	wear (hats)
かお	face	かべ	wall
かかります	take time/cost money	かみ	paper
かがく、 か学	Science	かみ（のけ）	hair
かきごおり	shaved ice treat	かみなり	lightning
かきます	draw	かみます	chew
かきます、 書きます	write	ガム	chewing gum
かくこと	drawing	カメラマン	photographer/camera operator
かくします	hide		
がくせい、 学生	student	かもく、 か目	subject
がくれき、 学れき	school history	かよいます	commute
かけじく	hanging scroll	から	from/because
かけます	wear (glasses)	カラオケパーティー	karaoke party
かさ	umbrella	からだ	body
かさたて	umbrella stand	からだにいい	good for your body
かざん、 火山	volcano	からて、 から手	karate
かしこまりました。	Certainly.	カリフォルニアロール	California roll
かします	lend	カレーうどん	curry noodles
カジノ	casino	かわ、 川	river
かしゅ、 か手	singer	がわ	side
かぜ	wind	かわいい	cute/pretty
かぜがつよい	windy	かわいそう	poor/pitiful
かぞえます	count	かん、 間	period of time
かぞく、 家ぞく	family	かんがえます	think/consider
ガソリンスタンド	petrol station	かんごふ	nurse
かた	shoulder	かんぱい。	Cheers!
かちます	win	がんばって!	Good luck!
カチンコチン	freezing up	かんじ	kanji
がつがつ	eating greedily/craving something	がんばります。	I will try my best.
がっき	musical instrument		
かっこいい	attractive/trendy	**き**	
がっこう、 学校	school	きいろ（い/の）	yellow
かっこわるい	unattractive/not trendy	きおん	air temperature
		きかせていただいて	letting me hear
カップ	cup	ききます、 聞きます	listen/hear

ISBN 9780170198271

きこえます、 聞こえます	audible
ぎし	engineer
きじ	article
ぎじゅつ	Design and Technology
きせつ	seasons
きそく	rules
きた、 北	north
きたぐち、 北口	north entrance
きたない	dirty
きっさてん	coffee shop
きてください。来てください。	Please come.
きてね。来てね。	Come, won't you.
きのう	yesterday
きびしい	strict
きぼう	request/desire
きます、 来ます	come
きます	put on (top half or general clothing)
きませんか、 来ませんか	Won't you come?
きもち	feeling
きもちがいい	feels good
ギャーギャー	sound of screaming loudly
キャプテン	captain
きゅうしょく、 きゅう食	school lunches
きゅうどう	Kyudo (archery)
きゅうり	cucumber
きょう、 今日	today
きょうがく、 きょう学'	co-educational
きょうぎ	event
きょうし	teacher
きょうしつ	classroom
きょうと	Kyoto
きょねん、 きょ年	last year
きらい（な）	dislikable
ぎらぎら	pulsating heat from the sun
きります	cut
きれい（な）	pretty/clean
キロ	kilograms
きをつけてください。	Please take care.
きんぎょ、 金ぎょ	goldfish
ぎんこう、 ぎん行	bank

ぎんこういん、ぎん行いん	bank employee
きんちょうします	nervous
きんぱつ（の）、金ぱつ（の）	blond (hair)
きんメダル、 金メダル	gold medal
ぎんメダル	silver medal

く

くうこう	airport
くすりや	pharmacy
ください	please give me
くち、 口	mouth
ぐちゃぐちゃ	soft and soggy/in disarray
くつ	shoes
くつや	shoe shop
くに、 国	country
くび	neck
くま	bear
くもり	cloudy
くらい	dark
ぐらい	about
クリケット	cricket
くるまいす、 車いす	wheelchair
くろ（い）	black
クラブかつどう	club activity
グラム	gram

け

けいかん	police officer
けいざい	Economics
けいじばん	bulletin board
げいじゅつか、げいじゅつ家	artist
けいたいでんわ、けいたい電話	mobile phone
けいれき	background/career
けしき	scenery
けしゴム	eraser
けします	turn off
けしょう	make-up
けしょう（を）します	wear make-up
げたばこ	shoe box
ゲラゲラ	a cackling laugh

二百十一

ISBN 9780170198271

けります	kick	ごちゃごちゃ	a jumble/a mess
~けん	counter for buildings and houses	こと	matter/thing
		ことし、 今年	this year
げんかん	entrance	ことしも よろしく おねがいします。 今年もよろしく おねがいします。	Remember me this year too.
げんき（な）	lively/spirited		
げんこう	manuscript		
けんこうじょうたい	medical conditions (serious only)		
		ことば	word
けんちくか、 けんちく家	architect	こども	child
げんざい	at present	こどものとき、 子どもの時	when I was a child
けんどう	kendo		
		この	this ...
		このへん	around here
こ		ごはん	cooked rice/meal
~こ	counter for small, round items	コマーシャル	commercial (TV)
		こまったとき、 こまった時	when (you are) in trouble
~ご、~語	language		
こうえん	park/playground	ごみ	rubbish
こうこう、 高校	senior high school	ごみばこ	rubbish bin
こうこうせい、 高校生	high school student	コミュニケーション	communication
こうこく	advertisement/publicity	こめ	rice (uncooked)
こうさてん	intersection	コメディー	comedy
こうそく、 校そく	school rules	ごめん	sorry
こうてい、 校てい	school yard	ごめんなさい。	I am sorry.
こうばん	police box	ゴルフ	golf
こうよう	autumn colours on leaves	これ	this one
こうりつ	public	これで	at/with this
コート	coat	ごろ	around (time)
ごがく、 語学	Language study	ごろごろします	lie around/loaf about
ごかぞくに どうぞ よろしく。 ご家ぞくに どうぞ よろしく。	Give my regards to your family.	こわい	scary
		こんげつ、 今月	this month
		こんこん	sound of heavy snow
ごがつにんぎょう、 五月人ぎょう	Children's Day decorative dolls	こんしゅう、 今週	this week
		こんど、今ど	this time
こくご、 国語	national language	こんばん、 今ばん／こんや、 今や	tonight
こくりつこうえん、 国りつこうえん	national park		
		コンビニ	convenience store
ここ	here (near the speaker)	コンピューター	computer
ごご	p.m.	コンピューター プログラマー	computer programmer
ここのつ、 九つ	nine		
ごぜん、 ご前	a.m.		
ごぜんちゅう、 ご前中	during the morning	**さ**	
こたつ	Japanese heater	ざあざあ	sound of heavy rain
ごちそうさま（でした）。	I have finished eating./ Thank you for the meal.	サイクリング	cycling
		さいこうきおん	highest temperature
こちらへどうぞ。	This way, please.	さいしょ	first

ISBN 9780170198271

さいていきおん	lowest temperature
ざいりょう	ingredients
さきます	bloom
さくひん	art work
さくぶん	essay
さくら	cherry blossom
さしばし	stabbing chopsticks
さしみ	sashimi
~さつ	counter for books and magazines
サッカー	soccer
ざっし	magazine
さっぽろ	Sapporo
さとう	sugar
さびしい	sad/lonely
さびしそう	seems sad
ざぶとん	Japanese-style cushion
さむい	cold
さむざむ	chilly/wintry
さゆう、 左右	left and right
さわります	touch
さんかげつかん、 三か月間	period of three months
さんかします	participate
サングラス	sunglasses
ざんねんでした。	It was unfortunate./It was disappointing.
さんばんめ、 三ばん目	the third one
さんぽ（を）します	go for a walk/stroll

し

~じ、~時	-o'clock
しあい	match/tournament
シーン	silence
ジーンズ	jeans
シェフ	chef
しお	salt
じかん、 時間	hour/time
じかんめ、 ～時間目	period/class
じかんわり、 時間わり	timetable
じきゅう、 時きゅう	hourly rate
シクシク	sound of sweeping
じこしょうかい	give a self-introduction
しごと	work
しごとづくえ	work desk

じしょ、 じ書	dictionary
じしょけい、 じ書けい	dictionary form
じしん	earthquake
しずか（な）	quiet
しぜん	nature
した、 下	below/under
じだいげき、 時だいげき	period drama/film
したがき、 下書き	draft/sketch
しつもん	question
しつれいします。	Excuse me./Goodbye (polite on phone).
しつれいですが…	Excuse me, but …
しています	wear (additional clothing)
じてんしゃ、 じてん車	bicycle
しとしと	sprinkling rain
しぼうのどうき	reason for applying
じぶんで、 じ分で	by oneself
じぶんばっかり、 じ分ばっかり	thinking of yourself
じまく	subtitles
します	do/play/order/put on (accessories)
しまった!	Oops!
しまります	to close (it closes)
しめい、 し名	full name
しめきり	deadline
しめます	close (I close)
じゃあ、 またね。	See you later.
Jポップ	J-Pop music
しゃかい、 社会	society
しゃかいがく、 社会学	sociology
ジャケット	jacket
しゃしん	photo
しゃちょう、 社ちょう	company president
シャツ	shirt
しゃべります	chat
シャワー	shower
しゅう、 週	week
じゅうい	veterinarian
しゅうがくりょこう、 しゅう学りょ行	school trip/excursion
じゆうこうどう、 じゆう行どう	free-time activities
じゅうしょ，住しょ	address/place of residency

ISBN 9780170198271

じゅうどう	judo
しゅうにいっかい、週に一かい	once a week
しゅうまつ、週まつ	weekend
じゅぎょう	lessons
じゅぎょうちゅう、じゅぎょう中	during lessons
しゅくだい	homework
しゅっぱつ、出ぱつ	departure
しゅっぱんしゃ、出ぱん社	publishing company
しゅふ	housewife/househusband
しゅわ、手話	sign language
じゅんびします	prepare
じゅんびたいそう	warm-up
しょうかい	introduction
しょうがく、小学	primary school
しょうがっこう、小学校	primary school
しょうじ	paper screen door
しょうしょうおまちください。	Please wait a moment.
じょうず(な)、上手(な)	good at
じょうば	horseriding
しょうゆ	soy sauce
しょうらい、しょう来	future
しょうわ	Showa reign (used for giving dates)
ジョギングします	jog
しょくじつき、食じつき	meals included
しょくれき	work history
じょしこう、女子校	girls' school
しょしんしゃ	beginner
しょどう、書道	calligraphy
じょゆう、女ゆう	actress
しりつ、私りつ	private
しりつがっこう、私りつ学校	private school
しります	know
しりませんよ。	I don't know.
しろ(い)	white
しんかんせん	bullet train/shinkansen
しんごう	traffic lights
じんこう、人口	population
しんしつ	bedroom
じんじゃ、じん社	Shinto shrine

しんしゃ、新車	new car
しんせつ(な)	kind
しんちょう	height
しんねん、新年	new year
しんぶん、新聞	newspaper

す

す	vinegar
すいえい、水えい	swimming
すいじょうスキー、水上スキー	waterskiing
すうがく、すう学	Mathematics
スースー	sound of sleeping
スーツ	suit
スーパー	supermarket
スカート	skirt
スキー	ski
すき(な)、好き(な)	like/likeable (favourite)
すきます	empty
すぐに	immediately
スケート	skating
すごい	amazing
すこし	a little
すごろく	Sugoroku (a Japanese variety of Parcheesi)
すずしい	cool (weather)
ずっと	all the way
ステーキ	steak
すてき(な)	nice/wonderful
スノーボード	snowboard
スニーカー	sneakers/runners
すばらしい	wonderful
スポーツインストラクター	sports instructor
ズボン	trousers/pants
すみます、住みます	live
すみません。	I am sorry./Excuse me./Thank you.
すもう	sumo
すもうべや	sumo stable/school
すらすらかきます、すらすら書きます	write fluently
スリッパ	slippers
すわります	sit
すんでいます、住んでいます	live ...

ISBN 9780170198271

せ

せいかくがいい	nice-natured
せいじ	politics
せいじか、 せいじ家	politician
せいと、 生と	student
せいねんがっぴ、生年月日	date of birth
せいびし	mechanic
せいふく	uniform
せいぶつ、 生ぶつ	biology
セーター	sweater/jumper
せがたかい、 せが高い	tall
せがひくい	short (height)
せきにんしゃ	company manager
せなか、 せ中	back
ぜひきてください。ぜひ来てくださ。	Please make sure to come.
せまい	narrow
せん、 千	one thousand
せんげつ、 先月	last month
せんじつ、 先日	the other day
せんしゃ、 せん車	car wash
せんぷうき	fan
ぜんぶ	all
せんしゅ、 せん手	athlete
せんしゅう、 先週	last week
せんせい、 先生	teacher
ぜんぜん	not at all
ぜんそく	asthma

そ

そう	yes, that's right
そうじ	clean up
そうじ（を）します	clean
そうすると	when you do that
そうですか。	Is that so?
そうですね	that's right isn't it
そうでもない	not so
ぞうり	thongs
そこ	there (near the listener)
そつぎょう	graduation
そと、 外	outside
その	that ...
そのあとで	after that

そば	noodles
そふ、 そ父	grandfather (*humble*)
ソフトボール	softball
そぼ、 そ母	grandmother (*humble*)
それ	that one ...
それから	after that (at start of sentence)

た

～だい	counter for machinery
たいいく	physical education
たいかい、 大会	competition/congress
だいがく、 大学	university
だいがくせい、 大学生	university student
だいく、 大く	carpenter
たいじゅう	weight (body)
だいじょうぶ、大じょうぶ	all right/OK
だいすき、 大好き	love
たいせつ（な）、大せつ（な）	important
たいそう	gymnastics
だいどころ	kitchen
たいふう	typhoon
たいへんです。大へんです。	It is hard/difficult.
たかい、 高い	expensive/high
たかすぎます、高すぎます	too expensive
だから	therefore
たくさん	many/much/a lot
タクシーのうんてんしゅ、タクシーのうんてん手	taxi driver
タクシーのりば	taxi stand
たくはいびん	home delivery
だけ	only
だします、 出します	put out
ただいま。	I am home.
たたみ	tatami
たたみのへや	tatami room
たちます	stand/pass time
だっこ	cuddle
たとえば	for example
たなばた	Star Festival
たのしい	enjoyable/fun
たのしみです。	I can't wait/ I look forward to it.

ISBN 9780170198271

たのしみにしています。	I am looking forward to it.	つかいます	use
たべます、 食べます	eat	つかうのは	using
たべもの、 食べ物	food	つかれます／つかれています	tired
たまがわ、 たま川	Tama River	つぎ（の）	next
たまご	egg	つきます	arrive
ためします	try	つくえ	desk
たらたら	sweating	つくります	make
だらだらします	dawdle/slow	つくろう!	Let's make it!
だれが	who	つけます	turn on
だれと	who with	つけます	wear/put on (jewellery or items you attach)
たんご	vocabulary	つづけます	continue
だんしこう、 男子校	boys' school	つなみ	tsunami/tidal wave
		つまらない	boring
ち		つゆ	rainy season
ちいさい、 小さい	small	つよい	strong
チーム	team	つり	fishing
ちかい	close	つれませんでした。	I couldn't catch it (fish).
ちかく	nearby		
ちかてつ、 ち下てつ	subway	**て**	
ちこく	late	て、 手	hand
ちこくします	late	Tシャツ	T-shirt
ちち、 父	father (*humble*)	DVDプレーヤー	DVD player
ちゃいろ（い／の）	brown	ていじせい、 てい時せい	part-time (high school)
ちゃしつ	tea ceremony room	テーブル	table
ちゃんこなべ	hot pot (sumo wrestlers' dish)	でかけましょう。出かけましょう。	Let's go out.
チャンピオン	champion	でかけます、出かけます	go out
ちゅうい!	Attention!	できます	able to do/can do
ちゅうおうぐち、中おう口	central exit	できるかな	I wonder if I can ...
ちゅうがく、 中学	junior high school	でぐち、 出口	exit
ちゅうごく、 中国	China	テクノロジー	technology
ちゅうしん、 中しん	centre	〜でした	it was
ちり	geography	〜でしょう	don't you think?/It probably will ...
ちります	fall (flowers/leaves)	です	is/are
チャット	chat	てつだいます、手つだいます	help
		てつだってください、手つだってください。	Please give me a hand.
つ		テニス	tennis
〜つ	counter for general items	デパート	department store
ツアーガイド	tour guide	てまきずし、 手まきずし	hand-rolled sushi
ついています	included/attached, (comes with a complementary gift)	でます、 出ます	go out/leave/exit/particpate
つうきんじかん、つうきん時間	commuting time		

ISBN 9780170198271

でます、 出ます	have (an idea)/appear
～でも	even now/if/now
でも	but/even/if/now
テレビ	television
テレビきょく	television station
てん	points/score
てんいん	shop assistant
てんき	weather
でんき、 電気	electricity/light
でんきスタンド、電気スタンド	lamp stand
でんきせいひん、電きせいひん	electrical product
でんしゃ、 電車	train
でんとうてきな	traditional
でんわします、電話します	telephone

と

と	and
ど	degree
ドア	door
ドイツご、 ドイツ語	German language
トイレ	toilet
～とう	counter for larger animals
とうき、 冬き	winter season
とうきょう、 東京	Tokyo
とうげいか、 とうげい家	potter
どうして	why
どうぞ	Here it is. (when passing things to someone)/ Go ahead.
どうですか。	How is it?
どうぶつえん	zoo
とうほく、 東北	north-eastern district of Japan
どうメダル	bronze medal
とお、 十	ten
とおい	far
とおります	pass by
とき、 時	time
ときどき、 時々	sometimes
どきどきします	excited/nervous
とくい（な）	good at/proud
どくしょ、 読書	reading
とけい、 時けい	clock/watch

どこ	where
どこで	where
とこのま、 とこの間	alcove
としょかん、 と書かん	library
どちらが／どれが	which one
とても	very
となり	next to
どの	which
どのぐらい	how long
とびこみ	diving
とまります	stop
ともだち、 友だち	friend
ドライブ	drive
ドラマ	drama shows
トランプをします	play cards
とりにいきます、とりに行きます	go and collect
とります	take
どれ	which one
ドレス	dress
どんな	what kind of
どんなもの	what kind of things

な

なか、 中	inside
ながい	long
ながぐつ	gumboots
なげます	throw
なごや、 名古屋	Nagoya
なぜ	why
なつ、 夏	summer
なつやすみ、 夏や休	summer holiday
など	etcetera
ななつ、 七つ	seven
なべもの	hot pot dishes
なにか、 何か	something
なにを、 何を	what
なまえ、 名前	name
なりたい	want to become
なります	become
なんじ、 何時	what time
なんせい、 南西	south-west
なんど、 何ど	what temperature

なんとう、 南東	south-east
なんねんかん、 何年間	how many years
なんねんせい、 何年生	what year level
なんばい、 何ばい	how many cups
なんようび、 何曜日	what day of the week

に

にかい、 二かい	second floor (first floor in Australia)/two times
にがて（な）、 にが手(な)	bad at
にぎやか（な）	lively
にくや	butcher
にこにこします	smile radiantly/beaming
にし、 西	west
にしぐち、 西口	west entrance
にちじ、 日時	date and time
～について	about
にています	looks alike
にばんめ、 二ばん目	second (one)
にほんご、 日本語	Japanese language
ニャーニャー	meow (cat)
ニューイヤーパーティー	New Year's party
にゅうがく、 入学	entering school
ニュース	news
にわ	garden
にわし	gardener
にんきがあります、 人気があります	popular

ぬ

| ぬいぐるみ | stuffed toy |
| ぬぎます | take off (clothing) |

ね

ねえ	hey
ネクタイ	tie
ねてしまった	fell asleep
ネットボール	netball
ねます	sleep
ねんがじょう、 年がじょう	New Year's card
ねんせい、 年生	year level
ねんねん、 年々	year by year

の

のせます	place
のち	after/later
のみます、 飲みます	drink
のみもの、 飲みもの	drinks
のり	seaweed
のりかえます	change (transport)
のります	ride
のんき（な）	easy-going

は

は	tooth/teeth
バーベキュー	barbeque
～はい ～ばい ～ぱい	counter for liquid in cups and bowls
はい	yes
はいいろ（の）	grey
ハイキング	hiking
はいく	haiku (short poem)
はいぐうしゃ	spouse
はいしゃ	dentist
はいゆう	actor
はいります、入ります	enter/belong
パイロット	pilot
ばか	silly/idiot
はがき	postcard
はきます	wear/put on (bottom half of clothing)
はくぶつかん	museum
はこ	box
はさみ	scissors
はし	bridge
バシッ	sound of knocking
はしります	run
はじまります	start (it starts)
はじめて	the first time
はじめまして。	I am pleased to meet you.
はじめます	start (I start)
パジャマ	pyjamas
ばしょ	place
はずかしい	embarrassing
はずかしかった	it was embarrassing
バスてい	bus stop
はたらきたいです。	I want to work.

ISBN 9780170198271

はたらきます	work
はな	flower
はな	nose
はなし、 話	story
はなします、 話します	speak/talk
はなせます、 話せます	can speak/talk
はなび、 はな火	fireworks
はなみ、 はな見	flower viewing
はなみツアー、 はな見ツアー	flower-viewing tour
はなや	florist
はは、 母	mother (*humble*)
はやい	fast/quick
はやく	quickly
はやくおへんじを かいてください。 はやくおへんじを 書いてください。	Please write back soon.
バラエティーショー	variety show
はる、 春	spring
はるいちばん、春一ばん	first storm of spring
はるかぜ、 春かぜ	spring wind
はれ	fine weather
はん、 半	half/half-past
ばん	number
ばんぐみ	TV or radio program
ハンサム（な）	handsome
ハンマー	hammer
パンや	bakery

ひ

ピアス	piercings/earrings
ヒーター	heater
ひがし、 東	east
ひがしぐち、 東口	eastern entrance
~ひき ~びき ~ぴき	counter for small animals
ひきます	play a musical instruments (stringed or keyboard)
ひげ	beard/moustache
ひこうき、 ひ行き	aeroplane
ひざ	knee
ひさしぶりですね。	It has been a long time.
ひじ	elbow
びじゅつ	visual arts

びじゅつかん	art gallery
ひしょ	personal assistant
びしょびしょ	sopping wet/soaking through
ひだり、 左	left
ひだりがわ、 左がわ	left-hand side
ひだりて、 左手	left hand
ひだりめ、 左目	left eye
ひっこしをします	move house
ひと、 人	person
ひとり、 一人	one person
ひどい	awful
ひとつ、 一つ	one
ひとつめ、 一つ目	first
ひとびと、 人々	people
ひなにんぎょう、 ひな人ぎょう	Hina dolls
ひび、 日々	day by day
ひまですか。	Are you free?
ひま（な）	free
ひゃく、 百	one hundred
ひゃくえんショップ、 百円ショップ	100 yen shop (discount shop)
びゅーびゅー	strong wind
ヒューマノイドロボット	humanoid robot
びょういん	hospital
びょうきのとき、 びょうきの時	when you are sick
びようし	beautician/hairdresser
ビル	building
ひるね	nap
ひるメロ	soap opera
ひるやすみ、 ひる休み	lunchtime/lunchbreak
ひろい	spacious
ピンク（の）	pink

ふ

ブーツ	boots
プール	swimming pool
ふうん。	I see. (*casual*)
フォーク	fork
ふきかえ	dubbing
ふたつ、 二つ	two

ISBN 9780170198271

ふたつめ、 二つ目	second
ぶちょう	company manager
フットボール	football
ブティック	boutique
ふでばこ	pencil case
ふとります／ ふとっています／ふとい	fat/thick
ふとん	Japanese bed
ふぶき	blizzard
ふみきり	railway crossing
ふゆ、 冬	winter
ふようかぞく、 ふよう家ぞく	dependents
プラットフオーム	platform
ぶらぶらします	dawdle/hang around
フランスご、 フランス語	French language
フリーマーケット	market/stall
ふりがな	*kanji* reading in *hiragana*
ブリスベン	Brisbane
ふります	fall (rain/snow)
ふるい	old (for objects)
ぶるぶる	shivering
ふろば	bathroom
プロフィール	profile
ふん/ぷん、 分	minute
ぶんか	culture
ぶんかさい	cultural festival
ぶんぽう	grammar

～へ	to …
へいせい	Heisei reign (used for giving dates)
へえ!	Wow! (*casual*)
ぺきん、 北京	Beijing
ぺこぺこ	hungry/starving
へた (な)、 下手 (な)	bad at
ベッド	bed
へや	room
ぺらぺらはなします、 ぺらぺら話します	speak fluently
へん	area/vicinity
ペン	pen
へん (な)	strange

べんきょうします	study
べんきょうになります	will help (me) learn/ my learning
べんごし	lawyer
へんじ	answer/reply
へんじかいてね! へんじ書いてね。	Write me a reply! (*casual*)
べんり (な)	convenient/handy

ほう	towards
ぼうえきがいしゃ、 ぼうえき会社	international trading company
ほうがく	Japanese music
ほうかご	after school
ぼうし	hat
ほうそうします	broadcast
ボート	boat
ホーム	platform
ホームステイ	homestay
ホームルーム	homeroom
ほくせい、 北西	north-west
ほけん	personal development
ほし	stars
ホストシスター	host sister
ホストします	host
ホストファミリー	host family
ほそい	skinny/thin
ぽつぽつ	light drops of rain
ホテル	hotel
ほん、 本	book
~ほん ~ぼん ~ぽん、 本	counter for long items or bottles
ほんせき、 本せき	place of permanent residence
ほんとうですか? ／ ほんとうに? 本とうですか。	Really?
ほんにん きぼうきにゅうらん、 本人きぼうき入らん	special requests for the position
ほんばこ、 本ばこ	bookcase
ほんや、 本や	bookshop

ISBN 9780170198271

ま

まあ	well then
まあ	Oh! (female)
まい、 毎	every
まい	counter for flat items
まいあさ、 毎あさ	every morning
まいしゅう、 毎週	every week
まいつき、 毎月	every month
まいとし、 毎年	every year
まいにち、 毎日	every day
まいばん、 毎ばん	every evening
まえ、 前	before/in front of
まがります	turn
まきじゃく	metal tape measure
まきす	sushi mat
まきます	roll
まけます	lose
まじめ（な）	serious
まずい	awful/bad taste
まぜます	mix
また	again
まだ	not yet/still
まだまだ	no/not at all
まち、 町	town/city
まちのちゅうしん、 町の中しん	centre of town
まちます	wait
まっすぐ	straight
まっすぐいきます、 まっすぐ行きます	go straight ahead
まっています。（まってます。）	I am waiting!
まってるよ。	I am waiting! (casual)
まつり	festival
まで	until/by
まど	window
マナー	manners
マニキュア	manicure/nail polish
まもります	protect
まよい ばし	wandering chopsticks
マラソン	marathon
マヨネーズ	mayonnaise
まるい	round
まわり	around

まん、 万	ten thousand
まんが	comics
まんがか、 まんが家	cartoonist
まんがきっさ	manga café
マンション	apartment/building

み

みえます、 見えます	visible/I can see …
みがきます	brush/polish
みぎ、 右	right
みぎがわ、 右がわ	right-hand side
みぎて、 右手	right hand
みぎめ、 右目	right eye
みじかい	short
みずぎ、 水ぎ	bathers/swimwear
みせ	shops
みせます、 見せます	show
みち	street/road
みっかかん、三日間	period of three days
みつけます、見つけます	find
みっつ、 三つ	three
みっつめ、 三つ目	third
みてください、見てください	please look
みどり（の）	green
みなとまち、 みなと町	port town
みなみ、 南	south
みなみぐち、 南口	southern entrance
みます、 見ます	see/watch/look
みみ、 耳	ear
みみがとおい、耳がとおい	difficulty hearing
みらい、 み来	future
みんな	everyone
みんなで	by everyone

む

むかえにいきます、むかえに行きます	go and pick someone up
むしあつい	humid
むずかしい	difficult
むすめ	daughter
むっつ、 六つ	six
むらさき（の）	purple

ISBN 9780170198271

め

め、目	eye
めいじん、名人	expert/master/professional
めがね	glasses
めそめそします	sob/whimper
メディア	media
メニュー	menu
めのまえ、目の前	right in front (of your eyes)
メモをとります	take a memo or note
メルマガ	mail magazine
めんせつ	interview
めんぜいてん	duty-free shop

も

も	also
もう	already
もういちど	once more
もういちどいってください。もうーど言ってください。	Please repeat it.
もうすぐ	soon
もうちょっと…	A little more …
モグモグ	sound of chewing
もしもし	hello (on the phone)
もちかた	way to hold
もちます	carry/hold
もちろん	of course
もってくるもの、もって来るもの	things to bring
もどします	return
もの	thing
ものいれ、もの入れ	storage
ものさし	ruler
もみじのはっぱ	maple leaves
ももいろ（の）	peach-coloured
もらいました	received
もん	gate

や

や	and … etc.
〜や	shop
やおや	greengrocer
やきいも	baked sweet potato

やきとり	yakitori/chicken skewers
やくざいし	pharmacist
やさかじんじゃ、やさかじん社	Yasaka Shrine
やさしい	kind/gentle/easy
やさしそう	looks kind
やすい、安い	cheap/less expensive
やすみ、休み	holiday
やせます／やせています	thin/slim/skinny
やっつ、八つ	eight
やま、山	mountain
やまぐち、山口	Yamaguchi (surname)
やまのぼり、山のぼり	mountain climbing
やめます	quit

ゆ

ゆうこう、友好	friendship
ゆうじん、友人	friend
ユーチューブ	YouTube
ゆうびんきょく	post office
ゆうめい（な）、ゆう名な	famous
ゆき	snow
ゆきだるま	snowman
ゆっくり	slowly
ゆび	fingers
ゆびわ	ring

よ

ようがく	Western music
ようしつ	Western-style room
ようしょく、よう食	Western food
よいやさ、よいさ	heave ho
よかった。	It was good./It is a relief./Great!
よく	often
よこ	next to
よやく	reservation
よせばし	pulling chopsticks
よっかかん、四日間	four days
よっつ、四つ	four
よびます	call out/call for

ISBN 9780170198271

よみかき、　読み書き	reading and writing
よみかた、　読みかた	way of writing
よみせ	night-time stalls
よみます、　読みます	read
より	from/than
よろしくおねがいします	Please remember me favourably.
よんコマまんが、四コマまんが	four-frame comic

ら

ラーメン	hot noodle soup (Chinese style)
らいげつ、　来月	next month
らいしゅう、　来週	next week
らいねん、　来年	next year
らくがき	graffiti
ラグビー	rugby
ラサールこうこう、　高校	La Salle High School
ラジオ	radio
らんぼう（な）	rough/violent

り

りきし	sumo wrestler
リサイクルします	recycle
りっぱ（な）	great/large/fine
りゅうがくせい、りゅう学生	exchange student
りょうり	cooking
りょかん	Japanese-style inn
りょこうがいしゃ、りょ行会社	travel agent
りょこうします、りょ行します	travel
リラックスします	relax
りれきしょ、　りれき書	personal history form

る

るすばんでんわ、るすばん電話	answering machine

れ

れいか、　れい下	below zero degrees
れいど	zero degrees
れきし	history
レジ	register/cashier
レポート	report
れんあい	love (romance)
れんしゅうします	practise

ろ

ローイング	rowing
ローラーブレード	rollerblading
ろくおんします	record
ロッカー	locker
ろてんぶろ	outdoor bath

わ

わあー。	Wow!
ワーワー	sound of loud crying
わかい	young
わがまま（な）	spoilt/selfish
わかりました。分かりました。	I understand. (I have understood.)
わかります、　分かります	understand
わくわく	exciting
わくわくする	excited/thrilled
わさび	wasabi
わしつ	tatami room (traditional style)
わしょく、　わ食	Japanese food
わすれないで！	Don't forget!
わすれます	forget
わたしたち、　私たち	we
わたしの、　私の	my
わたります	cross
ワハハハ	sound of laughing
わるい	bad
ワンピース	one-piece (day) dress

ISBN 9780170198271

Vocabulary list
英語一日本語

A

able to do/can do	できます
about	ぐらい
about	～について
accessory/jewellery	アクセサリー
accountant	かいけいし
actor	はいゆう
actress	じょゆう、 女ゆう
address	アドレス
address/place of residency	じゅうしょ、 住しょ
adult	おとな、 大人
advertisement/publicity	こうこく
aeroplane	ひこうき、 ひ行き
after/later	あとで、 のち
after school	ほうかご
after that	そのあとで
after that (at start of sentence)	それから
again	また
aikido	あいきどう
air conditioner	エアコン
air temperature	きおん
airport	くうこう
Akihabara/(abbreviation)	あきはばら／アキバ
alcove	とこのま、 とこの間
a little	すこし
a little more …	もうちょっと…
all	ぜんぶ
all the way	ずっと
already	もう
all right/OK	だいじょうぶ、 大じょうぶ
also	も
always	いつも
a.m.	ごぜん、 ご前
amazing	すごい、 すばらしい
and	と

and … etc.	や
animation/cartoons	アニメ
answer/reply	へんじ
answering machine	るすばんでんわ、 るすばん電話
anytime	いつでも
apartment	アパート
apartment (building)	マンション
appear/perform	～にでる、 ～出る
architect	けんちくか、 けんちく家
Are you free?	ひまですか。
area/vicinity	へん
arm	うで
around	まわり
around (a certain time)	ごろ
around here	このへん
arrive	つきます
art gallery	びじゅつかん
art work	さくひん
article	きじ
artist	げいじゅつか、 げいじゅつ家
asthma	ぜんそく
at/with this	これで
athlete	せんしゅ、 せん手
Attention!	ちゅうい!
attracted by	あこがれます
attractive/trendy	かっこいい
audible	きこえます、 聞こえます
aunt (*humble*)	おば
aunt (*polite*)	おばさん
autumn	あき、 秋
autumn festival	あきまつり、 秋まつり
autumn colours on leaves	こうよう
avocado	アボカド
awful/bad taste	まずい

二百二十四

ISBN 9780170198271

B

back	せなか、 せ中
background/career	けいれき
bad	わるい
bad at	にがて（な）、 にが手（な）／へた（な）、 下手（な）
bag	かばん
baked sweet potato	やきいも
bakery	パンや
bank	ぎんこう、 ぎん行
bank employee	ぎんこういん、 ぎん行いん
barbeque	バーベキュー
bathers/swimwear	みずぎ、 水ぎ
bathroom	おふろば、 おふろ
bear	くま
beard/moustache	ひげ
beautician/hairdresser	びようし
beautiful	うつくしい
because	から
become	なります
bed	ベッド
bedroom	しんしつ
before/in front of	まえ、 前
beginner	しょしんしゃ
behind	うしろ
Beijing	ぺきん、 北京
below/under	した、下
below zero degrees	れいか、 れい下
bicycle	じてんしゃ、 じてん車
big/large	おおきい、 大きい
biology	せいぶつ、 生ぶつ
birthday (date of birth)	せいねんがっぴ、 生年月日
black	くろい
blizzard	ふぶき
blond (hair)	きんぱつ（の）、 金ぱつ（の）
bloom	さきます
blue	あおい
boat	ボート
body	からだ
book	ほん、 本
bookcase	ほんばこ、 本ばこ
bookshelf	ほんだな、 本だな

bookshop	ほんや、 本や
boots	ブーツ
boring	つまらない
bottom	おしり
boutique	ブティック
box	はこ
boy	おとこのこ、 男のこ
boys' school	だんしこう、 男子校
bridge	はし
bright/light	あかるい
Brisbane	ブリスベン
broadcast	ほうそうします
bronze medal	どうメダル
brown	ちゃいろ（い/の）
brush/polish	みがきます
Buddhist temple	おてら
building	ビル
bullet train/shinkansen	しんかんせん
bulletin board	けいじばん
bus stop	バスてい
busy	いそがしい
but/even/if/now	でも
butcher	にくや
buy	かいます、 買います
by everyone	みんなで
by oneself	じぶんで、 じ分で

C

cackling laugh	ゲラゲラ
cafe	カフェ
California roll	カリフォルニアロール
call (a name)	いいます、 言います
call out/call for	よびます
calligraphy	しょどう、 書どう
can speak/talk	はなせます、 話せます
captain	キャプテン
car wash	せんしゃ、 せん車
cards (play)	トランプ（をします）
carpenter	だいく
carry/hold	もちます
cartoonist	まんがか、 まんが家
casino	カジノ
catch/receive	うけます

ISBN 9780170198271

central exit	ちゅうおうぐち、 中おう口	communication	コミュニケーション
centre	ちゅうしん、 中しん	commute	かよいます
certainly	かならず	commuting time	つうきんじかん、つうきん時間
Certainly.	かしこまりました。	company	かいしゃ、 会社
chair	いす	company employee,	かいしゃいん、 会社いん
champion	チャンピオン	company manager	ぶちょう／せきにんしゃ
change	おつり	company president	しゃちょう、 社ちょう
change (transport)	のりかえます	competition/congress	たいかい、 大会
chat	しゃべります／チャット	computer	コンピューター
cheap/less expensive	やすい、 安い	computer programmer	コンピューター プログラマー
Cheers!	かんぱい。	continue	つづけます
chef	シェフ	convenience store	コンビニ
cherry blossom	さくら	convenient/handy	べんり（な）
chew	かみます	conversation	かいわ、 会話
chewing gum	ガム	cooked rice/meal	ごはん
chicken skewers	やきとり	cooking	りょうり
child	こども	cool (weather)	すずしい
Children's Day decorative dolls	ごがつにんぎょう、五月人ぎょう	corner	かど
chilly/wintry	さむざむ	count	かぞえます
China	ちゅうごく、 中国	counter for books and magazines	～さつ
chopsticks	おはし	counter for buildings and houses	～けん
cinema/movie theatre	えいがかん	counter for general items	～つ
classroom	きょうしつ	counter for flat items	～まい
clean	そうじ（を）します	counter for floors	～かい
clean up	そうじ	counter for larger animals	～とう
clock/watch	とけい、 時けい	counter for long items or bottles	～ほん／～ぽん／～ぽん、～本
close	ちかい	counter for machinery	～だい
close (I close)	しめます	counter for small animals	～ひき／～びき／～ぴき
close (it closes)	しまります	counter for small round items	～こ
cloudy	くもり	counter of liquid in cups and bowls	～はい／～ばい／～ぱい
club activity	クラブかつどう		
coat	コート	country	くに、 国
co-educational	きょうがく、 きょう学'	cousin (humble)	いとこ
coffee shop	きっさてん	cousin (polite)	いとこさん
cold	さむい	cow	うし
colours	いろ	crab fish cake	かにかまぼこ
come	きます、 来ます		
come here	おいで		
Come, won't you.	きてね。 来てね。		
comedy	コメディー		
comics	まんが		
commercial (TV)	コマーシャル		

ISBN 9780170198271

cricket	クリケット	don't you think/ it probably will ...	〜でしょう
cross	わたります	door	ドア
cry loudly	ワーワー	draft/sketch	したがき、 下書き
cucumber	きゅうり	drama shows	ドラマ
cuddle	だっこ	draw	かきます
cultural festival	ぶんかさい	drawing	かくこと
culture	ぶんか	dress (one-piece)	ドレス、 ワンピース
cup	カップ	drink	のみます、 飲みます
curry noodles	カレーうどん	drinks	のみもの、 飲みもの
cushion (Japanese-style)	ざぶとん	drive	うんてんします
cut	きります	drop off	おろします
cute/pretty	かわいい	dubbing	ふきかえ
cycling	サイクリング	duration/between	あいだ、 間
		during lessons	じゅぎょうちゅう、 じゅぎょう中

D

dance	おどります
dangerous	あぶない
dark	くらい
date and time	にちじ、 日時
date of birth	せいねんがっぴ、生年月日
daughter	むすめ
dawdle/hang around	ぶらぶらします
dawdle/slow	だらだらします
day by day	ひび、 日々
degree	ど
delicious	おいしい、 うまい
dentist	はいしゃ
department store	デパート
departure	しゅっぱつ、 出ぱつ
dependents	ふようかぞく、 ふよう家ぞく
Design and Technology	ぎじゅつ
desk	つくえ
dictionary	じしょ、 じ書
dictionary form	じしょけい、 じ書けい
difficult	むずかしい
difficulty hearing	みみがとおい、耳がとおい
dirty	きたない
dislikable	きらい（な）
dive	とびこみ
do/play	します
doctor	いしゃ
Don't forget!	わすれないで!

during the morning	ごぜんちゅう、 ご前中
duty-free shop	めんぜいてん
DVD player	DVDプレーヤー

E

ear	みみ、 耳
earrings	イヤリング
earthquake	じしん
east	ひがし、 東
eastern entrance	ひがしぐち、 東口
easy-going	のんき（な）
eat	たべます、 食べます
eat out	がいしょくします、 外食します
eating greedily/craving something	がつがつ
economics	けいざい
egg	たまご
eight	やっつ、 八つ
elbow	ひじ
electrical product	でんきせいひん、 電きせいひん
electricity/light	でんき、 電気
email	イーメール、 Eメール
embarrassing	はずかしい
empty	すきます
engineer	ぎし ／エンジニア
English conversation	えいかいわ、 英会話

ISBN 9780170198271

English language	えいご、 英語
enjoyable/fun	たのしい
enter/belong	はいります、 入ります
entering school	にゅうがく、 入学
entrance	いりぐち、 入り口、 げんかん
eraser	けしゴム
essay	さくぶん
etcetera	など
every	まい、 毎
even now	〜でも
every day	まいにち、 毎日
every evening	まいばん、 毎ばん
every month	まいつき、 毎月
every morning	まいあさ、 毎あさ
every week	まいしゅう、 毎週
every year	まいとし、 毎年
everyone	みんな
excited/nervous/thrilled	どきどきします
exciting	わくわく
Excuse me./Goodbye.	しつれいします。
exercise	うんどう
exit	でぐち、 出口
expensive/high	たかい、 高い
expert/master/professional	めいじん、 名人
eye	め、 目

F

face	かお
fall (flowers/leaves)	ちります
fall (rain/snow)	ふります
family	かぞく、 家ぞく
famous	ゆうめい（な）、 ゆう名な
fans	うちわ
far	とおい
Farewell./Take care.	いってらっしゃい。
fast/quick	はやい
fat/thick	ふとります／ふとっています／ふとい
father (*humble*)	ちち、 父
father (*polite*)	おとうさん、 お父さん

feeling	きもち
feels good	きもちが いい
fell asleep	ねてしまった
festival	（お）まつり
find	みつけます、 見つけます
fine and later cloudy	はれのちくもり
fine weather	はれ
fingers	ゆび
finish	おわります
fireworks	はなび、 はな火
first	ひとつめ、 一つ目、 さいしょ
first (one)	いちばんめ、 一ばん目
first storm of spring	はるいちばん、 春一ばん
full name	しめい、 し名
first period	いちじかんめ、 一時間目
first time	はじめて
fishing	つり
five	いつつ、 五つ
floor	かい
florist	はなや
flower arranging	いけばな
flower viewing	おはなみ、 おはな見
flower-viewing tour	はなみツアー、 はな見ツアー
flower	はな
food	たべもの、 食べもの
football	フットボール
for example	たとえば
foreign language	がいこくご、 外国語
foreigner	がいこくじん、 外国人
forget	わすれます
fork	フォーク
four	よっつ、 四つ
four days	よっかかん、 四日間
four-frame comic	よんゴムまんが、 四ゴムまんが
free	ひま（な）
free-time activities	じゆうこうどう、 じゆう行どう
freezing up	カチンコチン
French language	フランスご、 フランス語
friend	ともだち、 友だち、 ゆうじん、 友人

ISBN 9780170198271

friendship	ゆうこう、　友好
from	から
from now	いまから、　今から
from when	いつから
from/than	より
full name	しめい、　し名
funny	おかしい
future	しょうらい、　しょう来／ みらい、　み来

G

garden	にわ
gate	もん
gardener	にわし
geography	ちり
German language	ドイツご、　ドイツ語
get off	おります
get up	おきます
girl	おんなのこ、　女のこ
girls' school	じょしこう、　女子校
Give my regards to your family.	ごかぞくにどうぞよろしく。 ご家ぞくにどうぞよろしく。
glasses	めがね
go	いきます、　行きます
go and collect	とりにいきます、 とりに行きます
go and pick someone up	むかえにいきます、 むかえに行きます
go for a walk/stroll	さんぽ（を）します
go home/return	かえります
go out	でかけます、　出かけます
go out/leave/exit/ pacticipate	でます、　出ます
go straight ahead	まっすぐいきます、 まっすぐ行きます
go up	あがります
goal	ゴール
gold medal	きんメダル、　金メダル
goldfish	きんぎょ、　金ぎょ
golf	ゴルフ
good	いい
good at	とくい（な）／じょうず（な）、 上手（な）
good for your body	からだにいい

Good luck!	がんばって！
Good night.	おやすみなさい。
Grade 1/Year 1	いちねんせい、　一年生
graduation	そつぎょう
graffiti	らくがき
gram	グラム
grammar	ぶんぽう
grandfather (*humble*)	そふ、　そ父
grandmother (*humble*)	そぼ、　そ母
grandfather (*polite*)	おじいさん
grandmother (*polite*)	おばあさん
great/large/fine	りっぱ（な）
green	みどり（の）
green apple	あおりんご
green bamboo	あおたけ
green caterpillar	あおむし
greengrocer	やおや
green leaves/foliage	あおば
green paddy/rice field	あおた
green seaweed	あおのり
green traffic light	あおしんごう
grey	はいいろ（の）
gumboots	ながぐつ
gymnastics	たいそう

H

haiku (short poem)	はいく
hair	かみ（のけ）
half/half past	はん、　半
hammer	ハンマー
hand	て、　手
hand-rolled sushi	てまきずし、　手まきずし
handsome	ハンサム（な）
hanging scroll	かけじく
happy/glad	うれしい
hat	ぼうし
have (an idea)/appear	でます、　出ます
have/be/there is (for inanimate objects)	います
have/be/there is ... (for inanimate objects)	あります
have a bath	おふろにはいります

ISBN 9780170198271

head	あたま
heater	ヒーター
heave ho	よいやさ／よいさ
heavy rain	おおあめ、　大あめ
height	しんちょう
Heisei reign (used for giving dates)	へいせい
hello (on the phone)	もしもし
help	てつだいます、手つだいます
here (near the speaker)	ここ
Here it is. Go ahead.	どうぞ。
hide	かくします
hey	ねえ
high school student	こうこうせい、　高校生
highest temperature	さいこうきおん
hiking	ハイキング
Hina dolls	ひなにんぎょう、ひな人ぎょう
History	れきし
holiday	やすみ、　休み
home delivery	たくはいびん
Home economics	かていか、　家ていか
homeroom	ホームルーム
homestay	ホームステイ
home tutor	かていきょうし、家ていきょうし
homework	しゅくだい
horseriding	じょうば
hospital	びょういん
host	ホストします
host family	ホストファミリー
host sister	ホストシスター
hot	あつい
hot noodle soup (Chinese style)	ラーメン
hot pot (sumo wrestlers' dish)	ちゃんこなべ
hot pot dishes	なべもの
hotel	ホテル
hour/time	じかん、　時間
hourly rate	じきゅう、　時きゅう
house/home	いえ、うち、　家
housewife/	しゅふ

househusband	
How are you?	おげんきですか
How is it?	どうですか。
how long	どのぐらい
how many cups	なんばい、　何ばい
how many years	なんねんかん、　何年間
how much	いくら（ですか。）
How old are you?	おいくつですか。
humanoid robot	ヒューマノイドロボット
humid	むしあつい
hungry/starving	ぺこぺこ

I

I am full.	おなかがいっぱいです。
I am home.	ただいま。
I am hungry.	おなかがすきました。
I am looking forward to it.	たのしみにしています。
I am looking forward to your reply.	おへんじをたのしみにしています。
I am pleased to meet you.	はじめまして。
I am sorry.	ごめんなさい。
I am sorry./Excuse me./Thank you.	すみません。
I am starving. (casual)	おなかがペコペコです。
I am teaching.	おしえています。
I am waiting!	まっています／まってます。
I am waiting! (casual)	まってるよ。
I can't wait./I look forward to it.	たのしみです。
I couldn't catch (fish).	つれませんでした。
I don't know.	しりませんよ。
I will be back.	いってきます。
important	たいせつ（な）、大せつ（な）
included/attached	ついています
ingredients	ざいりょう
inside	なか、　中
instructor	インストラクター
intelligent	あたまがいい
interesting/funny	おもしろい
international trading company	ぼうえきがいしゃ、ぼうえき会社

ISBN 9780170198271

Internet	インターネット
Internet site	インターネットサイト
intersection	こうさてん
interview	インタビュー、 めんせつ
introduction	しょうかい
irritated/nervous	いらいらする
is/are	～です
Is that so?	そうですか。
I see. (casual)	ふうん。
Italian language	イタリアご、 イタリア語
it is all down to you/ thanks to you	おかげ
It is hard/difficult.	たいへんです。 大へんです。
It has been a long time.	ひさしぶりですね。
It is time.	時間です。
it was	～でした
it was embarrassing	はずかしかった
It was good./It is a relief./Great!	よかった。
It was unfortunate./It is disappointing.	ざんねんでした。
I understand (I have understood).	わかりました。 分かりました。
I have finished eating./ Thank you for the meal.	ごちそうさま　（でした）。
I want to meet you.	あいたいです。 会いたいです。
I want to work.	はたらきたいです。
I want to write.	かきたいんです。 書きたいんです。
I will try my best.	がんばります。
I wonder if I can ...	できるかな

J

J-Pop music	Jポップ
jacket	ジャケット
Japanese bed	ふとん
Japanese food	わしょく、 わ食
Japanese heater	こたつ
Japanese language	にほんご、 日本語
Japanese music	ほうがく
Japanese-style inn	りょかん
jeans	ジーンズ
jewellery	アクセサリー

jog	ジョギングします
judo	じゅうどう
jumble/a mess	ごちゃごちゃ
junior high school	ちゅうがく、 中学
just lucky/it just happened	たまたま

K

kanji	かんじ
kanji reading in hiragana	ふりがな
karaoke party	カラオケパーティー
karate	からて、 から手
kendo	けんどう
kick	けります
kilograms	キロ
kind	しんせつ（な）
kind/gentle/easy	やさしい
kitchen	だいどころ
knee	ひざ
know	しります
Kyoto	きょうと、 京都
Kyudo (archery)	きゅうどう

L

lamp stand	でんきスタンド、 電気スタンド
language	～ご、 ～語
language study	ごがく、 語学
La Salle High School	ラサールこうこう、 高校
last month	せんげつ、 先月
last week	せんしゅう、 先週
last year	きょねん、 きょ年
late	ちこくします
lawyer	べんごし
leave/participate	でます
left	ひだり、 左
left and right	さゆう、 左右
left eye	ひだりめ、 左目
left hand	ひだりて、 左手
left-hand side	ひだりがわ、 左がわ
leg/foot	あし

ISBN 9780170198271

lend	かします
lessons	じゅぎょう
Let's eat. I accept the meal/drink. (said before eating)	いただきます。
Let's go out.	でかけましょうか。 出かけましょうか。
Let's make it!	つくろう。
letting me hear	きかせていただいて
library	としょかん、 と書かん
lie/fib	うそ
lie around/loaf about	ごろごろします
light drops of rain	ぽつぽつ
lightning	かみなり
like/likeable (favourite)	すき（な）、 好き（な）
listen/hear	ききます、 聞きます
live	すみます、 住みます
live ...	すんでいます、 住んでいます
lively/sprited	にぎやか（な）、 げんき（な）
living room	いま
locker	ロッカー
long	ながい
looking forward to seeing	あえるのをたのしみにしています
looks alike	にています
looks kind	やさしそう
lose	まけます
love	だいすき、 大好き
love (romance)	れんあい
lowest temperature	さいていきおん
lunchtime/lunchbreak	ひるやすみ、 ひる休み
lunch box	おべんとうばこ

M

magazine	ざっし
mail magazine	メルマガ
make	つくります
make a telephone call	でんわをします、 電話をします
make-up	けしょう
man	おとこのひと、 男の人
manga café	まんがきっさ

manicure/nail polish	マニキュア
manners	マナー
manuscript	げんこう
many/much/a lot	たくさん
maple leaves	もみじのはっぱ
marathon	マラソン
market/stall	フリーマーケット
match/tournament	しあい
Mathematics	すうがく、 すう学
matter/thing	こと
mayonnaise	マヨネーズ
meals included	しょくじつき、 食じつき
mechanic	きかいこう／せいびし
media	メディア
medical conditions (serious only)	けんこうじょうたい
meet	あいます、 会います
meeting	かいぎ、 会ぎ
menu	メニュー
metal tape measure	まきじゃく
meow (cat)	ニャーニャー
minute	ふん/ぷん、 分
mix	まぜます
mobile phone	けいたいでんわ、 けいたい電話
money	おかね
moon viewing	おつきみ、 お月見
mother (*humble*)	はは、 母
mother (*polite*)	おかあさん、 お母さん
mountain	やま、 山
mountain climbing	やまのぼり、 山のぼり
mouth	くち、 口
move house	ひっこしをします
movie	えいが
museum	はくぶつかん
music	おんがく
musical instrument	がっき
my	わたしの、 私の

N

Nagoya	なごや、 名古屋
name	なまえ、 名前

二百三十二

232

ISBN 9780170198271

nap	ひるね
narrow	せまい
national language	こくご、 国語
national park	こくりつこうえん、 国りつこうえん
natural hot springs	おんせん
nature	しぜん
navel	おへそ
nearby	ちかく
neck	くび
necktie	ネクタイ
need	いります
nervous	きんちょうします
netball	ネットボール
new	あたらしい、 新しい
new car	しんしゃ、 新車
New Year	おしょうがつ、 おしょう月
new year	しんねん、 新年
New Year's party	ニューイヤーパーティー
New Year's card	ねんがじょう、 年がじょう
New Year's food	おせちりょうり
news	ニュース
newspaper	しんぶん、 新聞
next	つぎ（の）
next month	らいげつ、 来月
next to	となり、 よこ
next week	らいしゅう、 来週
next year	らいねん、 来年
nice/wonderful	すてき（な）
nice-natured	せいかくがいい
night-time stalls	よみせ
nine	ここのつ、 九つ
noisy	うるさい
noodles	そば
north	きた、 北
north-eastern district of Japan	とうほく、 東北
north entrance	きたぐち、 北口
northwest	ほくせい、 北西
nose	はな
not at all	まだまだ／ぜんぜん
not really/not very often/not well	あまり、 あんまり

not so	そうでもない
not yet/still	まだ
now	いま、 今
number	ばん
number one/the most ...	いちばん、 一ばん
nurse	かんごふ

○

o'clock	じ、 時
of course	もちろん
often	よく
Oh! (female)	まあ
Oh, really is that so?	ああ、 そうですか。
old (for objects)	ふるい
older brother (*humble*)	あに
older brother (*polite*)	おにいさん
older sister (*humble*)	あね
older sister (*polite*)	おねえさん
the Olympics	オリンピック
on foot	あるいて
on/above	うえ、 上
once a week	しゅうにいっかい、 週に一かい
once more	もういちど
one	ひとつ、 一つ
one hundred	ひゃく、 百
100 yen shop (discount shop)	ひゃくえんショップ、 百円ショップ
one person	ひとり、 一人
one-piece (day) dress	ワンピース
one thousand	せん 、 千
only	だけ
open	あけます
orange	オレンジ（の）
origami	おりがみ
outdoor bath	ろてんぶろ
outside	そと、 外
over there (away from both the speaker and listener)	あそこ
overcoat	コート
overseas	かいがい、 海外、 がいこく， 外国

ISBN 9780170198271

P

pants/trousers	ズボン
paper	かみ
paper screen door	しょうじ
park/playground	こうえん
participate	さんかします
part-time (high school)	ていじせい、　てい時せい
part-time job	アルバイト
pass by	とおります
peach-coloured	ももいろ（の）
pen	ペン
pencil	えんぴつ
pencil case	ふでばこ
people	ひとびと、　人々
period/class	〜じかんめ、　〜時間目
period drama/film	じだいげき、　時だいげき
period of three days	みっかかん、　三日間
period of three months	さんかげつかん、 三か月間
period of time	かん、　間
participate	さんかします
person	ひと、　人
person with a cheerful personality	あかるいせいかくの人
personal assistant	ひしょ
personal development	ほけん
personal history form	りれきしょ、　りれき書
petrol station	ガソリンスタンド
pharmacist	やくざいし
pharmacy	くすりや
photo	しゃしん
photographer/camera operator	カメラマン
physical education	たいいく
pick up	むかえに行きます
picture	え
piercing/earrings	ピアス
pilot	パイロット
pink	ピンク（の）
place	ばしょ
place	のせます
place (e.g. 3rd place)	い（三い）
place of permanent residence	ほんせき、　本せき

platform	ホーム／プラットフオーム
play	あそびます
play a musical instrument (stringed or keyboard)	ひきます
play cards	トランプをします
please (give me)	おねがい（します）／ （ください）
Please come and play.	あそびにきてください。 あそびに来てください。
Please come.	きてください。 来てください。
Please give me a hand.	てつだってください。 手つだってください。
Please look.	みてください。 見てください。
Please make sure to come.	ぜひきてください。　ぜひ 来てください。
Please remember me.	よろしくおねがいします。
Please repeat it.	もういちどいってください。 もう一ど言ってください。
Please take care.	きをつけてください。
Please wait a moment.	しょうしょうおまちください。
Please write back soon.	はやくおへんじを かいてください。 はやくおへんじを 書いてください。
p.m.	ごご
points/score	てん
police box	こうばん
police officer	けいかん
politician	せいじか、　せいじ家
politics	せいじ
poor/pitiful	かわいそう
popular	にんきがあります、 人気があります
population	じんこう、　人口
port town	みなとまち、　みなと町
postcard	はがき
post office	ゆうびんきょく
potter	とうげいか、　とうげい家
practise	れんしゅうします
prepare	じゅんびします
presently	げんざい
pretty/clean	きれい（な）
primary school	しょうがく、　小学

ISBN 9780170198271

primary school	しょうがっこう、 小学校
private	しりつ、 私りつ
private school	しりつがっこう、 私りつ学校
profile	プロフィール
protect	まもります
public	こうりつ
publishing company	しゅっぱんしゃ、 出ぱん社
pulling chopsticks	よせばし
pulsating heat from the sun	ぎらぎら
purple	むらさき（の）
push	おします
put it	いれます、 入れます
put out	だします、 出します
pyjamas	パジャマ

Q

question	しつもん
quickly	はやく
quiet	しずか（な）
quit	やめます

R

radio	ラジオ
railway crossing	ふみきり
rain	あめ
rainy season	つゆ
read	よみます、 読みます
reading	どくしょ、 読書
reading and writing	よみかた、 読みかた
Really?	ほんとうですか。／ ほんとうに？
reason for applying	しぼうのどうき
received	もらいました
recommendation	おすすめ
record	ろくおんします
recycle	リサイクルします
red	あか（い）
register/cashier	レジ
relax	リラックスします

remember	おぼえます
report	レポート
request/desire	きぼう
reservation	よやく
retired	いんたいしています
return	もどします／もどります／ かえります
rice (uncooked)	こめ
rice cake	おにぎり
rice cakes for New Year	おもち
ride	のります
right	みぎ、 右
right eye	みぎめ、 右目
right hand	みぎて、 右手
right-hand side	みぎがわ、 右がわ
right in front (of your eyes)	めのまえ、 目の前
ring	ゆびわ
rise	あがります
river	かわ、 川
roll	まきます
rollerblading	ローラーブレード
room	へや
rough/violent	らんぼう（な）
round	まるい
rowing	ローイング
rubbish	ごみ
rubbish bin	ごみばこ
rude	しつれい（な）
ruler	ものさし
rugby	ラグビー
rules	きそく
run	はしります

S

sad/lonely	さびしい
salt	しお
Sapporo	さっぽろ
sashimi	さしみ
say	いいます、 言います
scary	こわい
scenery	けしき

ISBN 9780170198271

school	がっこう、　学校	silly/idiot	ばか	
school trip/excursion	しゅうがくりょこう, しゅう学りょ行	silver medal	ぎんメダル	
school history	がくれき、　学れき	sing	うたいます	
school lunches	きゅうしょく、　きゅう食	singer	かしゅ、　か手	
school rules	こうそく、　校そく	singing show	うたばんぐみ	
school yard	こうてい、　校てい	sit	すわります	
Science	かがく、　か学	six	むっつ、　六つ	
science fiction	エスエフ（SF）	skating	スケート	
scissors	はさみ	sketch	したがき、　下書き	
sea	うみ	ski	スキー	
seasons	きせつ	skinny/thin	ほそい	
seaweed	のり	skirt	スカート	
second (one)	ふたつめ、　二つ目	sleep	ねます	
second floor (first floor in Australia)/two times	にかい、　二かい	slippers	スリッパ	
		slowly	ゆっくり	
See you later.	じゃあ、　またね。	small	ちいさい、　小さい	
see/watch/look	みます、　見ます	smile radiantly/beaming	にこにこします	
seems sad	さびしそう	snack	おやつ	
self-introduction	じこしょうかい	sneakers/runners	スニーカー	
Send me an email.	Ｅメールしてね。	snow	ゆき	
senior high school	こうこう、　高校	snowboard	スノーボード	
serious	まじめ（な）	snowman	ゆきだるま	
seven	ななつ、　七つ	soap opera	ひるメロ	
shaved ice treat	かきごおり	sob/whimper	めそめそします	
Shinto shrine	じんじゃ、　じん社	soccer	サッカー	
shirt	シャツ	society	しゃかい、　社会	
shivering	ぶるぶる	Sociology	しゃかいがく、　社会学	
shoe shop	くつや	socks	くつした	
shoe box	げたばこ	soft and soggy/ in disarray	ぐちゃぐちゃ	
shoes	くつ			
shop	〜や	softball	ソフトボール	
shop assistant	てんいん	something	なにか、　何か	
shopping	かいもの、　買いもの	sometimes	ときどき、　時々	
shops	みせ	song	うた	
short (height)	せがひくい、　みじかい	soon	もうすぐ	
shoulder	かた	sopping wet/soaking through	びしょびしょ	
show	みせます、　見せます			
Showa reign (used for giving dates)	しょうわ	sorry	ごめん	
		sound of chewing	モグモグ	
side	がわ	sound of knocking	バシッ	
sign language	しゅわ、　手話	sound of laughing	ワハハハ	
silence	シーン	sound of heavy rain	ざあざあ	
		sound of heavy snow	こんこん	

ISBN 9780170198271

sound of screaming loudly	ギャーギャー
sound of sleeping	スースー
south	みなみ、 南
south-east	なんとう、 南東
south-west	なんせい、 南西
southern entrance	みなみぐち、 南口
souvenir	おみやげ
souvenir shop	おみやげや
soy sauce	しょうゆ
spacious	ひろい
speak/talk	はなします、 話します
speak fluently	ぺらぺらはなします、 ぺらぺら話します
special requests for the position	ほんにんきぼうきにゅうらん、 本人きぼうき入らん
spoilt/selfish	わがまま
sports day	うんどうかい
sports instructor	スポーツインストラクター
spouse	はいぐうしゃ
spring	はる、 春
spring wind	はるかぜ、 春かぜ
sprinkling rain	しとしと
stabbing chopsticks	さしばし
stairs	かいだん
stand/pass time	たちます
Star Festival	たなばた
stars	ほし
start (I start)	はじめます
start (it starts)	はじまります
station	えき
steak	ステーキ
stomach	おなか
stop	とまります
storage	ものいれ、 もの入れ
stormy	あらし
story	はなし、 話
straight	まっすぐ
strange	へん（な）
street/road	みち
strict	きびしい
strong	つよい

strong wind	びゅーびゅー
student	せいと、 生と／ がくせい、 学生
study	べんきょうします
stuffed toy	ぬいぐるみ
subject	かもく、 か目
subtitles	じまく
subway	ちかてつ、 ち下てつ
sugar	さとう
sugoroku (a Japanese variety of parcheesi)	すごろく
suit	スーツ
summer	なつ、 夏
summer holiday	なつやすみ、 夏休み
sumo	すもう
sumo stable/school	すもうべや
sumo wrestler	りきし
sunglasses	サングラス
supermarket	スーパー
sushi mat	まきす
sweater/jumper	セーター
sweating	たらたら
sweets	おかし
swim	およぎます
swimming	すいえい、 水えい
swimming pool	プール

T

table	テーブル
take	とります
take (a shower)	あびます
take a memo or note	メモをとります
Take care of yourself.	おからだにきをつけて。
take off (clothing)	ぬぎます
take time/cost money	かかります
tall	せがたかい、 せが高い
Tama River	たまがわ
tatami	たたみ
tatami room	たたみのへや
tatami room (traditional style)	わしつ

ISBN 9780170198271

taxi driver	タクシーのうんてんしゅ、 タクシーのうんてん手
taxi stand	タクシーのりば
tea	おちゃ
tea ceremony room	ちゃしつ
tea cup/bowl	おちゃわん
team	チーム
teach/tell	おしえます
teacher	きょうし
teacher	せんせい、 先生
technology	テクノロジー
telephone	でんわします、 電話します
television	テレビ
television station	テレビきょく
ten	とお、 十
tennis	テニス
ten thousand	まん、 万
Thank you for waiting.	おまたせしました。
Thank you for the meal.	ごちそうさま（でした）。
that …	その
that one	それ
that one over there	あれ
that … over there	あの
that's right isn't it	そうですね
the first day	いちにちめ、 一日目
the first time	はじめて
the other day	せんじつ、 先日
there (near the listener)	そこ
therefore	だから
thin/slim/skinny	やせています／やせます／ほそい
thing	もの
things to bring	もってくるもの、 もって来るもの
think/consider	おもいます、 かんがえます
thinking of yourself	じぶんばっかり、 じ分ばっかり
third	みっつめ、 三つ目
this …	この
this month	こんげつ、 今月
this one	これ
This way, please.	こちらへどうぞ。

this week	こんしゅう、 今週
this year	ことし、 今年
third (one)	さんばんめ、 三ばん目
throw	なげます
thongs	ぞうり
three (counter)	みっつ、 三つ
tie	ネクタイ
time	とき、 時
timetable	じかんわり、 時間わり
tired	つかれます／つかれています
to …	〜へ
today	きょう、 今日
together	いっしょに
toilet	おてあらい、 お手あらい／トイレ
Tokyo	とうきょう／東京
tomorrow	あした
tonight	こんばん、 今ばん/こんや／今や
too expensive	たかすぎます、 高すぎます
tooth/teeth	は
touch	さわります
tour guide	ツアーガイド
towards	ほう
town/city	まち、 町
traditional	でんとうてきな
traffic lights	しんごう
train	でんしゃ、 電車
train station	えき
travel	りょこうします、 りょ行します
travel agent	りょこうがいしゃ、 りょ行会社
trousers	ズボン
try	ためします
try hard	がんばります
T-shirt	Tシャツ
tsunami/tidal wave	つなみ
tummy/stomach	おなか
turn	まがります
turn off	けします
turn on	つけます

ISBN 9780170198271

tutor	かていきょうし
TV or radio program	ばんぐみ
two (counter)	ふたつ、 二つ
typhoon	たいふう

U

udon noodles	うどん
umbrella	かさ
umbrella stand	かさたて
umm	えーと、 ええと
unattractive/not trendy	かっこわるい
uncle (*humble*)	おじ
uncle (*polite*)	おじさん
understand	わかります、 分かります
uniform	せいふく
university	だいがく、 大学
university student	だいがくせい、 大学生
unpleasant	いや（な）
until/by	まで
use	つかいます
using	つかうのは

V

variety show	バラエティーショー
various	いろいろ（な）
verandah	えんがわ
very	とても
veterinarian	じゅうい
vinegar	す
visible/I can see ...	みえます、 見えます
visual arts	びじゅつ
vocabulary	たんご
volcano	かざん、 火山

W

wait	まちます
waiter	ウェイター
waitress	ウェイトレス
wake up	おきます
wall	かべ
wandering chopsticks	まよいばし

want to become	なりたい
warm	あたたかい／ぽかぽか
warm-up	じゅんびたいそう
was nervous	きんちょうしました
was often attracted by	（～に）よくあこがれました
wasabi	わさび
wash	あらいます
waterski	すいじょうスキー、 水上スキー
way of moving	うごかしかた
way of writing	よみかた、 読みかた
way of holding	もちかた
we	わたしたち、 私たち
wear (hat)	かけます
wear (glasses)	かぶります
wear make-up	けしょう（を）します
wear/put on (accessory/jewellery)	します
wear/put on (bottom half of clothing)	はきます
wear, put on (jewellery or item you attach)	つけます
wearing (additional clothing)	しています
wear/put on (top half or general clothing)	きます
weather	てんき
week	しゅう、 週
weekend	しゅうまつ、 週まつ
weeping/sobbing	シクシク
weight (body)	たいじゅう
Welcome home.	おかえりなさい。
welcome/May I help you?	いらっしゃいませ
well then	まあ
west	にし、 西
west entrance	にしぐち、 西口
Western food	ようしょく、 よう食
Western music	ようがく
Western-style room	ようしつ
what	なに/なん、 何
what day of the week	なんようび、 何曜日
what kind of	どんな
what kind of things?	どんなもの

二百三十九

ISBN 9780170198271

what temperature	なんど、 何ど
what time	なんじ、 何時
what year level	なんねんせい、 何年生
wheelchair	くるまいす、 車いす
when	いつ
when (you are) in trouble	こまったとき、 こまった時
when I was a child	こどものとき、子どもの時
when you are sick	びょうきのとき、びょうきの時
when you do that	そうすると
where	どこ
where (at)	どこで
which	どの
which one	どちらが／どれ
white	しろ（い）
who	だれが
who with	だれと
why	どうして／なぜ
will help (me) learn/ my learning	べんきょうになります
win	かちます
wind	かぜ
window	まど
windy	かぜがつよい
winter	ふゆ、 冬
winter season	とうき、 冬き
with all one's might	いっしょうけんめい
woman	おんなのひと、 女の人
Won't you come?	きませんか、 来ませんか
Won't you come and play?	あそびにきませんか。あそびに来ませんか。
wonderful	すばらしい
word	ことば
work	しごと
work	はたらきます
work desk	しごとづくえ
work history	しょくれき

Wow!	わあー。
Wow! (casual)	へえ!
write	かきます、 書きます
write fluently	すらすらかきます、すらすら書きます
Write me a reply! (casual)	へんじかいてね。へんじ書いてね。

Y

yakitori	やきとり
Yamaguchi (surname)	やまぐち、 山口
Yasaka Shrine	やさかじんじゃ、やさかじん社
year by year	ねんねん、 年々
year level	～ねんせい、 ～年生
yellow	きいろ（い/の）
yen	えん、 円
yes	はい。
yes (casual)	うん。
yes, that's right	そう
yesterday	きのう
you	あなた
young	わかい
younger brother (humble)	おとうと
younger brother (someone else's)	おとうとさん
younger sister (humble)	いもうと
younger sister (someone else's)	いもうとさん
YouTube	ユーチューブ

Z

zero degrees	れいど
zoo	どうぶつえん

ISBN 9780170198271

Notes

ISBN 9780170198271

漢字

Unit 1	何	時	分	半				
Unit 2	上	下	中	前				
Unit 3	学	校	年	生				
Unit 4	春	夏	秋	冬				
Unit 5	百	千	万	円				
Unit 6	手	目	耳	口				
Unit 7	食	飲	行	買	安	高	大	小
Unit 8	私	男	女	書	見	聞	父	母
Unit 9	右	左	入	出	東	西	南	北
Unit 10	毎	今	週	先	来	住	好	名
Unit 11	語	英	家	友	会	社	間	町
Unit 12	新	読	電	車	外	国	話	々